D0996816

The
COUNTRYMAN'S
Pocket Book

Garth Christian
Over 500 Drawings By C. Dampier Freeman

Bounty Books

First published in Great Britain in 1967

This edition published in 2011 by Bounty Books
a division of Octopus Publishing Group Ltd
Endeavour House, 189 Shaftesbury Avenue
London WC2H 8JY
www.octopusbooks.co.uk

An Hachette UK Company
www.hachette.co.uk

Copyright © Garth Christian 1967

ISBN 978-0-753721-96-4

Printed & bound in China

Contents

Foundations of Landscape

*Age of the Earth – Dating the Geological Past –
Bedded Rocks – Igneous Rocks – Metamorphic Rocks –
What the Countryman Sees*

The process of reconstructing the past, repeatedly asking ourselves why a portion of landscape differs from that of a neighbouring plain or valley, can add a whole dimension to the understanding and enjoyment of the countryside. No landscape in the world contains such diversity of structure or more variety of scenery within a limited area than the land of Britain. This is due to the tilted strata of the underlying rocks which enable the traveller in the course of a few miles to pass from chalk or limestone to sands and clays of widely different origin and age, each with its own typical configuration of the ground and distinctive vegetation. The landscape as we know it was mainly shaped by agricultural man between about 2000 B.C. and A.D. 1830; but his treatment of the land depended upon the quality of the different soils and the nature of the local moist, temperate climate.

Equipment. Geology in the field, which is the proper place to study it, demands little equipment but a notebook, pencil and a geological hammer, the latter weighing up to a pound, with a square head at one end and a tapering chisel-like edge at the other. A haversack and small boxes or plastic bags are useful for specimens, when collecting is considered essential.

Age of the Earth. We know from a study of the radioactive minerals in rocks forming the earth's crust that our planet is at least a thousand million years old, and it is probably nearer twice that amount.

7

Dating the Geological Past. In the absence of precise data, the immense stretches of geological time are divided into Eras, and these are subdivided into Periods or Systems, all with their own smaller divisions. Fossils forming the remains or impressions of ancient plants and animals, and found in vast numbers in deposits laid down as sediments, differ so much from one series of rocks to another that it is possible to distinguish one rock-bed from its neighbours by this means alone. Each fossil zone has its own distinctive fauna. It is even possible in successive beds of the Wealden chalk to trace the evolutionary development of the form and detail on shells of the sea urchin *Micraster*. A single fragment of fossil may sometimes reveal not only the faunal zone but a particular section of it.

Unlike these BEDDED ROCKS derived from sediments, the older IGNEOUS ROCKS of north and west Britain, formed from molten material thrown up by volcanoes and other eruptions, generally contain no fossils. It is more difficult, therefore, to estimate their approximate age. But in all geological periods sedimentary rocks were formed at the same time as the igneous rocks, and in many instances, the erupting volcanic material spread over them. Elsewhere it penetrated between layers of the sediments with their fossils; thus enabling us to gauge a rough idea of the date of origin. A journey from North Wales to Kent takes the traveller in successive stages from the ancient Pre-Cambrian rocks to the recent rocks of South-East England, and it is doubtful if there is anywhere else in the world where so much variety can be found in such a limited area.

BEDDED ROCKS

These comprise parallel layers or *strata* formed by the stiffening of sediments thrown upon the shores or formed at the bottom of lakes or seas. An early stage in their formation can be seen by visiting the mud-flats or sand-dunes around our low-lying coasts. Great rivers like the Thames or Humber carry huge quantities of detritus down to the estuaries where mud and sandbanks are created.

Yet even as new land is being formed around the Wash and many large estuaries, the sea is making heavy inroads into the sands, gravels and clays of glacial origin on the Norfolk and Suffolk coast, in south-east Yorkshire and in the boulder clay cliffs between Criccieth and Aberystwyth. As this material crumbles it may be carried out with the tides before sinking to form fresh deposits of clay or sand, while eroding limestone cliffs contribute to marine deposits formed from the shells of lime created by innumerable sea creatures.

Dips, Folds and Faults. The beds in this great class of sedimentary rocks may be in horizontal or vertical layers, or they may slope in what is called a *dip*, or be contorted into *folds*— twisted out of their original position during subsequent movements of the earth's crust. The clays and chalk of the London Basin form a gentle saucer-shaped *syncline*, a dip with twin limbs or sides. By contrast the Wealden beds of Sussex form an *anticline*, an arch-like structure in which the two limbs slope away from each other. Cracks in the earth's crust are called *faults*, when the beds of the strata, subject as they are to tremendous pressures, fall out of alignment. (See diagram of Hog's Back.)

The presence of any rock-bed on the surface is known as its *out-crop*. We should not under-estimate the influence of the weather in shaping these surface rocks over vast periods of time. The dramatic nature of Snowdonia owes less to the rocks that remain than to others that have eroded away. But for erosion, the Wealden anticline would form an outcrop of chalk and red sand rising 2,500 feet above sea level.

CHALK, confined to south and east England, was created within the past 120 million years, a vast Wealden dome being worn away by weathering even as it formed. It is composed of tiny white grains of calcite, a mineral made of calcium carbonate

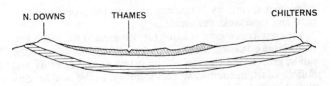

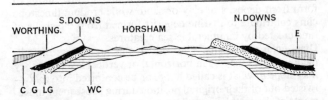

TOP: **The London Basin,** with Chalk beneath the Gault Clay, linking the North Downs and Chilterns. BOTTOM: **Main folds of the Weald.** E. Eocene; C. Chalk; G. Gault; L.G. Lower Greensand; W.C. Weald Clay.

blended with crumbs of shell from myriad marine animals of some shallow sea.

FLINT. Silica probably derived from the skeletons of sponges dwelling in the shallow seas where the chalk was formed.

CONGLOMERATES. Coarser fragments and pebbles of almost any rock, under heavy pressure, may be welded by natural cement into a solid substance sometimes known as 'Pudding-stone'. The ingredients may range in size from tiny specks of dust and grains of sand to quite large boulders, and they may be arranged in neat layers or form a disorderly mixture of shapes, sizes and materials. The natural cement may be composed of limestone, ironstone, or some sort of sand or clay. Our ancestors of prehistoric times knew the conglomerates of the Wye Valley as vast 'standing stones', while those of the

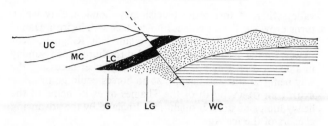

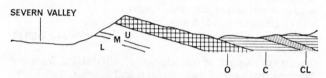

TOP: **The Hog's Back, Surrey,** where the upward thrust on the south side has created a fault. U.C. Upper Chalk; M.C. Middle Chalk; L.C. Lower Chalk; G. Gault; L.G. Lower Greensand; W.C. Wealden Clay. BOTTOM: **Cotswold Hills,** showing Lower (L), Middle (M) and Upper (U) Lias. O. Oolites; C. Clay; C.L. Corallian Limestone (derived from coral reefs).

summit of the Brecon Beacons comprise silica known as QUARTZ, an ingredient of granite and other igneous rocks. GRITS. Angular sand grains, as distinct from smooth ones. Millstone grit, long used for the grinding of corn, hence its name, is the dark stubborn rock that gives grandeur to so much of the Pennines of North Derbyshire and Yorkshire.

CLAY. Potter, brickmaker and metallurgist could not manage without this rock, and tiny portions of the unusually pure China clay or kaolin even find a place in chocolate cream! Few visitors to France realise that the 'Paris Clay' in the valley of the Seine continues northwards beneath the Channel to the Thames

11

valley where it forms the blueish-grey London Clay which turns brown as the air comes into contact with its iron. Daniel Defoe recorded how a 'lady of quality' at Ringmer, near Lewes, on the Wealden clay, travelled to church each Sunday in a coach drawn by six oxen, this being 'meer necessity, the way being so stiff and deep, that no horses could go in it.'

BOULDER CLAY north of the Thames owes its name to the heavy lumps of stone brought into England by the advancing glaciers of the Ice Age.

LOAM. A blending of clay and sand much liked by farmers and gardeners.

MARL. A mixture of clay and limestone.

SHALE (shell or scale). A slender layer of clay.

MUDSTONE. Clay welded into firm rock that reveals no sign of layers.

OIL SHALE. Source of our deposits of oil, distilled from the decaying remnants of ancient plants and animals.

BLUE LIAS. A corruption of layers, comprising shales particularly rich in ammonites and the fossil remains of prehistoric reptiles. The famous Blue Lias shales of the Lyme Regis area of Dorset are the source of many of the remains of giant reptiles contained in our museums.

COAL. An early stage in the transformation of decaying vegetation into fuel is demonstrated in the PEAT which covers extensive tracts of northern Britain, Ireland and our south country heathlands. All bogs are of podsolised peat, and the different layers of their rotting fibre possess a remarkable capacity for retaining intact the pollen grains deposited by trees thousands of years ago. Good use has been made of this discovery in assessing the origin and development of the vegetation in prehistoric times.* Water flowing from the peat bogs of the Chailey Common Local Nature Reserve in Sussex, and from many north country bogs, is a rich brown colour. This

* See pages 99–101.

points to the presence of limonite, or bog iron ore, a hydrated oxide of iron formed from the decaying plants deep in the soil. LIGNITE marks the second stage of the development of coal, and it is known as 'brown coal' and has some limited use as a source of industrial heat. BITUMINOUS COAL—which contains no bitumen or pitch!—is the fuel commonly used for domestic heating, and ANTHRACITE, with its high carbon content, is a valuable steam coal.

GRAPHITE. Natural carbon, source of the lead for lead-pencils, formerly mined at Borrowdale in the Lake District.

IRONSTONE. The clay ironstones of Northamptonshire, Lincolnshire and Yorkshire may date from the Jurassic period 140 million years ago. They can also be found, as in parts of Yorkshire, in the Upper Jurassic Oolitic beds.

IGNEOUS ROCKS

These *Massive* or *Igneous Rocks*, which are the source of many of our minerals, comprise *Plutonic Rocks* like *Granite*, formed deep in the crust of the earth, and *Volcanic Rocks* such as *Basalt*, cast up by repeated eruptions. This is not the place to linger over details of their origin and nature, except to add that their source lay in subterranean reservoirs of molten material differing widely in their mineral silica content, and in the speed with which they cooled and hardened after pouring out on to the earth's surface.

GRANITE, so familiar to visitors to Dartmoor, Land's End, and parts of the Lake District and Scotland, is much the most common of these rocks.

BASALT, which cooled more rapidly than granite, hence the general absence of visible crystals, can be seen in large parts of the Inner Hebrides and Northern Ireland, and it is never more impressive than in the walls of Fingal's Cave on the Island of Staffa.

DYKES AND SILLS. Molten material flowing upwards from

13

the subterranean reservoirs sometimes formed a vertical DYKE, easily recognisable as a wall of Igneous Rock cutting through the Bedded Rocks. Elsewhere it squeezed between the layers of rock to form a SILL, lacking the slaglike appearance of volcanic lava, and burning and transforming the rocks with which it made contact.

METAMORPHIC ROCKS

The immense pressures exerted by movements of the earth at various periods, and particularly in Caledonian times, and the heat transferred from the fiery Igneous rocks to the sedimentaries often transformed their nature, limestone being turned into MARBLE, sandstone into QUARTZITE, a hard, gleaming rock, while clay and shale became SLATE. Granite was often transformed into the sparkling GNEISS (pronounced 'nice').

WHAT THE COUNTRYMAN SEES

A visitor to Charnwood Forest in Leicestershire, with its marls and sandstones dating from TRIASSIC times nearly 170 million years ago, may be startled by the ridges of PRE-CAMBRIAN rocks that have survived a thousand million years or more of weathering. More remnants of this remote period can be seen in all their grandeur in the Highlands and western corners of Scotland, the Western Isles, and in Anglesey and a few other places. These rocks of the ARCHAEAN era—from the Greek term for 'ancient' or 'beginning'—contain no true fossils.

Palaeozoic Rocks, of the second era which was known to the older geologists as the Primary, lie beside the pre-Cambrian rocks near Loch Carran in north-west Scotland, around Skiddaw in the Lake District, in the Isle of Man and in North and Central Wales where they were first studied. They can be seen again in Shropshire beside the pre-Cambrian rocks of the Longmynd.

The first firm evidence of living things can be traced to the

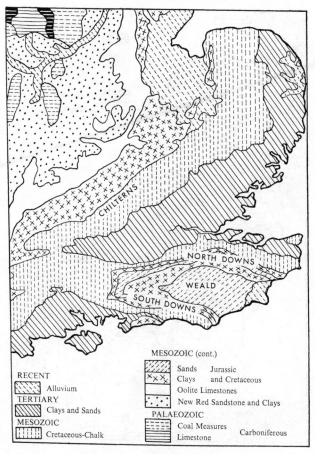

RECENT

Alluvium

TERTIARY

Clays and Sands

MESOZOIC

Cretaceous-Chalk

MESOZOIC (cont.)

Sands — Jurassic
Clays — and Cretaceous
Oolite Limestones
New Red Sandstone and Clays

PALAEOZOIC

Coal Measures
Limestone — Carboniferous

15

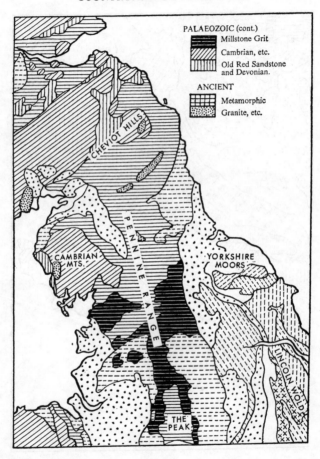

PALAEOZOIC (cont.)

Millstone Grit

Cambrian, etc.

Old Red Sandstone
and Devonian.

ANCIENT

Metamorphic

Granite, etc.

CHEVIOT HILLS

PENNINE RANGE

CAMBRIAN
MTS.

YORKSHIRE
MOORS

LINCOLN WOLD

THE
PEAK

CAMBRIAN ROCKS, probably formed nearly 500 million years ago, and surviving in the Malvern Hills, in Merionethshire and beside the Menai Straits of North Wales, in north-west Scotland and the countryside of Shropshire. There, too, as in much of Wales, the Lake District, southern Scotland and eastern Ireland, we find the ORDOVICIAN ROCKS, sandstones, grits, shales and rather less limestone, with traces of the earliest fish that inhabited the shallow Ordovician seas or those deeper waters of Galloway. It was in Ordovician times that the Cambrian and pre-Cambrian crust of North Wales was pierced by the molten outpourings that were to form what we know today as Snowdonia and Cader Idris.

Silurian and Devonian Periods. (350–285 million years ago?) The great Caledonian folding of the Highland valleys and ridges occurred, and there were numerous intrusions of granite. The Devonian Rocks of North and South Devon—mainly sandstones, shales, grits and slates, with limestone in the neighbourhood of Plymouth and Torquay—appear to have been formed in the depths of the sea, whereas the Old Red Sandstone, also dating from Upper Palaeozoic times, was deposited in lakes and shallow coastal waters. Many fossil fish new to science have been found in the Old Red Sandstone of Scotland which form the basis for much fertile soil of the Lowlands and some of the Scottish glens. These rocks also yield the rich red soil of Herefordshire and Breconshire.

Carboniferous Period. (285–210 million years ago?) No birds sang in this remote period, but before its close the first amphibia had appeared. It was in the warm seas of the Lower Carboniferous period that the Mountain Limestone formed, while the Millstone Grit and Coal Measures date from the Upper Carboniferous period. Impressions of fossilised insects, molluscs, fish, amphibians or plants are frequently found embedded in the coal.

The close of this period was marked by the second great

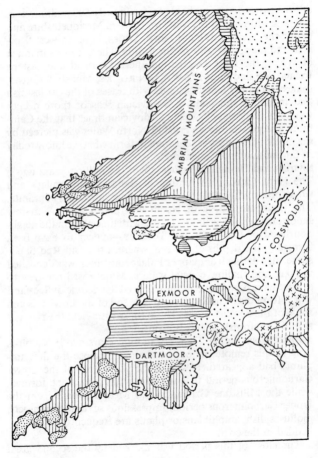

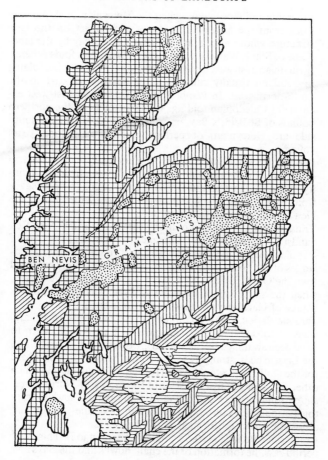

mountain building phase, when the Hercynian or Armorican folds from the south inflicted a sharp impact on the land structure whose effects are demonstrated today by the landscape of South Wales, Devon and Cornwall. The folds generally run in an east-west direction whereas the Caledonian folding in Scotland usually runs from the south-south-east to the north-north-west. In Pembrokeshire we find an east-west example of Caledonian folding. While the cliffs on the northern bounds of St Bride's Bay are Caledonian, those on the south side are Hercynian, or perhaps a hundred million years younger.

Permian Period. (210–170 million years ago?) A narrow strip of Dolomite or Magnesian Limestone running from the vicinity of Nottingham to the Durham coast seems to be a legacy from this period. Much red marl and conglomerates of the New Red Sandstone were also laid.

Triassic Period. (170–145 million years ago?) More New Red Sandstone dates from the Mesozoic Era, known as the 'Age of Reptiles', which includes this period. The light Bunter Sandstones of the north-west Midlands, even more vividly coloured than the Old Red Sandstone, were laid in the Triassic Period, when the salt lakes of Cheshire and deposits of gypsum—a source of blackboard chalk—were also formed.

Jurassic Period. (145–120 million years ago?) Most of Britain, other than the Highlands and parts of East Anglia, seem to have been swamped by the sea during this period. It left behind the Liassic beds, strangely soft and muddy, and forming a base for the Oolitic limestones which form the Cotswolds and much other fine country from Dorset to the moors of North Yorkshire. Some of the clays of the Midland plain also date from this period when our land abounded in crocodiles, turtles and a host of giant reptiles such as the dinosaurs.

Cretaceous Period. (120–75 million years ago?) This vast period saw the formation of the chalk downs and the clays and sandstones of the Wealden beds, the Lower Greensand—which owes its name to the tiny grains of greenish glauconite in the sand—and the Blue Gault Clay. The top layers of this gault, like the Upper Greensand, and the Chalk, belong to the Upper Cretaceous Period.

Eocene Period. (75–45 million years ago?) The leaves of tropical evergreens and palm trees found embedded in the cliffs of

Chipping Campden: typical Cotswold buildings. Oolitic limestones shaped the Cotswolds.

Bournemouth and the Isle of Wight show that in Eocene times, when the London Clay was laid, our climate was tropical. Fruits of Nipa palms, now associated with the Malayan swamps, have been found in the London Clay deposited as mud in the Isle of Sheppey. This Period belonged to the Tertiary Era.

Oligocene Period. (45–25 million years ago?) The word means 'few recent', and it is a period which saw the start of the great

GEOLOGICAL TIME SCALE

Age in Millions of Years	Periods (Maximum thicknesses in feet)	Mountain Building	Igneous Activity	Time Ranges of Life Groups	
1					
	PLIOCENE 18,000 ft.				
15					
	MIOCENE 21,000 ft.			TERTIARY	
25		Main Alpine Folds	Outflow of Basalts in N.W. Scotland		
	OLIGOCENE 15,000 ft.				
45					
	EOCENE 23,000 ft.				Mammals
75					Birds
	CRETACEOUS 64,000 ft.			MESOZOIC (SECONDARY)	Reptiles
120					
	JURASSIC 22,000 ft.				Land Plants
145			Many Lavas, Sills in North; Granites in S. West		Amphibia
	TRIASSIC 25,000 ft.				
170					
	PERMIAN 18,000 ft.	Main Hercynian Folds			

Age in Millions of Years	Periods	Mountain Building	Igneous Activity	Time Ranges of Life Groups	
210			Basaltic Rocks in Mid-Scotland		Seaweeds and invertebrates Fishes
	CARBONIFEROUS 40,000 ft.			PALAEOZOIC	
285					
	DEVONIAN 37,000 ft.	Main Caledonian Folds	Much Granite appears		
325					
	SILURIAN 20,000 ft.				
350					
	ORDOVICIAN 40,000 ft.		Much volcanic activity. Rocks of Lake District and Snowdonia formed		
410					
	CAMBRIAN 40,000 ft.				
500		Pre-Cambrian Folds	More Granite intrusions		
1,000– 2,000 ?	PRE-CAMBRIAN			ARCHAEAN	

Alpine mountain building storms of Europe, when ripples reaching Britain raised the chalk deposits of southern England.

Miocene Period. (25–15 million years ago?) This 'middle recent' period saw more effects of the ripples from the Alpine mountain activity of the Continent. Besides the raising of the south country chalk, cracks appeared in the ancient rocks of North-West Scotland, releasing an outflow of Basalts and the Lake District may have reached its final form. There are no Miocene deposits in Britain, as the land was not submerged in this Period.

Pliocene Period. (15–1 million years ago) The main structure of our land was settled by the dawn of this period, though the retreating seas were now to leave behind the shelly sand-beds of East Anglia and the North Downs of Surrey. Indeed, land and sea have repeatedly changed places, and mountains and plains, for all their vast ages, are the most impermanent of structures, subject as they are to movements of the earth's crust and to the endless eroding influence of the weather.

Pleistocene Period. This 'most recent' period forms part of the Quarternary era that began a mere million years ago. Rocks of the period include the Boulder Clay, deposited in so many areas north of the Thames during the Great Ice Age.

Holocene Period. This second Quarternary system includes the peat bogs now forming, the silts left behind by our rivers, the sands and pebbles brought ashore by the sea. Creation is a continuous process and we can observe it happening.

BIBLIOGRAPHY

Condry W. M. *The Snowdonia National Park*. Collins, New Naturalist Series, London, 1966.

Evans, I. O. *The Observer's Book of Geology*. Frederick Warne, London, N.D.

Hawkes, Jacquetta. *A Land*. Cresset Press, London, 1951.

Steers, J. A. *The English Coast and the Coast of Wales.* The Fontana Library, Collins, London, 1966.

Steers, J. A. *The Coastline of England and Wales.* Cambridge University Press, Cambridge, 1948.

Trueman, A. E. *Geology and Scenery in England and Wales.* Penguin Books, London, 1963 ed.

Wild Flowers

Ecology of Plants – Naming Flowers – Reproduction –
Classification – Glossary – Flower Families

ECOLOGY OF PLANTS

On finding a wild flower, the first question to ask is 'Why is it growing here?' The answer involves a consideration of the geological factors discussed in the last section, the amount of light and moisture reaching it, the nature of the climate and micro-climate—and temperature is particularly important—the acidity or alkalinity of the soil, the supply of mineral salts in the ground and the size of the soil particles, for water is much more readily retained by the small particles of clay, of course, than by the larger grains of sand.

Distribution. A glance at the great *Atlas of the British Flora* raises more questions of a fascinating kind. The lesser gorse, *Ulex minor*, so abundant on the heaths of the Weald, where it flowers brilliantly in July and August, proves to be absent from Ireland and the English Midlands, and strangely rare in the West. The half-evergreen under-shrub hairy greenweed, *Genista pilosa*, that grows on the Lizard Peninsula in Cornwall, appears to be absent from every other corner of Britain except West Wales, now that heath fires have destroyed the last surviving specimens in Ashdown Forest, Sussex. It may not seem odd that the mountains of Snowdonia possess a rich alpine flora reminiscent of the Scottish Highlands hundreds of miles to the north; it is surely surprising that a familiar common flower like the red campion, *Melandrium rubrum*, proves to be an extreme rarity in Cambridgeshire.

The botanist soon begins to distinguish the calcicoles or

lime-loving plants from the calcifuges or lime-haters; and the species which do well on both types of soil. The fragrant orchid, *Gymnadenia conopsea*, flourishes on the chalk downs and on the acid sandy heaths—though plants in the various habitats may differ much in size and depth of colouring. Species growing on the outskirts of their range tend to be much more particular about soil and situation. The little alpine fern, green spleenwort, *Asplenium viride*, is confined to the limestone hill rocks of northern and western Britain and south and west Ireland. Yet within the heart of its range in the Alps, it prospers on acid granitic rocks. A vast field for exciting research lies open to the ecologically-minded botanist with an understanding of geology.

Climate and plant ecology. It is hard to over-estimate the influence on plants of the weather, including the micro-climate. In a corner of Ashdown Forest, Sussex, there is a colony of the leafy liverwort, *Nardia compressa*, that is clearly a legacy from the last Ice Age which ended 10,000 years ago. It survives only because of the cold, damp atmosphere preserved around them by overhanging rocks moistened by a fast-flowing stream. Near at hand is the hay-scented fern that is thought to have thrived on the same spot for 8,000 years, thanks to the moist micro-climate similar to that which must have existed throughout the area around 6000 B.C. Studies of this subject are still only in their infancy, and the influence of climate on plant ecology may gain mounting economic importance, especially as man begins to manipulate the local weather—and this is a topic of which much may be heard during the next few decades.

The influence of man. Many most attractive plant communities would soon disappear if it were not for regular grazing which keeps down the scrub. Yet a balance between over- and under-grazing is needed if the biological capital of the soil, the quality of the grass crop and the richness of the flora are to be maintained. Many wild flowers of the pastures and meadows benefit, too, from the demand for hay; for during the vital periods of rapid growth in late spring and early summer the grass is protected from trampling and grazing, while the cutting of the crop halts the natural succession and thus prevents invasion by ranker growths.

The presence of particular plants is often suggestive of past actions by man. Plants formerly used as medicinal herbs or for the dye they produced—dyer's greenweed, *Genista tinctoria*, which yielded a yellow dye from the flower is an example— tend to occur in the neighbourhood of old-established villages. Bluebells, *Endymion non-scripta*, yellow archangel, *Gale-obdolon luteum*, and wood anemone, *Anemone nemorosa*, are species of open woodland and their presence may imply that the underwood was formerly coppiced, being cut every ten or twelve years. Rosebay willow herb, *Epilobium angustifolium*, rapidly colonises ground frequently ravaged by fire; and abundant stinging nettles, *Urtica dioica*, on a roadside verge implies that the ground, rich in nitrogen, may have been disturbed by roadworks. Ragwort, *Senecio jacobaea*, is often most abundant where the farmer has failed to call in the rabbit-clearance society, for it fares best in soil scratched by these animals. The increasingly common pineapple weed, *Matricaria matricarioides*, offers proof of heavy trampling, though many other plants, including bluebells, are vulnerable to the pressure of human feet.

Trampling and collecting. The point is important, for the pressures on the countryside are rapidly mounting. Botanical students trampling through a bog can all too easily wreck the old-established water system and transform the whole nature of the plant community. Collecting has gravely damaged the status of many of the rarer plants. No sensible person wants to prevent primrosing by children—though even the common primrose has been picked out of existence in Leicestershire, and it has also vanished from Middlesex.

Some limited collecting of the more common wild flowers may be essential for teaching purposes. But it must be done with a thought for the future. The gathering of annuals and biennials, by preventing them from seeding, ensures their absence in future years. Perennials, such as the orchids, may continue for a time to come up every year; but eventually each plant must die and if no seed has been deposited in the soil, none will take their place.

Practical conservation. Judicious intervention by man can do much to increase the variety and abundance of our wild flowers. Sometimes the interference, and its beneficial consequences, may be quite accidental. Mining at Alvecote, near Tamworth, Staffordshire, which caused subsidence of a portion of the Anker Valley, and the consequent flooding of 120 acres, resulted in an invasion of waders and wildfowl who brought with them the seeds of aquatic plants. Again, by allowing a drainage ditch to become choked, a south country parish council inadvertently enabled the rare and beautiful meadow thistle, *Cirsium dissectum*, which only grows in acid mud, to colonise a fresh site.

More often man's intervention, if it is not to prove harmful, must be carefully planned in the light of ecological understanding. Thanks to strict conservation by the Kent Trust for Nature Conservation, the extremely rare monkey orchid, *Orchis simia*, increased from a single plant in 1955 to 285 plants in 1966.

Schoolboys cutting bracken in a Sussex nature reserve enabled the beautiful saw-wort, *Serratula tinctoria*, to multiply ten-fold. After they had cut two and a half lorry loads of birch scrub from an area of damp heath, there was a dramatic increase in the sphagnum moss, sedges and other species in a peat bog that had dried out a hundred yards away.

All the time our wild flowers are multiplying and declining, extending their range or retreating under the impact of ecological changes which are generally—but not always—the result of man's intervention. In recent years many attractive plants like the corncockle, *Agrostemma githago*, have become rare owing to more intensive methods of farming. Improved drainage has harmed the status of many beautiful plants of the wet habitats. But our flora is still very rich. More than 5,000 wild plants have been found in Britain, and a typical English parish may even now contain 400 or 500 different species.

NAMING FLOWERS

A Chinese or Brazilian botanist may shake his head in bewilderment if asked about autumn crocus or yellow stonecrop; and their difficulties increase if one is so unkind as to mention any of the local names—Naked Nannies for the autumn crocus and Welcome-home-husband-though-never-so-drunk for the yellow stonecrop. Talk to them of *Crocus nudiflorus* or *Sedum acre*, and they may well comprehend. Latin, the international language of the civilised world for hundreds of years, enables the botanist of every nation to identify at once plant names of any other country.

These may reveal much. While most buttercups have yellow flowers and the water crowfoot white ones, the generic name *Ranunculus* discloses their relationship as members of the same family. Alba or album shows that the flower is white, while no one would doubt that *Viola hirta* is a hairy plant, or *V. odorata* a sweet-smelling one. The fly orchid's character is clearly revealed in the scientific name, *Orchis insectifera*, the rare soldier orchid—now confined to a site in the Chilterns and another in Suffolk—is *O. militaris*, while the bee orchid has the specific name *apifera*.

Some species are named after the botanists who discovered them. Honeysuckle reminds us of the German scientist Lonitzer, and our only perennial goosefoot, Good King Henry, is granted the odd specific names *bonus-henricus*. The dandelion, *Taraxacum officinale*, much used in olden times for medicinal purposes, gains its specific name from *officina*, the medicine room of the medieval monastery.

REPRODUCTION

Many flowers such as the buttercup and the violet produce both eggs and sperm and are thus hermaphrodite. Others such as the oak, hazel and cuckoo pint are unisexual, producing male and female flowers on the same plant, while some unisexual species such as the willow and the hop produce blooms of the two sexes on different plants.

Pollination. Fusion between the male and female gamete—fertilisation—depends for a large number of plants on a visiting insect. Bees and wasps, moths and butterflies, beetles and flies are the prime agents of pollination. An insect attracted to a bloom by its attractive colours or, more often, its perfume, flies from flower to flower in search of nectar. Many of the most effective insect pollinators such as the social bees, which systematically work a species of flower until all the nectar is harvested, have legs or abdomen well clothed with hairs which collect large quantities of pollen. One species of German bee has been proved to carry an amount of pollen equal to half the full weight of the insect. Pollen brushed on to an insect's hairs in one flower soon falls on to the sticky stigma of the next.

Fertilisation. The pollen grain, having dropped on to the stigma, produces a pollen tube which grows down the style into the cavity of the ovary containing the passive female gametes, or eggs. The male gamete or sperm flows down the tube into the ovary and fuses with the egg, which may then produce an embryonic plant.

Flowers and insects. Some wild flowers secrete their nectar only at a particular hour of the day. The bees, with their acute sense of time, have learned to visit them at the right moments. They are particularly fond of 'labiate' type flowers with a lower and upper lip, like yellow archangel and other members of the snapdragon family. In its native Peru our familiar nasturtium, *Tropaeolum majus*, mainly depends for pollination on the humming birds, which are adept at finding their way to the nectar hoarded in the spur deep within the flower. Our short-tongued humble bees cannot emulate this feat, so they have devised a way of gaining entry by cutting a hole in the wall of the spur. This gives them access to the nectar, but they do not assist pollination in any way. Some honey bees have developed the same method of biting their way by the backdoor into the heart of the bluebell, while other domestic bees enter through the main entrance. The whole process has recently been filmed by Dr F. R. Philps and is shown in his film 'The Wood'.

Flowers which openly display their nectar such as ivy are particularly attractive to flies and wasps. Bogbean attracts the pearl-bordered and marsh fritillary butterflies, while hogweed, hemlock, cow parsley and other umbellifers are pollinated by hover-flies, drone-flies and many predatory beetles. The vast compositae family, which includes the daisies and mayweed, are also much visited by these insects.

Much remains to be discovered about the whole remarkable process. We still do not know what insects pollinate certain plants, such as the monkey orchid, nor whether the process occurs by day or at night.

The pollination of the cuckoo pint or wild arum, *Arum maculatum*, is as well documented as any. The plant throws off an unwholesome smell which entices insects associated with decaying matter. The visiting insects slip on the damp, smooth surface of the flower's inner tube and fall into a neat 'moth and beetle' trap beneath. A ring of stiff spines prevents release and the insects are trapped for the night. They stumble through the male part of the flower down into the female section below where any pollen they may have collected falls on to the stigma. Next morning the flower has begun to shrivel and the ring of downward curving spines become limp. The walls of the flower can now be climbed with little difficulty. On the way up the insect returns through the male sector, which has now ripened, and which usually deposits a load of pollen grains on the visitor's back or legs. Soon the creature escapes into the sunlight; but before long it may be tempted to enter another wild arum and the whole process is repeated.

Self-fertilisation. Violets are among a number of plants which produce special flowers that fail to open, remaining in bud while their stamens and carpels ripen. The pollen then showers down upon the stigma without any outside intervention.

Wind pollination. The flowers of many British grasses and trees are most unobtrusive, for they have no need to display bright colours, relying for pollination on the wind. The prospects for wind-blown pollen grains in search of a waiting stigma must be exceedingly poor. Hence the vast quantity of pollen that a single specimen must yield to the wind if it is to succeed in reproducing its own kind.

Vegetative reproduction. Many plants such as the crocus and the bluebell can reproduce themselves by developing new corms at the base during the growing season. The young corm grows into a new plant early in the following spring. Some aquatic plants extend their range by the ability of any part to grow into a new plant if separated from the parent. The underground stems of grasses and the rhizomes of bracken possess this same capacity. Layering, when a shoot strikes root while attached to the parent plant, is another form of vegetative reproduction. Even a beech tree will occasionally do this, as examples at Kew and in the New Forest show.

CLASSIFICATION

The world of plants comprises a number of major groups. These are—1, Fungi: moulds, mushrooms, and toadstools; 2, Algae: seaweeds; 3, Mosses and liverworts; 4, Ferns and horsetails; 5, Conifers and flowering plants. These groups are divided into classes and families mainly based upon their evolutionary sequence, beginning with the most simple and ascending to the more complex. One hesitates to be dogmatic, but the table below probably represents the facts, and all of them have to be taken into account when plants are classified.

PRIMITIVE	HIGHER FORMS
Hermaphrodite flowers	Unisexual flowers
Solitary flower	Inflorences (e.g. Dandelions and daisies)
Many-parted flowers	Few parts to a flower
Petalled flowers	No petals
The regular flower	Irregular flower
Free carpels	Fused carpels
Many carpels	Few carpels
Single fruit	Aggregate fruits

Monocotyledons. The first tiny leaf within the embryonic plant inside the seed is termed the cotyledon or seed-leaf. Monocotyledons—grasses, sedges, water plantain family and others—usually have only one cotyledon, and are parallel-veined in the leaves. The parts of their flowers are usually in threes or multiples of three.

Dicotyledons. The leaves of these plants—which have two cotyledons—are usually net-veined, frequently broad and often stalked. Their flower parts are generally in multiples of four or five, and they range from the buttercup family to the daisy family.

Family Groups. Species with several characters in common are placed together in family groups. Lady's smock, shepherd's purse and charlock all produce flowers with 4 petals and 2 short and 4 long stamens, and they are therefore classified as members of the same cabbage family. Plants with flowers possessing 5 petals, 5 sepals often with a bristle, and prominent stamens, and fruits with 5 segments issuing out into a long pointed beak, are cranesbills, placed together in the geranium family. If a plant has square stems, paired leaves, two-lipped snapdragon type flowers, and fruit comprising 4 small nuts within the calyx, it is bound to be a member of the thyme family, *Labiatae*. The more primitive families, such as the buttercups or Rancunculaceae, vary greatly not merely from species to species but from one specimen to another.

GLOSSARY

Acid: of soils, lacking lime.

Alkaline: of soils with lime or chalk.

Alternate: not opposite or whorled.

Annual: a plant with a life cycle of a year.

Anther: portion of stamen housing pollen grains.

Biennial: a plant completing its life cycle within two years. Flowers only in second year.

Bract: a small modified leaf, at base of flower stalk or just below flower-head.

Calyx: the sepals fused at the base, sometimes forming a tube to protect the bud, sometimes separate.

Capsule: dry fruit that splits to release seed.

Carpel: one or more units comprising the stigma, style and ovary forming the female part of the flower.

Corolla: the petals joined at the base, sometimes into a tube.

Deciduous: leaves fall each autumn.

Filament: stalk of stamen.

Half-evergreen: keeping some leaves through winter.

Node: point on stem where the leaf grows.

Ovary: young seed-vessel below the style in which female eggs are produced.

Pappus: feathery or hairy 'parachute' on fruits of dandelions and other species.

Perennial: a plant living for more than two years.

Perianth: the sepals and petals together

Petals: Usually the brightly coloured part of the flower, and may attract insects. Some flowers do without them.

Pistil: female part of the flower.

Pollen: small grains from the anthers containing the male cells required for fertilizing the egg.

Receptacle: swollen head of the flower-stalk.

Rhizome: the underground rooting stem persisting for more than one season.

Sepals: the outer parts of the flower, often green, but looking like petals when coloured.

Spore: minute fruiting body on back of fern fronds and their relatives.

Stamen: the male part of the flower comprising the filament with pollen-producing anther.

Stigma: the top of the style where pollen grains arrive.

Stipules: two tiny leaf-like objects at base of leaf-stalk.

Style: the stalk linking stigma and ovary in the female flower.

Sucker: shoot growing from roots of tree or shrub.

Tendril: thin twining outgrowth.

Whorl: 3 or more flowers or leaves around a stem.

FLOWER FAMILIES

Buttercup Family *Ranunculaceae*

Marsh Marigold, *Caltha palustris* (Kingcup and May Blobs). Hairless tufted perennial. Widespread, on marshy ground. March–June.

Wood Anemone, *Anemone nemorosa.* Solitary white flowers with many yellow anthers. Sometimes tinged pink or purple beneath. Widespread in and around open woodland, roadside banks. March–May.

Lesser Celandine, *Ranunculus ficaria.* Appears before the swallows which inspire its name—from the Greek *chelidon*—swal-

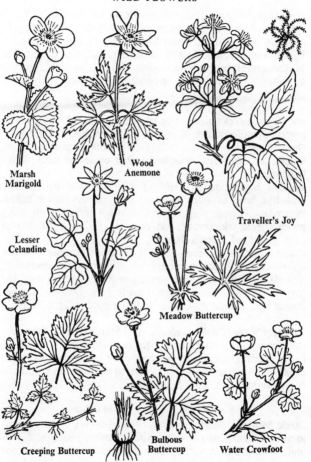

Marsh
Marigold

Wood
Anemone

Lesser
Celandine

Traveller's Joy

Meadow Buttercup

Creeping Buttercup

Bulbous
Buttercup

Water Crowfoot

low. Hairless perennial, shining glossy yellow petals. Widespread and abundant in moist shady sites. March–May.

Meadow Buttercup, *R. acris.* Much disliked, like its relatives, by cattle on account of its bitter flavour. Tallest of the familiar buttercups. Hairy perennial 1–3 ft. high. No runners; erect or spreading sepals, many flower-heads, stalk smooth. Widespread and common in damp meadows. May–July.

Creeping Buttercup, *R. repens.* Resembles bulbous buttercup, but larger leaves and erect or spreading sepals. Leafy runners emerge from juncture of leaves with stem and readily root, thereby developing new plants. Widespread and common, verges, and in moist woodland, often on heavy soils. May–September.

Bulbous Buttercup, *R. bulbosus.* Distinguished by swollen, bulk-like base of stem. Slighter and hairier than meadow buttercup. Orange tinge of pollen often reflected on shiny petals. Most widespread and common yellow buttercup of drier grassland. March–June.

Water Crowfoot, *R. aquatilis.* All the 13 British species of Water crowfoot have white buttercup-type flowers, often present in abundance, and their size—together with the shape of the leaves—are the main distinguishing feature. Different species favour fast flowing water, still water or mud. March–September.

Traveller's Joy, *Clematis vitalba* (Old Man's Beard). Our only climber with opposite pinnate leaves, white woolly, feathery fruits, dominates miles of south-country hedgerows on chalk. Small green-white flowers attractive to flies and bees. Rare in N.; abundant in S. July–September.

Cabbage Family *Cruciferae*

Black Mustard, *Brassica nigra.* Stalked leaves and pods adjoining stem distinguish from rape and other relatives. 2–3 ft. high. Mustard and oil for soap and medicines derived from

Black Mustard

Charlock

Jack-by-
the-hedge

Lady's Smock

Whitlow Grass

Shepherd's Purse

Watercress

Hairy Rock Cress

seeds, hence cultivation through centuries. Common in waste corners, stream banks, cliffs. May–August.

Charlock, *Sinapis arvensis* (Wild Mustard, Runch). Annual yellow crucifer, 6–18 in. high, usually bristly on lower parts. Less divided leaves than white mustard. Declining through weedkillers, but still much too common on farms. Seeds will germinate after more than a decade in soil. May–July.

Jack-by-the-Hedge, *Alliaria petiolata* (Garlic Mustard). Hedge garlic, as it may be called, betrays itself by the smell of garlic when rubbed. White flowers, often on unbranched stem, growing abundantly in light shade of walls, hedges and woods. April–June.

Lady's Smock, *Cardamine pratensis* (Cuckoo Flower). Perennial, 10–18 in. high, with graceful flowers ranging in shade from rich lilac to white. 4 sepals and petals, 6 stamens,* of which 2 are short, anthers yellow. Widespread and numerous in damp places throughout Britain. April–June.

Whitlow Grass, *Erophila verna.* A slender, hairy annual, less than 3 in. high, with deeply cleft white flowers with 4 petals divided into two lobes. Common on sandy ground, walls, rocks all over Britain. March–June.

Shepherd's Purse, *Capsella bursa-pastoris.* Most common of the crucifers, with triangular or heart-shaped seed-pods. 3–18 in. high, variable leaves, small white flowers, in every month.

Watercress, *Nasturtium officinale. Rorippa nasturtium aquaticum.* Hairless, creeping, aquatic perennial, still widely cultivated, but also growing in ditches and streams throughout Britain. Typical white flowers of Cabbage family, with 4 petals, 4 long and 2 short stamens. May–October.

Hairy Rock Cress, *Arabis hirsuta.* Hairy biennial, 6–18 in. leaves and seed pods pointing skywards. Widespread and fairly common on limestone rocks, chalk grassland. May–August.

---

* This applies to all the family.

Violet Family *Violaceae*

Common Dog Violet, *Viola riviniana.* The most common of our violets. Pointed sepals, hairless, heart-shaped leaves, as broad as they are long, issuing from side branches. Lowest petal forms a pale, curved spur for nectar, notched at tip. Abundant in woods, on heaths and mountains. April–June.

Heath Dog Violet, *V. canina.* Bluer flowers, longer, slightly hairy leaves. Heaths, dunes. April–June.

Wild Pansy, Heartsease, *V. tricolor.* A variable annual, with leafy, deeply cut stipules at base of leaf stalks. Flowers vary in colour from purple to yellow. Frequent in cornfields and grass. April–September.

Sweet Violet, *Viola odorata.* The only scented British violet. Heart-shaped leaves, which, like the flowers, grow from the base. Varies in colour from violet to white, or even pink, yellow or apricot. Long runners. Common on hedge banks, woods, especially on chalk. February–April.

Wood Dog Violet, *V. reichenbachiana.* Smaller, narrower, paler than dog violet, with more pointed leaves and flowers that have straight, thin, unnotched spurs a shade darker than the petals. Flowers lilac to purplish. Common in southern woods, hedges. Rare in N. March–May.

Hairy Violet, *V. hirta.* Like an unscented sweet violet, hairy leaves, no runners, pale blue flowers. Common on chalk grassland and in woods. Rare Ireland. March–May.

Marsh Violet, *V. palustris.* Small creeping plant with rounded leaves, pale lilac flowers with rounded end to sepals. Acid marshes, fens, bogs, wet woods. April–July.

Milkwort Family *Polygalaceae*

Common Milkwort, *Polygala vulgaris.* Our most abundant milkwort, with alternate pointed leaves and flowers that may be blue, mauve, pink, white, and with a ripe capsule less

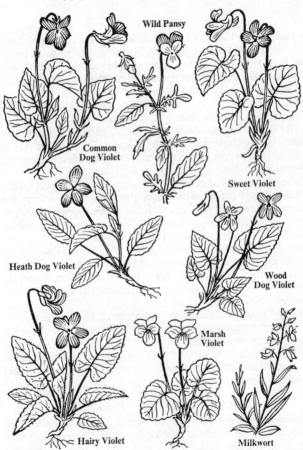

Wild Pansy

Common
Dog Violet

Sweet Violet

Heath Dog Violet

Wood
Dog Violet

Marsh
Violet

Hairy Violet

Milkwort

broad than that of the heath milkwort. Common especially on chalk grassland. May–September.

St John's Wort Family   *Hypericaceae*

Common St John's Wort, *Hypericum perforatum.* A hairless perennial, 1–2 ft. tall, with a specific name derived from the tiny transparent dots—oil-producing cells—on the leaves. 'Wort' means 'plant' or 'herb'. Most common member of its family. Black dots on yellow petals and often on pointed sepals. Common in hedge banks, thin scrub in S. Rare in N. July–September.

Slender St John's Wort, Elegant St John's Wort, *H. pulchrum.* A graceful plant of acid heathland; flowers tinged with red behind, and semi-heart shaped leaves in pairs. July–August.

Goosefoot Family   *Chenopodiaceae*

Fat Hen, *Chenopodium album.* Our most abundant Goosefoot, with toothed lower leaves, and flowers in spikes on an upright stem that may be tinged red. 1–3 ft. tall. Common on waste land. July–September.

Pink Family   *Caryophyllaceae*

Bladder Campion, *Silene vulgaris, S. cucubalus.* Distinguished by the hairless swollen calyx, net-veined, beneath the white—or occasionally pink—flowers, with 5 small deeply-cleft petals. Abundant in grassland and verges especially in the south. June–September.

Red Campion, *S. dioica, Melandrium dioicum, Lychnis dioica.* Unscented hairy perennial, with cluster of large bright pink flowers, short-toothed calyx. Common on roadside verges, in woods, cliffs, mountains. Rare East Anglia. April–late autumn.

Ragged Robin, *Lychnis flos-cuculi.* Easily identified by the divided red petals with 4 narrow, uneven lobes. Common on moist ground. May–July.

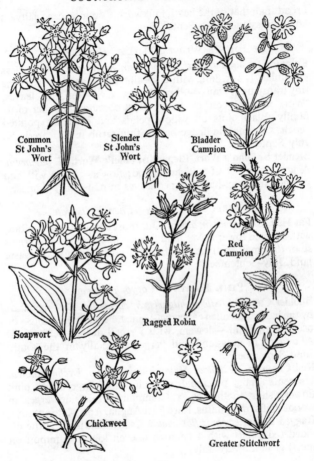

Common
St John's
Wort

Slender
St John's
Wort

Bladder
Campion

Soapwort

Ragged Robin

Red
Campion

Chickweed

Greater Stitchwort

44

Soapwort, *Saponaria officinalis* (Bouncing Bett). Perennial with creeping rhizome producing flowering stems 1–3 ft. high, with pink blooms one in. across. Common beside road-verges and streams.

Chickweed, *Stellaria media*. A common pest of gardeners, an annual, with small white flowers containing 3 to 7 stamens with red anthers and 5 sharply divided petals. A line of hairs down one side of rounded stem. Abundant where ground has been disturbed. January–December.

Greater Stitchwort, *S. holostea*. Prominent spring hedgerow plant with large white flowers containing petals cleft almost half way; 1–2 ft. high, unstalked narrow leaves with rough edges. Abundant in open woods, hedges. April–June.

MALLOW FAMILY *Malvaceae*

Common Mallow, *Malva sylvestris*. Attractive hairy perennial, 1–3 ft. high, ivy-like leaves sometimes with tiny black spot at base. Pink-purplish petals and numerous stamens joined in heart of flower, which may be over 1 in. broad, 'Cheese'-shaped fruits. Common in south by roadsides. June–September.

Musk Mallow, *Malva moschata*. Deeply divided leaves make identification simple. Pleasant pink flowers may be 2 in. broad. Hedge banks and verges. June–September.

GERANIUM FAMILY *Geraniaceae*

Meadow Cranesbill, *Geranium pratense*. Hairy perennial, 1–2 ft. high, with flowers a much brighter blue than those of other cranesbills. Reddish stalks to long deeply-lobed leaves. Upper stem leaves shorter, almost unstalked. Fairly common by roadsides. Rare Ireland and N. Scotland. June–September.

Bloody Cranesbill, *G. sanquineum*. Large crimson flowers on hairy stems, petals slightly notched, leaves deeply cut. Not

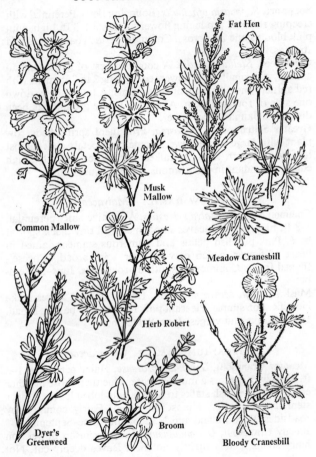

Fat Hen

Musk
Mallow

Common Mallow

Meadow Cranesbill

Herb Robert

Dyer's
Greenweed

Broom

Bloody Cranesbill

46

common. Prefers dry limestone rocks or sand. June–August.

Herb Robert, *Geranium robertianum.* This annual is a familiar occupant of semi-shaded hedge banks, woods and stony sites throughout Britain. Hairy stems and green leaves may be reddish-tinged and produce an unattractive smell. Distinguished from other cranesbills by triangular fernlike leaves and rounded edge to petals. April–October.

Pea Family *Papilionaceae*

Dyer's Greenweed, *Genista tinctoria.* Attractive undershrub about 12 in. tall, often found on verges, heaths and other grassy places on chalk or clay in England, Wales or, less often, in Scotland. Not in Ireland. Formerly cultivated in Britain for its green-yellowish dye. Small slender leaves; smaller flowers than broom. June–August.

Broom, *Sarothamnus scoparius.* Like a miniature prickless gorse, with small, often three-lobed leaves that may drop early in the year. Bears a dense mass of brilliant yellow flowers, often two to a stem; hairy pods; angular stems. Much used through the centuries for broom-making, medicine, and as an antidote to witches. Visited by bees for its pollen, but harbours no honey. After the insect has flown, the petals remain apart with withered style and stamens exposed—a sign that no pollen remains for other visitors. Acid soils, May–June.

Dwarf Furze or Lesser Gorse, or Petty Whin, *Ulex minor.* Shorter, softer and less prickly spines than *Ulex europaeus*, and smaller flowers which appear in July, August and September. Heaths and moors in E. Rare in W; not in Ireland.

Gorse, *Ulex europaeus.* This common prickly shrub will grow as high as 8 ft., forming a useful barrier against encroachment on vulnerable sites such as sandhills or wet heathland. Winter food for New Forest ponies. Sound of hairy pods exploding can often be heard in summer heat. Does well on Downs, but prefers light, lime free soils. Blaze of yellow flowers in March–June said to have brought Linnaeus to his knees in thanksgiving to God.

Petty Whin or Needle Furze, *Genista anglica*. A smaller spiny undershrub, with attractive yellow flowers in spikes; spines on stem; small oval leaves; edge of wet habitats on acid heaths and moors, but uncommon; not in Ireland. May–July.

Common Bird's-foot, *Ornithopus perpusillus*. A slender downy annual with groups of beaked pods not unlike a bird's claw, hence the name. Leaves and pale shade of the yellow flowers distinguish from bird's-foot trefoil. Widespread and common on dry gravel and sandstone sites. May–August.

Bird's-foot Trefoil, *Lotus corniculatus* (Bacon-and-eggs, Fingers and Thumbs, Lady's Slipper, Tom Thumb, Lady's Fingers, and 60 other local names!) Easily distinguished from its relatives, as our drawings show. Abundant in dry grassland. May–September.

Rest-harrow, *Ononis repens*. The specific name reveals it as a creeping plant. It is also tough, 'arresting the harrow' with its stems. Flowers pink, with 10 stamens joined. Common on chalk grassland, where the pink pea-like flowers lie within 12 in. of the ground. June–September.

Tufted Vetch, *Vicia cracca*. An attractive hairy perennial with long stalks bearing tendrils and, on one side, abundant bright blue-violet flowers. Common on grassy sites throughout the country. June–August.

Red Clover, *Trifolium pratense*. Our most common red clover, with upper leaves—but not the lower ones—almost without stalks. Large stipules at base of leaves. Sweet scented flowers attract many bees which find good nectar for honey. Abundant in grassland. May–October.

White Clover, or Dutch Clover, *Trifolium repens* (Kentish Clover). Small, low, hairless perennial, with pale band across the finely toothed leaflets. White flowers, though they some-

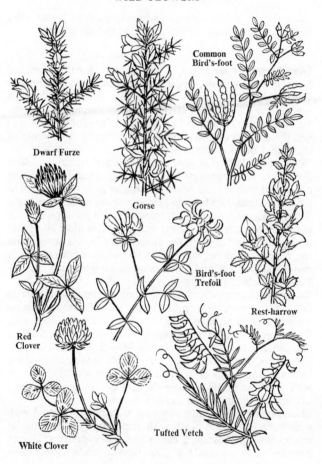

Dwarf Furze

Common Bird's-foot

Gorse

Red Clover

Bird's-foot Trefoil

Rest-harrow

White Clover

Tufted Vetch

times show a pinkish shade and normally turn brown after blooming. Abundant on grasslands. May–September.

ROSE FAMILY *Rosaceae*

Herb Bennet, Wood Avens, *Geum urbanum.* A hairy perennial found in damp ground, especially near woods and hedgebanks. Green lobes alternating with the sepals, which are about as long as the 5 spreading petals. Red styles and many stamens. Hooks on each fruit tend to be caught in the fur of mammals and the feathers of birds, thereby assisting the distribution of the seed. Common. June–August.

Silver-weed, *Potentilla anserina.* No other common yellow flower has silvery pinnate leaves. Among a number of plants associated with ground heavily grazed by geese. Much used in past as medicinal herb. Even placed in shoes to keep feet comfortable! Roots, treated like roasted or boiled parsnips, eaten in the Hebrides. I find it puzzling that while it is often silvery on both sides of leaves or on the underside only, it is never so on the upper part alone. Some good textbooks say 'Common in damp grassy places' and others insist that it likes a dry habitat. Both are right. May–August.

Tormentil, *P. erecta.* A slender, trailing perennial whose stems fail to form roots, with an attractive yellow flower containing 4 sepals and petals compared with 5 on Creeping Cinquefoil. Roots were once a favoured cure for diarrhoea among children and cattle. Abundant on acid soils. May–September.

Creeping Cinquefoil, *P. reptans.* Palmate leaves all on long stalks, and generally deserving its name 'five-leaved'. Flowers, with 5 yellow petals, double the size of Tormentil blooms. Common in waste places. June–September.

Meadowsweet, *Filipendula ulmaria.* A hairless perennial with strong stems, 2–4 ft. tall, with dense upright clusters of creamish-white flowers. 5 petals and many stamens. Silvery complexion to underside of green pinnate leaves. Sweet scent

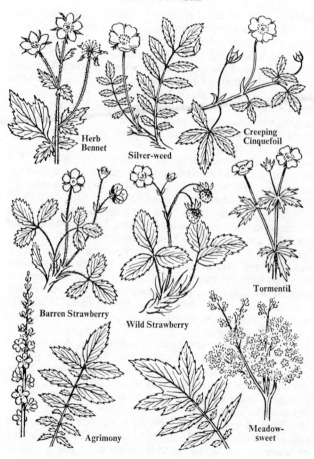

Herb
Bennet

Silver-weed

Creeping
Cinquefoil

Barren Strawberry

Wild Strawberry

Tormentil

Agrimony

Meadow-
sweet

51

attractive to insects. Frequent in damp meadows, woods, fens, ill-drained verges of country roads. June–September.

Barren Strawberry, *Potentilla sterilis.* Generally smaller than the wild strawberry, with space between the white petals, whereas those of the wild strawberry seem to touch. Dull, dry fruits. Earlier than wild strawberry. Common on dry hedgebanks, in woods and scrub. February–May.

Wild Strawberry, *Fragaria vesca.* Perrennial, like a miniature garden strawberry, with pleasant juicy fruits much liked by birds and children. Common in open woods and around hedgerows. April–July.

Agrimony, *Agrimonia eupatoria.* A tall, slender perennial, 1–2 ft. high, with pinnate leaves and small yellow flowers in tapering spikes, and lacking the green lobes alternating with the sepals-epicalyx—characteristic of the rose family. Like those of herb bennet, the fruits have small hooks designed to aid distribution via animal fur and feathers. Long used as a cure for colds and adder bites! June–August.

Field Rose, *Rosa arvensis.* The long styles joined in the heart of the unscented, creamy-white flowers, with their many yellow stamens, ease the task of identification. Pinnate leaves and hooked prickles on trailing stems. No sepals on smooth red hips which are smaller than those of the dog rose. Common in hedges, copses, open woodlands in S., local in N. and in Ireland. June–August.

Burnet Rose, *R. pimpinellifolia. R. spinosissima.* A shrub only 6–24 in. in height, sending out suckers that produce prickly branched stems. Creamy-white scented flowers usually borne singly, and the undivided sepals remain on the dark purple hips. Locally common on mountains, downs, dunes and heaths especially near the coast. Uncommon in S.E. May–September.

Dog Rose, *R. canina.* The most frequent, and variable, wild rose of S. England, standing 4–10 ft. high, with large pale pink or white flowers whose scent is attractive to many insects, though no nectar is produced. A pair of flat stipules with minute pin-shaped glands, on the bottom of the leaf stalk. Unlike the field rose, the styles are not joined. Red hips, shedding the sepals before ripening, a valuable source of vitamin C. Common in hedgerows, thickets south of the Border. June–July.

Sweet Brier, *R. rubiginosa.* An attractive small shrub with bright pink or occasionally white flowers, and leaves that produce a sweet fragrance w en rubbed. Common in woods, scrub and hedges on chalk or limestone in S; rare in Scotland, local in Ireland.

STONECROP FAMILY *Crassulaceae*

Yellow Stonecrop, Wall-pepper, *Sedum acre.* Our most abundant member of this family, with a mat of short stems, stout yellow-green leaves with a bitter, peppery taste, hence the specific name *acre* or 'bitter'. 2–4 in. high on walls, roofs, dunes, beaches and other dry sites. June–July.

Wall Pennywort, *Umbilicus rupestris.* A strange fleshy perennial—Dandy navelwort to some countrymen—2–12 in. high, with rounded, toothed leaves growing from stalk below a central dimple. Bell-shaped greenish flowers with 5 small sepals and 5 teeth on corolla tube. Not uncommon, especially near Western coasts, on rocks, walls, banks. June–August.

LOOSESTRIFE FAMILY *Lythraceae*

Purple Loosestrife, *Lythrum salicaria.* A beautiful water-side plant, not unlike rosebay willow herb, and no relation to yellow loosestrife, standing 2–4 ft. high. Slender-petalled, bright red-purple flowers arranged in whorls, some with style and stamens half of medium length and half short; another variety has a style of medium length with variable stamens; and others have short style and long or medium-sized stamens. Widespread especially in fens and marshes. June–August.

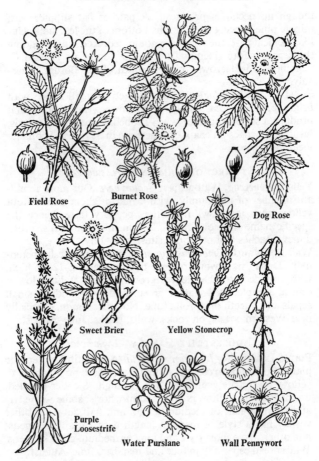

Field Rose

Burnet Rose

Dog Rose

Sweet Brier

Yellow Stonecrop

Purple
Loosestrife

Water Purslane

Wall Pennywort

54

Water Purslane, *Peplis portula.* A hairless annual, with creeping and rooting stems and thick leaves often faintly reddish like the stalks. Tiny unstalked green flowers produced in the leaf axils. 6-pointed calyx teeth, 6 pink petals—or none at all—and 6-12 stamens. Widespread and moderately common outside Scotland on damp sites. Not on chalk or limestone. June–September.

WILLOW HERB FAMILY *Onagraceae*

Broad-leaved Willow Herb, *Epilobium montanum.* Thin stem, 1–2 ft. high, broad lanceolate leaves and 4-lobed stigma. Sharply toothed leaves opposite. Flowers have 4 pink-purplish petals, 4 short and 4 long stamens, and 4 lobed stigma. Fruit splits into 4 parts when ripe, drifting with wind from woods, hedges and cultivated ground. June–August.

Rosebay Willow Herb, *E. angustifolium. Chamaenerion angustifolium.* Familiar perennial, up to 5 ft. high, narrow lanceolate alternate leaves, tapering spikes of pinkish-purple flowers; stamens long and drooping, petals unequal. Long capsules release fluffy seeds that carry far in wind to woodland clearings, waste and burnt ground. Often on bomb sites. July–September.

Great Hairy Willow Herb, *E. hirsutum* (Codlins and Cream). 4 ft. high, hairy, sessile leaves, all opposite, growing from near base of stem. Pollen dispersed before 4-lobed stigma is fully developed, hence need for cross-pollination by bees and hoverflies. Common in ditches, stream banks. July–August.

UMBELLIFER FAMILY *Umbelliferae*

Cow Parsley, *Anthriscus sylvestris,* Our most abundant springtime umbellifer of roadside verges and hedgerows. Perennial, 2–4 ft. tall, with hollow grooved stems, green pinnate, fernlike leaves, broader and more dissected than those of hedge parsley. Petals in outer flowers differ in size. April–June.

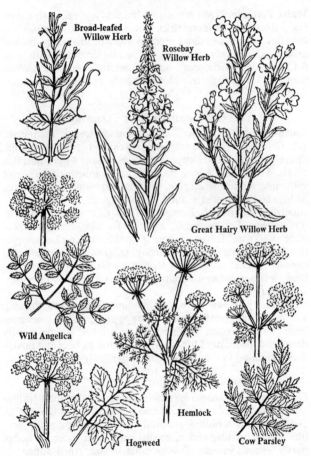

Broad-leafed Willow Herb

Rosebay Willow Herb

Great Hairy Willow Herb

Wild Angelica

Hemlock

Hogweed

Cow Parsley

Hemlock, *Conium maculatum.* Our only white umbellifer with hollow, purple-spotted—and very poisonous—stems and an unattractive smell. 3–7 ft. tall. Delicate-looking finely-cut 2–5 pinnate leaves. Frequent on damp roadsides, banks of streams, especially in S. May–August.

Wild Angelica, *Angelica sylvestris.* Stout perennial, 2–5 ft. tall larger lower leaves may have leaflets arranged in threes. Usually no bracts under compound umbels. 2–3 pinnate leaves downy below. Large umbels of white flowers may be softly tinged pinkish. Long stamens. Common in damp woods, fens, grassland. June–September.

Hogweed, *Heracleum sphondylium* (Cow Parsnip). Our most numerous white umbellifer of summer and autumn. 2–6 ft. high. Broad, hairy lobed leaflets on stalks with broad sheath. White or pinkish-tinged flowers with outer petals of various sizes. Roadsides, fields, open grassland. April–October.

Upright Hedge Parsley, *Torilis japonica.* A tall thin plant, last of the familiar medium-sized umbellifers to flower, which bears its long-stalked white flowers on solid, hairy stems. Common on roadsides and hedge banks. July–September.

Wild Carrot, *Daucus carota.* Feathery bracts below the compound umbels betray this typical carrot, with dense umbels of dark-white flowers, those in the centre tinged red. Fruits flattened, oval, and bristly. Common in fields and roadsides. June–September.

Fool's Water-cress, *Apium nodiflorum. A. repens* (Marshwort). A hairless perennial, 1–3 ft. tall, with white flowers in compound umbels without stalks, or with very short ones. Leaves resemble watercress. Egg-shaped fruit. Common in ponds, streams, ditches. June–September.

Ground Elder or **Goutweed,** *Aegopodium podograria.* A hairless creeping perennial, much disliked by gardeners. 1–2 ft. high, grooved hollow stems. Broad lanceolate leaflets. No bracts beneath umbels of white flowers. All too common in

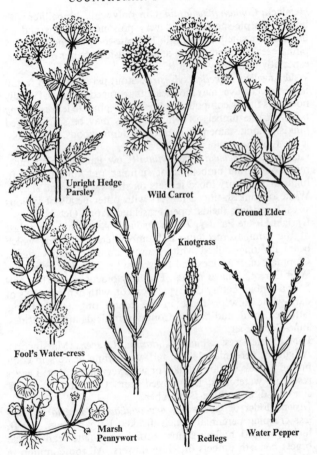

Upright Hedge
Parsley

Wild Carrot

Ground Elder

Knotgrass

Fool's Water-cress

Marsh
Pennywort

Redlegs

Water Pepper

shady places, roadside verges, throughout Britain. May–September.

Marsh Pennywort, *Hydrocotyle vulgaris*. Differs from other umbellifers in its undivided round leaves, joined in the centre to the stalk, and it is often classified in a separate family of its own. Inconspicuous whorls of tiny pink-white flowers sheltered by round slightly-lobed leaves. Widespread in bogs and marshes especially on acid heaths. June–August.

DOCK FAMILY *Polygonaceae*

Knotgrass, *Polygonum aviculare*. A thin much-branched annual 2–12 in. long, with unequal lanceolate leaves, white stipules encircling the prostrate or upright stem and the small pink or white flowers lurking between leaf and stalk. A common weed of waste places and the sea shore. June–September.

Redlegs or **Spotted Persicaria**, *P. persicaria*. An annual 6–18 in. tall, distinguished by its red stems and dark mark in the middle of the thin lanceolate leaves which are sometimes silky beneath. Flowering spikes frequently in pairs. Common on damp waste ground. June–September. *P. nodosum*, also sometimes called Spotted Persicaria, or Knotted P., is bushier, and has pink flowers, spotted stems and sometimes yellow glands on underside of leaves.

Water Pepper, *P. hydropiper*. A small semi-hairless annual, 9–24 in. high, which earns its name from the flavour of the leaves. Sheaths protect the stem where the slender leaves emerge. Small greenish-white flowers in a thin spike, with the 3 sepals dotted with yellow glands. Small dark fruits. Common in ditches except in N. Scotland. July–September.

Common Sorrel, *Rumex acetosa*. An erect perennial 6 in.–3 ft. tall, with slender arrow-shaped leaves on a long stalk that can be eaten in salads. Outer sepals of unisexual flowers reflexed. Common in meadows throughout Britain. May–July.

Sheep's Sorrel, *R. acetosella*. Much smaller than Common

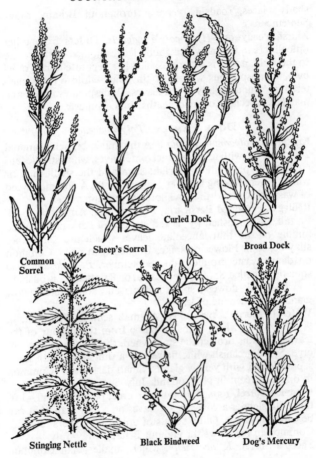

Curled Dock

Broad Dock

Sheep's Sorrel

Common Sorrel

Stinging Nettle

Black Bindweed

Dog's Mercury

Sorrel—3–10 in. high—with stalked spear-shaped leaves lobed at the base. Leafless flower spikes in whorls that redden as they age. Common on grassland and heaths, especially the poorer acid soils. May–August.

Curled Dock, *Rumex crispus.* Defined under the Agriculture Act, 1947 as an obnoxious weed—like the species below—this most common perennial has wavy lanceolate leaves, curled at the edges, and stands up to 3 ft. high. Oval fruit sepals with 1 wart—or 3 near coast. Abundant on waste lands. June–September.

Broad Dock, *R. obtusifolius.* The toughest of the two most common docks, 1–3 ft. tall, with big, broad leaves that are the country child's remedy for nettle stings. Formerly used by villagers as a cool wrapping for butter. Fruit sepals triangular, toothed, with a single wart. June–September.

Black Bindweed, *Polygonum convolvulus.* A prostrate or climbing annual which may grow 3 feet, twining clockwise whereas the true Bindweeds grow anti-clockwise. Heart-shaped leaves resemble those of the latter, but its flowers are utterly different, being small, pinkish-green and on short stalks. Dark triangular nuts. Common on waste ground and fields. June–October.

NETTLE FAMILY *Urticaceae*

Stinging Nettle, *Urtica dioica.* A familiar perennial of disturbed ground, with coarse stinging hairs housing an acid that inflicts a painful sensation if the protective tip is broken off. Male and female flowers on different plants. A useful substitute for spinach, if cooked when young, and the heart-shaped leaves are also a favourite food for some colourful butterflies. June–September.

SPURGE FAMILY *Euphorbiaceae*

Dog's Mercury, *Mercurialis perennis.* A hairy creeping perennial with unbranched stems issuing from a straggling rhizome.

Male and female flowers, greenish in shade, on different plants. Pollination by wind. Height varies from a few inches to several feet. Common in woods and hedgerows, including beechwoods. February–May.

Sun Spurge, *Euphorbia helioscopia.* A smooth yellow-green annual, 4–12 in. tall, and distinguished from its relatives by the toothed leaves. Bracts leaf-like. Yellow flowers protected by round green lobes. Rich in a milky juice. Common in fields, gardens, waste land. April–November.

Wood Spurge, *E. amygdaloides.* A familiar occupant of south-country woods, with slender lanceolate leaves, often faintly reddish, and flowers, which appear in the second year, massed in the middle of the stem. Crescent-shaped glands on each flower cup, composed of bracts joined together in pairs and protecting many yellowish-green male flowers together with one female flower. 1–2 ft. high. March–June. Common in S.

HEATH FAMILY *Ericaceae*

Ling, *Calluna vulgaris.* The familiar evergreen undershrub, less than 2 ft. tall, which adds so much beauty to our moorlands in late summer. Much visited by bees, which find flowers containing 8 stamens, each with a pair of tiny flaps at the base of the anthers. Dies off at about 24 years, after regenerating itself with new stock around the ageing plant. Successfully competes against most rival species, but too often dominated by bracken after heath fires. Abundant on heaths, moors and bogs. July–September.

Bell Heather, *Erica cinerea.* An evergreen undershrub up to 2 ft. high, with smooth leaves in whorls of 3 and smaller leaves bunched at the base. Bell-shaped corolla houses 8 stamens with 2 toothed flaps under the anthers. Flowers in long spikes, and a deeper pink than those of Cross-Leaved Heath. Abundant on drier moors. June–September.

Cross-leafed Heath, *Erica tetralix.* Distinguished from Bell

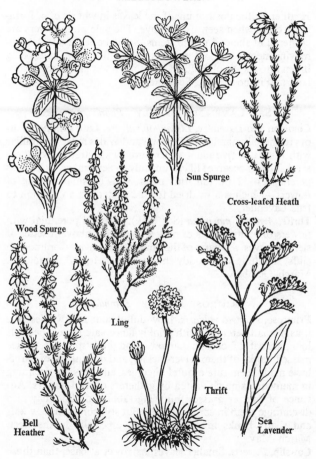

Wood Spurge

Sun Spurge

Cross-leafed Heath

Ling

Bell Heather

Thrift

Sea Lavender

Heather by the positioning of the leaves in whorls of 4, forming a cross when seen from above. The pale pink flowers are clustered at the end of the stems. Some bees are adept at removing nectar without pollinating the flower, a hole being bitten into the corolla tube. Common on wet and damp heathland and in bogs. June–September.

SEA-LAVENDER FAMILY *Plumbaginaceae*

Common Sea-Lavender, *Limonium vulgare*. Late summer visitors to the salt marshes of England and Wales must be familiar with this attractive plant which turns wide stretches of these areas into an ocean of lilac from July to September. A hairless perennial 4–12 in. tall, this plant, with its small throng of flowers—which can be dried for the winter—is no relation to true Lavender.

Thrift, *Armeria maritima* (Sea Pink). A tufted perennial with flowers of many shades of pink a few inches above rosettes of slender leaves. All parts of the flowers are in fives. Common on cliffs, sandhills and muddy shores, and on inland mountains. March–October.

PRIMROSE FAMILY *Primulaceae*

Primrose, *Primula vulgaris*. How dull it sounds if we describe it as a small perennial with crinkly lanceolate leaves, pedicels long, throat of corolla narrow. And how splendid to see massed banks of them. Over-picking and digging up of plants have made them rare around big cities, and they are declining in many areas much visited by gatherers of wild flowers. Advance of coarser grasses following rabbits' decline may also discourage them in some districts. But still common in woods and shady banks in most counties, especially in the west. March–May.

Cowslip, *P. veris*. Smaller leaves, narrower at base, than those

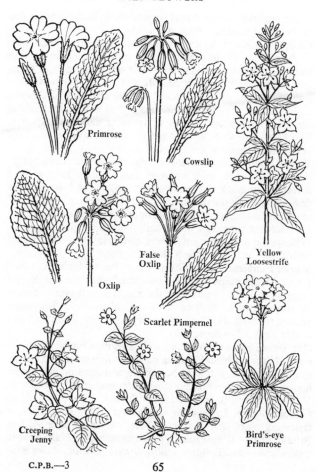

Primrose

Cowslip

Oxlip

False
Oxlip

Yellow
Loosestrife

Scarlet Pimpernel

Creeping
Jenny

Bird's-eye
Primrose

of the primrose. Small flowers in umbels on leafless stalks. Prefers chalk, limestone, clay. April–May.

Oxlip, *P. elatior*. Like a small primrose, with flowers drooping in the manner of the cowslip. They grow on a common stem that may be 12 in. tall. Damp woods on chalky clay of Cambridgeshire, Bedfordshire, Suffolk and Essex. April–May.

False Oxlip, *P. veris X vulgaris*. Hybrid offspring of Cowslip and Primrose. The flowers are bigger and paler than those of the true Cowslip, and the leaves are more hairy and tapering. The stem tends to be shorter and the flowers a richer shade of yellow than those of the true Oxlip.

Yellow Loosestrife, *Lysimachia vulgaris*. An attractive perennial, 2–4 ft. high, with opposite and whorled lance-shaped leaves, often black-dotted, on short stalks. The bright yellow flowers have five sepals united and revealing five teeth with red margins, and the red stamens are opposite the petals. Regarded since Roman times as a useful herb to ward off flies and gnats. Widespread and common in fens, riverside areas and around ponds, particularly in the S. July–August.

Scarlet Pimpernel, *Anagallis arvensis* (Poor Man's Weatherglass). An apt name for this little annual, since the red flowers close as soon as clouds hide the sun. These flowers—exceptionally white or various shades of blue—have 5 stamens around the style. Petals slightly hairy. Common in gardens and arable land. May–September.

Bird's-eye Primrose, *Primula farinosa* (Bonny Birdseye). A delightful little perennial bearing soft-pink flowers with a yellow eye in an umbel a few inches above a rosette of pale green leaves. Locally common on moist sites, generally limestone in N. England and S. Scotland. May–June.

Creeping Jenny, *Lysimachia nummularia* (Herb Tuppence). A charming plant that has never been known to bear seed in Britain. Leaves almost round, hence its name, for Nummularia means 'coin-like'. Bell-like yellow flowers on short stalks issuing from the runners that must be responsible for its reproduction. Damp woods and gardens. May–August.

Gentian Family *Gentianaceae*

Felwort, *Gentiana amarella*. A hairless biennial—or exceptionally an annual—2–12 in. tall, with spikes of purple, bell-shaped flowers. The calyx and corolla have 5, or occasionally 4, equal lobes. There is a fringe of hairs inside the corolla tube. Frequent on chalk and limestone turf in some districts. August–October.

Marsh Gentian, *Gentiana pneumonanthe*. A beautiful rare plant of damp acid heaths, liable to fluctuate in numbers on particular sites for reasons not adequately explained. A weak hairless perennial with opposite slender leaves, it bears a rich blue trumpet-shaped flower that may be 1–2 in. long. The flowers are usually carried singly on stems 3–9 in. tall, but I have known many individuals to bear five, six and seven blooms on a single stem, and one plant on a Sussex Naturalist's Trust Reserve bore 9 flowers on one stem. Local and declining in England and Wales. July–October.

Common Centaury, *Centaurium erythraea*. A charming hairless annual, 2–12 in. tall, with pink unstalked flowers in terminal clusters on short branches rising from a rosette of leaves. The latter have 3 distinct veins and are a trifle bigger than the stem leaves. A widespread and locally common species of dry grassland, woods, quarries, especially in the S. June–September.

Yellow-wort, *Blackstonia perfoliata*. An attractive species with bright yellow flowers, much larger than the pink blooms of centuary, and with up to 8 sepals, petals and stamens instead of the 4 or 5 that its relatives generally possess. Broad greygreen leaves joined at the base. Widespread but local on chalk and limestone grassland. June–October.

BORAGE FAMILY *Boraginaceae*

Small Bugloss, *Lycopsis arvensis*. Annual, 12–18 in. in height, with wavy spear-shaped leaves as rough and bristly as an ox's tongue—hence the name 'Bugloss' or 'ox-tongued'. Clusters of almost unstalked blue flowers which have their corolla-tube kinked at the base, unlike those of other members of this family. Common on sand-dunes, fields and other open light land all over Britain. May–September.

Water Forget-me-not, *Myositis scorpioides*. A light-green creeping perennial which sends short-haired leaves growing along damp, shady ground, and which produces little clusters of typically forgetmenot flowers, though larger than those of some of its relatives—¼ in. Their shade varies from pink to pale or deep blue. Common on wet sites. May–September.

Common Forget-me-not, *M. arvensis*. Small light-blue flowers, with coralla tubes shorter than the calyx, are produced by this familiar annual of dry or disturbed ground, particularly around woods and hedge banks. The flowering stem only gradually uncurls as the flowers begin to bloom, hence the local name Field Scorpion Grass—after the scorpion's curled tail. April–September.

Comfrey, *Symphytum officinale*. Yet another medicinal herb, as the specific name confirms. The roots of this perennial were long used for poultices and the leaves, made into a tea, were said to relieve bronchitis. It stands 2–4 ft. high, with broad spear-shaped leaves and bell-like flowers that may be pink, white, cream, mauve, blue or purple. It prefers damp shade in the vicinity of streams, rivers and ditches. May–July.

BINDWEED FAMILY *Convolvulaceae*

Small Bindweed, *Convolvulus arvensis*. The pink and white cone-shaped flowers, an inch in width, and the arrow-shaped leaves make this twining or prostrate perennial easily recog-

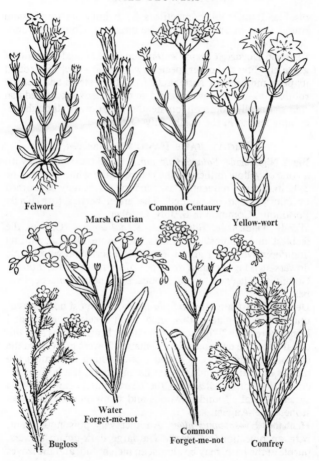

Felwort

Marsh Gentian

Common Centaury

Yellow-wort

Bugloss

Water
Forget-me-not

Common
Forget-me-not

Comfrey

69

nisable. It may kill competitors by twining its tough stem round them in an anti-clockwise direction. Common. June–September.

Common Dodder, *Cuscuta epithymum*. An annual parasite of gorse and ling and other species, twining anti-clockwise round its prey and drawing sustenance from their stems and not the roots. Pink-white flowers amid a thick network of reddish stems. Locally common on heaths and downs, though becoming less so in the north. July–October.

NIGHTSHADE FAMILY *Solanaceae*

Black Nightshade, *Solanum nigrum*. A small bushy annual with a cone of yellow anthers in the centre of the white flower. The 2–12 in. stem is frequently dark, and the leaves may be toothed or faintly lobed or pointed. The green berries turn black. Poisonous. Common in S. July–October.

Woody Nightshade, Bittersweet, *S. dulcamara*. 'One of the feeblest and poorest of twiners,' to quote Darwin, curling 'indifferently to the right or left.' It is a perennial with purple flowers strikingly similar to those of its relative, the potato. Common in hedgerows and woods. Poisonous. June–September.

Deadly Nightshade, *Atropa bella-donna*. The most notorious of our poisonous plants, this uncommon species is a tall and bushy perennial 2–6 ft. tall, sometimes bearing leaves of unequal size. The dark purple bell-shaped flowers grow from the end of the leaf stalks. It is most often found near ruins, the monks of medieval monasteries having found it a herb worth cultivating for its effects on the heart, muscles and nervous system. Usually found in woods and scrub on chalk or limestone. June–August.

Henbane, *Hyoscyamus niger*. Another very poisonous plant, with an objectionable smell. The large dark-cream flowers, purple at the base, may be almost an inch broad, and the leaves

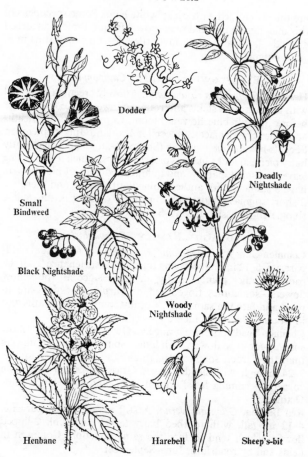

Dodder

Deadly
Nightshade

Small
Bindweed

Black Nightshade

Woody
Nightshade

Henbane

Harebell

Sheep's-bit

are thickly clothed with sticky white hairs. Some specimens of this uncommon biennial may grow 4 ft. tall. Prefers disturbed ground—farmyards are a favourite site—on sandy soils in S. June–August.

BELLFLOWER FAMILY *Campanulaceae*

Harebell, *Campanula rotundifolia.* A lovely creeping perennial with underground stems and rounded lower leaves that wither before the soft blue flowers bloom. Common on dry heaths and other grassy places. Bluebell in Scotland. July–September.

Sheep's-bit, *Jasione montana* (Sheep's Scabious). This slightly hairy biennial looks like a typical scabious, which it is not. The leaves are small, narrow and oblong, and the soft blue flowers have 5 stamens with anthers joined at the base, and there are 2 short stigmas. Widespread but local on acid heaths, cliffs, shingle and grassland. May–September.

SNAPDRAGON FAMILY *Scrophulariaceae*

Common Cow-Wheat, *Melampyrum pratense.* An annual semi-parasite, 6–12 in. tall, deriving much of its sustenance from the roots of other plants. Easily identified since all the yellow flowers—sometimes tinged red or purple or white—are in pairs and face the same way. Locally common on heaths and in woods. May–September.

Common Toadflax, *Linaria vulgaris.* Our most abundant yellow snapdragon-type flower, with longer spurs and smaller flowers than the garden snapdragon. A hairless perennial, it stands 9–24 in. high, with slender leaves. Grass banks and odd waste corners, becoming less frequent in N. and in Ireland. July–October.

Red Bartsia, *Odontites verna.* A stiff, straight semi-parasite, 4–12 in. tall, with toothed hairy leaves and pink 2-lipped flowers which tend to face the same direction. Common in fields and by roadsides. June–September.

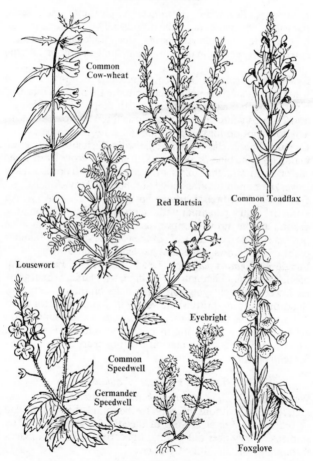

Common
Cow-wheat

Red Bartsia

Common Toadflax

Lousewort

Eyebright

Common
Speedwell

Germander
Speedwell

Foxglove

73

Lousewort, *Pedicularis sylvatica.* A pleasant small semi-parasitic perennial of damp heaths, usually no more than 6 in. high with toothed pinnate leaves. Deep pink flowers in leafy spikes. Fairly common on damp heathland and moors. April–July.

Eyebright, *Euphrasia nemorosa.* Another semi-parasite of heathland, a small annual often no more than an inch or two high—though it can grow 10 in.—with deeply-toothed leaves, and 2-lipped white flowers often flushed red or violet and with a yellow spot on lower lip. Common. June–September.

Common Speedwell, *Veronica officinalis.* A small hairy perennial. The light blue or near pinkish flowers grow from short stalks or in straight spikes in the leaf axils. Toothed hairy leaves. Common on grasslands and heaths. May–August.

Germander Speedwell, Birdseye Speedwell, *V. chamaedrys.* An attractive hairy perennial with stems that advance along the ground before growing upwards. Long-stalked bright blue flowers emerge from the axils of the toothed leaves. A familiar plant of hedgerows, fields and gardens. March–July.

Foxglove, *Digitalis purpurea* (Dead Man's Bells, Fairy Thimbles). An upright biennial, 2–5 ft. high, with large, broad, greyish lower leaves carrying soft white hairs on their underparts. Big drooping pink-purplish flowers, 2 in. long, with 2 long and 2 short stamens and a thin style. Widespread and abundant on acid soils, often appearing in cleared woodland. Poisonous. The drug digitalis much used in treating heart disease. June–September.

THYME FAMILY *Labiatae*

Water Mint, *Mentha aquatica.* A most common hairy perennial, identified without difficulty by the rounded heads of lilac or reddish flowers at the top of the stiff 9–24 in. stems. The stamens usually peer out beyond the corolla-tube. Wet places throughout Britain. July–October.

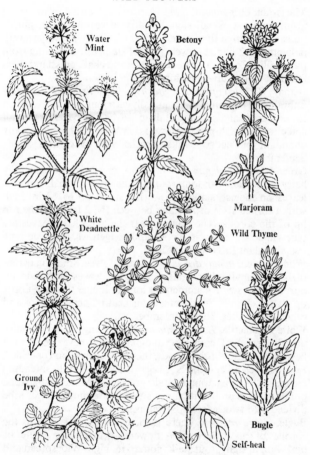

Water Mint

Betony

Marjoram

White Deadnettle

Wild Thyme

Ground Ivy

Self-heal

Bugle

Marjoram, *Origanum vulgare.* A perennial with a pronounced aromatic scent. Small slightly hairy leaves and dark purple buds at the top of the 1–2 ft. stem gradually giving way to very pale purple. 2-lipped flowers, with 4 stamens protruding from the corolla. Common in hedge banks and chalk grassland. Less frequent in N. July–September.

Betony, *Betonica officinalis, Stachys officinalis.* A faintly hairy unbranched perennial, 6–24 in. tall, with long, slightly toothed lower leaves, and small unstalked leaves just beneath the tall spike of reddish-purple flowers. Widespread and locally abundant on hedge banks, heaths and in woods. June–September.

Ground Ivy, *Glechoma hederacea.* A creeping and generally hairy perennial, with long rooting runners and small rounded leaves on longish stalks. Flowering stems up to 12 in. high with a forked style protruding between the 2 lobes of the top lip of the corolla. The flowers near the axil of the leaves are blue-violet. Common in woods and hedgerows, but becoming less abundant in N. March–June.

Wild Thyme, *Thymus drucei.* A prostrate sweet-smelling perennial with small, short-stalked opposite leaves and reddish-purple flowers with 4 stamens as long or longer than the upper lip of the corolla. Widespread on heaths, hedge banks and other grassy sites. June–September.

White Deadnettle, *Lamium album.* It is strange how this hairy upright perennial, common though it is, has never penetrated beyond the edges of the woods, though it thrives on roadsides. Local in Ireland and the N. of Scotland. 1–2 ft. tall, spreading by means of long tough, underground stems. Heart-shaped pointed leaves and white flowers with a prominent lower lobe divided into two. March–November.

Bugle, *Ajuga reptans.* There is virtually no upper lip to the corolla of these deep blue flowers—occasionally white or pink—on upright stout stalks some 6 in. high. Widespread and abundant in damp woods and commons all over Britain. May–July.

Self-heal, *Prunella vulgaris.* A short creeping perennial with an upright stem 4–12 in. high bearing violet—or pale pinkish—flowers, with hairs on the calyx and bracts. Long praised as a useful substitute for a doctor, hence the name. Very common—as the specific name *vulgaris* implies—in woods and grassland. June–September.

BEDSTRAW FAMILY *Rubiaceae*

Heath Bedstraw, *Galium hercynicum. G. saxatile.* A small creeping plant, barely six in. high, with whorls of 4–6 sharply pointed leaves, and small white flowers with a sickly fragrance. Abundant on acid sandy heaths, and on some grassland. June–August.

Goosegrass, *G. aparine* (Cleavers). A straggling annual, 1–4 ft. in length, that clings to its neighbours—and which distributes its fruit by attaching them to the fur of passing animals—which flourishes in hedgerows, fields and woods throughout Britain. Inconspicuous white flowers, with 4 petals, 4 corolla lobes and 4 stamens. Well liked by geese and other poultry, hence the name. May–August.

TEASEL FAMILY *Dipsacaceae*

Wild Teasel, *Dipsacus fullonum.* A handsome sturdy perennial beloved of goldfinches and marsh tits, with broad, prickly hollow stems that I have known to grow nearly 7 ft. high. The flowers of this biennial are pale purple and they often linger on the brown dead stems thoughout the winter. Locally common in wild corners of the S. July–September.

Devil's-bit Scabious, *Succisa pratensis.* A somewhat hairy perennial 1–3 ft. tall, with more or less untoothed leaves and florets of equal length, unlike the Field Scabious and Small Scabious. The lower leaves are long and narrow, the higher leaves small and slender. The rootstock is so short that country people of the past suspected it had been bitten off by the Devil, hence the plant's name. Attractive dark bluish-purple flowers protected by hairy bracts, and with purple or pink anthers. Abundant in damp grassland, heaths, and woods. July–October.

DAISY FAMILY *Compositae*

Golden Rod, *Solidago virgaurea.* A pleasant faintly downy perennial ranging in size from a few inches to 2 ft., with slender slightly toothed leaves and small yellow flowers in branched spikes. Locally common in dry woods, on heaths and hedge banks. Uncommon in S.E. July–September.

Common Ragwort, *Senecio jacobaea.* A perennial, up to 4 ft. tall, with many flower-heads each with some 15 ray florets. Distinguished from other ragworts by having two kinds of downy fruits—smooth or hairy. Widespread and abundant especially in dry chalk grassland, or sandy soils. June–October.

Common Groundsel, *S. vulgaris.* A familiar weed of disturbed ground, 3–14 in. tall, with two rows of bracts below the flower heads, the outer row being tipped black. January–December.

Coltsfoot, *Tussilago farfara.* A low perennial of ill-drained waste places, especially on clay, the yellow flowers with disk and ray-florets appearing in late winter and early spring before the large heart-shaped leaves. Very common. February–April.

Daisy, *Bellis perennis.* A plant that needs no description. The single flowerheads of this familiar perennial have yellow disk florets and white ray florets, frequently tipped with crimson. Throughout the British Isles in every month of the year.

Hemp Agrimony, *Eupatorium cannabinum.* A tall handsome perennial, often 4 ft. high, which might well be mistaken for a valerian. Hairy stems and small pale-pink flowers—or mauve, red or white—in thick clusters. Long white styles; and bracts

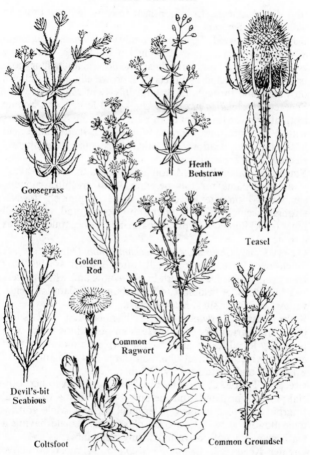

Goosegrass

Heath
Bedstraw

Teasel

Golden
Rod

Devil's-bit
Scabious

Coltsfoot

Common
Ragwort

Common Groundsel

tipped with purple. Common near fresh water, and in damp woods. July–September.

Scentless Mayweed, *Tripleurospermum maritimum. Matricaria maritima.* A scentless hairless annual, 6–24 in. high, with bushy 2–3 pinnate leaves and large daisy-like flowers an inch or more broad, and protected by bracts with brown edgings. Common on waste land throughout Britain. July–September.

Sneezewort, *Achillea ptarmica.* Undivided leaves with minute teeth distinguish this plant from Yarrow. Creamy-white flowers with 8 or more outer florets. Will grow 2 ft. in damp acid heathland, wet meadows and other moist sites, often slightly shaded. July–September.

Yarrow, *A. millefolium.* 'Milfoil', meaning 'a thousand leaves', is another name for this perennial with creeping runners, slender 2–3 pinnate leaves, and white or pinkish flowers, strongly scented, with 5 outer (ray) florets, and very small inner (disk) florets. A gypsy herbal remedy, once much used as a tonic.

Ox-eye Daisy, *Chrysanthemum leucanthemum* (Marguerite). A much-loved perennial 2 ft. tall, often known as the 'Dog Daisy' or 'Moon Daisy', with bright yellow and white flowers 1–2 in. broad. A widespread and abundant plant of fields, verges, and other sites. May–August.

Spear Thistle, *Cirsium vulgare.* A biennial that is classified under the Agriculture Act, 1947, as an obnoxious weed, with pinnately lobed leaves and reddish-purple flowers more than an inch wide. Our most abundant large-flowered thistle, on wasteland and pastures. July–October.

Creeping Thistle, *C. arvense. Carduus arvensis.* Another 'official pest' of farmland, and the only British thistle with small fragrant pale-lilac blooms in terminal clusters. Male and female flowers grow on separate plants, the female having a feathery pappus of brown hairs. July–September.

Greater Knapweed, *Centaurea scabiosa.* A most attractive

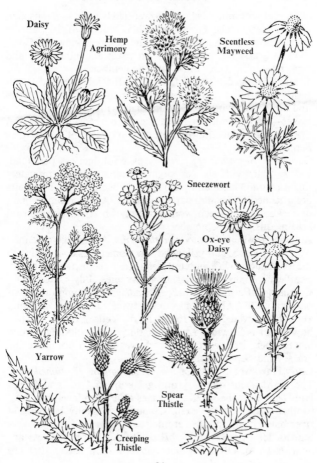

Daisy

Hemp
Agrimony

Scentless
Mayweed

Sneezewort

Ox-eye
Daisy

Yarrow

Spear
Thistle

Creeping
Thistle

perennial with purple showy flower-heads with 4–5 conspicuous slender petals. Green sepal-like bracts which, like the upper leaves, distinguish it from the Lesser Knapweed. Common in grassland, particularly on chalk and limestone, and especially in S. Rarer in N. July–September.

Lesser Knapweed, *C. nigra. C. obscura* (Black Knapweed,Hardhead). A familiar and well-liked perennial of roadside verges and other grassy places, 6–24 in. high, with slender lanceolate leaves—only the lower ones being toothed—that are not prickly. Many flat sepal-like bracts with a comb of teeth. June–September.

Saw-wort, *Serratula tinctoria.* A pleasant hairless perennial, 1–2 ft. tall, with slender slightly-toothed leaves, pinnately lobed or undivided, and purple thistle-like flowers. The fruits are attached to a rough pappus of hairs. An uncommon plant of meadows and open woods, mainly on chalk but also on acid heaths. July–September.

Autumn Hawkbit, *Leontodon autumnalis.* A variable perennial with shiny leaves and yellow flowers, sometimes confused with the dandelion, with outer florets often reddish underneath. Feathery pappus. Common in grassy sites. July–October.

Common Cat's Ear, *Hypochoeris radicata.* A common perennial, about 1 ft. high, or roughly twice the size of Autumn Hawkbit, covered with rough hairs. Yellow dandelion-like flowers an inch wide. Abundant on grass, including garden lawns where its low rosettes of leaves tend to dominate the grass. June–September.

Leafy Hawkweed, *Aphyllopoda. H. sabaudum. H. umbellatum.* The Hawkweeds of this group grow up to 4 ft., and flower late. They lack the rosette of leaves at ground level, but have toothed leaves on the stem. Common on sandy heaths and river banks. July to late autumn.

Smooth Hawk's Beard, *Crepis capillaris.* A thin hairless annual, 6–15 in. tall, with arrow-shaped stem leaves that are

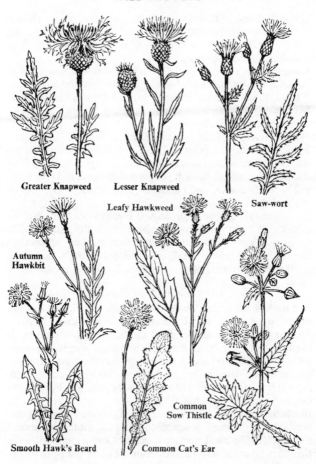

Greater Knapweed   Lesser Knapweed

Leafy Hawkweed   Saw-wort

Autumn
Hawkbit

Common
Sow Thistle

Smooth Hawk's Beard   Common Cat's Ear

shiny, and yellow flowers $\frac{1}{2}$ in. in diameter, on a stalk thinner than those of other hawkbeards. No stem leaves on many small forms of this plant growing on heaths. Common on grassland. June–November.

Common Sow Thistle, *Sonchus oleraceus* (Smooth Sow Thistle). An all too common annual of damp and cultivated land, 6 in.– 3 ft. high, with pinnately lobed lower leaves. Yellow flowers like miniature dandelions, and forming 'dandelion clocks' when seeding. May–October.

Wall Lettuce, *Mycelis muralis. Lactuca muralis.* A common hairless and slender perennial, 2–3 ft. tall, with smooth lower leaves on long stalks, and upper ones springing straight from the stem. 4–5 florets in each yellow flower-head. In hedgerows, walls, shady banks, and on the edge of woods, especially on chalk. July–September.

Dandelion, *Taraxacum officinale.* If these plants were rare we might well hail them as outstandingly beautiful flowers, with their dazzling yellow ray florets, deeply lobed or toothed leaves that can prove a useful addition to salads, and stout roots used as a medicine. Throughout the year in waste places.

LILY FAMILY *Liliaceae*

Bog Asphodel, *Narthecium ossifragum.* The specific name of this beautiful plant is the Latin for 'bone-breaking', peasant farmers grazing cattle on the wet heaths believing that it made the bones of their beasts brittle. The yellow star-like flowers, with white hairs on the 6 orange anthers turn an attractive orange shade when running to seed in autumn. Locally common in bogs and wet acid heaths in the N., and W., less numerous in S. and E. Late June–August.

Bluebell, *Hyacinthoides non-scripta. Endymion non-scriptus. Schilla nutans.* Since it is unable to stand the winters in Eastern Europe, this is a plant that most excites Continental visitors to Britain, who are amazed at the ocean of blue in our open wood-

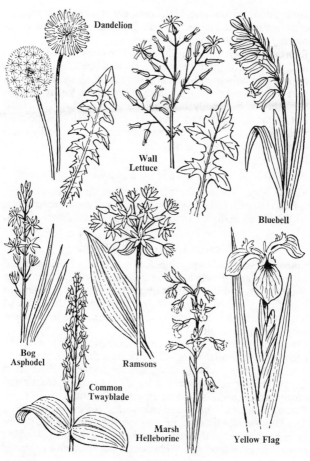

Dandelion

Wall
Lettuce

Bluebell

Bog
Asphodel

Ramsons

Common
Twayblade

Marsh
Helleborine

Yellow Flag

85

lands during April–June. Unfortunately, it takes a 100 years to establish a good bluebell wood; heavy trampling and over-picking can all too soon destroy it.

Ramsons, *Allium ursinum.* The smell of onions, which survives in the bulb throughout the winter, is often one's first introduction to our only broad-leaved garlic. The 2 shiny leaves with parallel veins are not unlike those of Lily of the Valley, though they should be readily distinguished by the sharply twisted leaf stalks. Long-stalked white flowers with slender pointed petals and bracts that wither and fall very early. Locally common in damp woods. April–June.

IRIS FAMILY *Iridaceae*

Yellow Flag, *Iris pseudacorus.* Our most common wild iris, 3–6 ft. tall, with brilliant yellow flowers and erect broad leaves with a raised midrib. Common by fresh water. June–August.

ORCHID FAMILY *Orchidaceae*

Marsh Helleborine, *Epipactis palustris.* The only English orchid with white and purplish-brown flowers. Narrow leaves, with pointed tips, and hairy sepals tinged green are other points to look for, and there is a yellow spot at the top of the 2-jointed lip. Rare in most areas; locally common in some fens, marshes and dune-slacks. June–August.

Common Twayblade, *Listera ovata.* Large oval stem leaves with conspicuous parallel veins—2 of them as the name implies—distinguish this orchid. 2 long slender segments hang from the yellowish-green flower. 1–2 ft. tall, common in woods and scrub and open grass all over Britain. May–July.

Butterfly Orchid, *Platanthera chlorantha. Habenaria virescens.* The long slender unlobed lip and lengthy spur are the distinguishing features of this elegant white flower, with a pair of big broad leaves at the base. Widespread, but local and probably declining. Mainly in southern woods and pastures, often on limestone and chalk. The **Lesser Butterfly Orchid**, *P. bifolia*, is equally graceful, but smaller, and with closely parallel pollen-masses in the heart of the whiter flowers. More uncommon. June–July.

Bee Orchid, *Ophrys apifera*. A favourite orchid, 6–18 in. tall, with narrow leaves pointed at the tips, and flowers with bright pink sepals, slender square-tipped green petals, and the broad velvety lip strikingly resembles a bee alighting on the flower. Some 2–5 flowers are usually borne. This somewhat rare plant of chalk grassland and the borders of woods appears to be declining. It has always been less common in the N. than in the S. June–July.

Fly Orchid, *Ophrys insectifera*. This rare plant is much taller than the Bee Orchid, growing up to 2 ft., and producing a long brown lip with a blue patch in the middle and 2 minute pointed petals; strikingly similar in appearance to the body and first pair of legs of an insect. It grows on chalk grassland and at the edge of woodland—generally downland or sites on limestone—and may easily be confused with a Bee Orchid, though it is much more slender. May–June.

Fragrant Orchid, Scented Orchid, *Gymnadania conopsea*. A delightful plant, generally about a foot high—though I have known it to vary in size from a few inches to 2 feet—which is easily recognised by the long slender spur reminiscent of the Pyramid Orchid. Long, narrow, unspotted leaves grow from the stem, and the bracts are as long as the sweet-scented, dark pink or purplish flowers. Widespread and not uncommon, mainly on chalk or limestone, sometimes on acid sandy heaths and pastures. June–August.

Heath Spotted Orchid, *Orchis maculata. O. ericetorum, Dactylorchis maculata*. A lovely and most variable orchid, 6–12 in. tall, with purplish-black spots on the leaves. The flowers vary in shade from purple or pink to white, with crimson dots. The

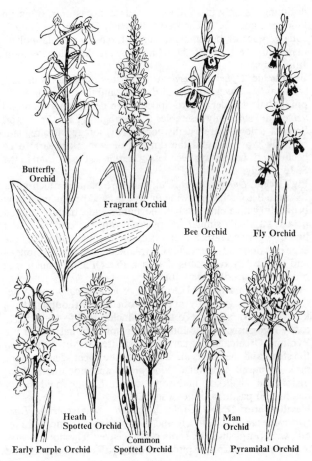

Butterfly Orchid

Fragrant Orchid

Bee Orchid

Fly Orchid

Heath Spotted Orchid

Early Purple Orchid

Common Spotted Orchid

Man Orchid

Pyramidal Orchid

sepals stand out on either side of the flower like a pair of wings and the broad lower lip has a short middle tooth, whereas the Common Spotted Orchis, *D. fuchsii*, has a pointed middle lobe as long as the two side wing-like ones. Widespread and common on damp acid heaths and in bogs in N.W. and S.E. England; rare in the Midlands. May–July.

Early Purple Orchid, *O. mascula.* One of the earliest of the orchises, with long leaves growing up from the base of the 12 in. stem, and flowers in a large loose spike, with notches in the middle lobes of the lips, and a long thick spur growing upwards. Some botanists insist that the plant gives off a scent indistinguishable from that of cats. Common in woods and meadows all over Britain. April–June.

Common Spotted Orchid, *Dactylorchis fuchsii. Orchys fuchsii. O. okellyi.* Taller and sturdier than the Heath Spotted Orchid with which it frequently hybridises, though the latter is usually found on acid heathland whereas *D. fuchsii* prefers chalk soils. A solid stem, long, lean, pointed leaves, heavily spotted, and flowers varying from light purple to white and forming a pointed spike, are all characteristic of this attractive species. Fens, woods and wet grassy sites, as well as downland. Largely concentrated in the S. and E. and in Ireland. May–August.

Man Orchid, *Aceras anthropophorum.* An extremely rare orchid, 6–18 in. tall, and the only one with yellow or brown-lipped flowers, this lip being strangely similar in shape to the form of a man. Unspotted leaves at the base and on the stem; flowers forming a long slender spike with green sepals and the chocolate-edged lip deeply lobed, as our illustration clearly shows. Confined to a few pastures, abandoned quarries and patches of scrub on chalk and limestone in S.E. England, particularly Kent and Surrey, and N. to Northamptonshire and Lincolnshire. June–July.

Pyramidal Orchid, *Anacamptis pyramidalis. Orchis pyramidalis.* Aptly named in view of the dense pyramid of light purple or deep pink flowers, with a 3-lobed lip and a long thin spur, curved as in our picture. Only the Fragrant Orchid shares this feature. The leaves are unspotted. Favours chalk or limestone, where it is not uncommon, though it also thrives on sand-dunes. Rarer in N. July–August.

GRASS FAMILY *Gramineae*

Sweet Vernal Grass, *Anthoxanthum odoratum.* One of the first grasses to flower, this sweet-scented species, on a slender stem about a foot high, is a widespread and common plant of grass-land and open woods. April–July.

Reed Grass, *Phalaris arundinacea. Digraphis arundinacea.* Reed Canary Grass. An attractive perennial, 3–6 ft. tall, favouring riversides and pond-banks and the margins of ditches. The Greek 'Phalaros' or 'brilliant' refers to the shining seeds. June–August.

Common Cat's-Tail Grass. *Phleum pratense* (Timothy Grass). One of the most familiar and useful species of pastures and meadows. It grows 9 in.–4 ft.—most often 1–2 ft.—and does well on dry sandstone or during periods of drought. Broad leaves, rough to the touch. June–August.

Slender Fox-tail, *Alopercurus myosuroides.* An annual with slender pointed panicle and short, sheathed leaves, thriving on dry soils in S. England, especially roadside verges. Mousetail. Blackbent. May–autumn.

Meadow Fox-tail, *A. pratensis.* Found almost everywhere, par-ticularly in wet meadows and on ill-drained verges, this hair-less perennial may grow 1–4 ft. tall, bearing a yellow-green panicle 2 in. in length. Relished by farm stock. April–July.

Marsh Fox-tail, *A. geniculatus* (Floating Fox-tail). This peren-nial is much smaller than the last species, though it grows up to 1–4 ft. in moist shady places. The stem bends sharply at the lower joints, making recognition simple. Though preferring wet sites, it will also prosper on dry ground. When growing in

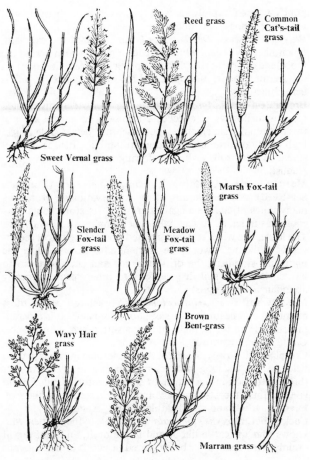

Reed grass

Common Cat's-tail grass

Sweet Vernal grass

Marsh Fox-tail grass

Slender Fox-tail grass

Meadow Fox-tail grass

Wavy Hair grass

Brown Bent-grass

Marram grass

ponds, where it rapidly spreads, the leaves lie on the surface of the water. June–September.

Wavy Hair Grass, *Deschampsia flexuosa.* An attractive plant, much liked by sheep, which spreads a glossy sheen across the moorlands of the north when the spikelets flower. Common on dry heaths, woods, moorland and mountains where the soil is acid. June–July.

Brown Bent-grass, *Agrostis canina.* Another widely distributed plant with flowers of a delicate beauty. The slender stem of this perennial, rising from a stout base, may be a couple of feet high in its favourite boggy haunts in the hills. It is also widespread on dry soils, while preferring acid heathland. June–August.

Marram Grass, Sea Matweed, *Ammophila arenaria* (Common Sea-Reed). A valuable ally of the conservationist, protecting many miles of coastline against erosion. Its stout roots may extend as much as 20 feet, while the stem may be 1–4 ft. tall. The leaves are wide, stiff and pointed, their margins curved inwards, while the flower is the shape of a fox's brush. Once the plant has stabilised the drifting sands and enabled them to harden into firm soil, it gives way to other species. Locally abundant. July–August.

Meadow Soft Grass, *Holcus lanatus* (Yorkshire Fog). A most abundant and beautiful grass of poor damp land. It is a perennial that grows 1–2 ft. high, and has a soft, downy appearance. Cattle tend to ignore it. May–Autumn.

Creeping Soft Grass, *H. mollis.* A troublesome intruder in corn fields, where its long runners may extend four or five feet through the soil in the course of a few months. Slenderer and greener than the last species, and less attractive to the eye. Favours woods and acid heathland. July–August.

Cock's-foot, *Dactylis glomerata.* Invaluable to the farmer, who knows that the cattle like it and thrive on it, and that it will rapidly grow again after being grazed or cut. It is also tolerant

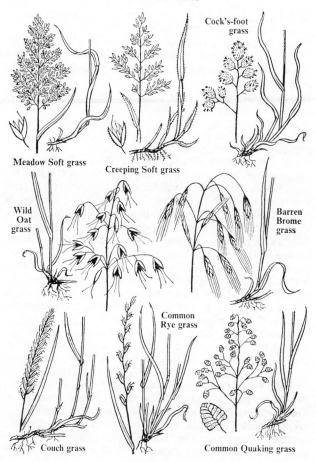

Cock's-foot grass

Meadow Soft grass

Creeping Soft grass

Wild Oat grass

Barren Brome grass

Common Rye grass

Couch grass

Common Quaking grass

93

of drought and will grow almost anywhere, hence its abundance. 6 in.–3 ft. tall. May–Autumn.

Wild Oat Grass, *Avena fatua.* An attractive-looking plant which the farmer prefers to see in a vase rather than in his fields, and it is a costly pest in the East Anglian corn belt. June–August.

Barren Brome Grass, *Bromus sterilis.* Another common grass of roadside verges, hedge banks and waste places, 6–18 in. high, with pale green spikelets that gradually become tinged with purple and then grey-green or brown. Attractive to the human eye, but not to the palate of farm stock. May–July.

Couch Grass, White Couch, Creeping Wheat, Twitch, *Agropyrum repens.* Every minute portion of the root of this troublesome perennial is liable to produce a new plant with such speed that it has earned the nickname Quick, Quich and Squitch, as well as those already listed. The shoots are well liked by cattle. Common in cultivated ground everywhere. June–September.

Common Rye Grass, Perennial Rye Grass, *Lolium perenne* (Beardless Darnel, Red Darnel). It does not always deserve the name 'Perennial Rye Grass', for on unfavourable ground it may become a biennial. There are several lines down the smooth, pointed leaves, and the plant may grow as much as 3 ft. or as little as 6 in. The spikelets grow alternately from the stem. Well liked by cattle. June–August.

Common Quaking Grass, *Briza media.* Well-named in view of its tendency to vibrate even before approaching footsteps or in the face of the gentlest of summer breezes. Widely distributed in dry or damp grassland when the soil is poor. June–August.

Annual Meadow Grass, *Poa annua* (Suffolk Grass). A light green hairless annual, 2–10 in. high, that grows almost everywhere. The flat leaves are hooded at the tip. January–December.

Wood Melick Grass, *Melica uniflora.* Though only local in Scotland, this plant can be frequently seen in woods and other shady places throughout England and Wales. It often stands

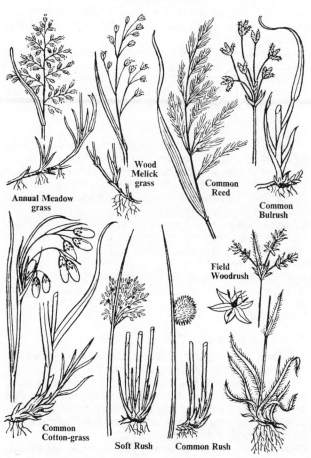

Annual Meadow
grass

Wood
Melick
grass

Common
Reed

Common
Bulrush

Field
Woodrush

Common
Cotton-grass

Soft Rush

Common Rush

95

9–18 in. high amid the bluebells, and it is well liked by farm stock. There are lines on both sides of the rich-green leaves. April–July.

Common Reed, *Phragmites communis.* A lovely perennial of river banks and shallow ponds, with deep green leaves, almost an inch broad, and abundant purplish flower spikelets that turn brown. Formerly much used in East Anglia and elsewhere for thatching. August–October.

SEDGE FAMILY *Cyperaceae*

Common Bulrush, *Scirpus lacustris.* The true Bulrush, a name so often wrongly applied to the familiar Reed-mace of garden ponds. A tough hairy perennial 3–8 ft. tall, it has long been much used in basket-making or for the seats of rush-bottomed chairs. The end panicle comprises a thick cluster of reddish-brown spikelets. June–August.

Common Cotton-grass, *Eriophorum angustifolium.* A delightful plant that displays heads of gleaming white down about the bogs and wet moorlands of Britain. The small flowers are brownish-green and have yellow anthers; then as the fruits develop, the strange white cotton-threads appear on every flower head. While more numerous in the N., it is locally common on acid soils in the S. April–May. The downy cotton-heads are displayed through the late summer.

RUSH FAMILY *Juncaceae*

Soft Rush, *Juncus effusus.* Probably our best known Rush, for it grows 1–4 ft. high, forming thickly matted pale-green tufts in moist ground over much of Britain. The light green glossy stems are thicker than those of Hard Rush; the flowers are brown, forming a panicle that may be two or three inches in diameter. The tough, pliant stems have long been used for mats and stools. July–August.

Common Rush, *Juncus communis. Juncus conglomeratus.* Another most abundant species where the ground is damp. This **Compact Rush**, as it may also be called, is very similar to the last species, differing in the neater, rounded form of the flowers which tend to be a deeper brown. The pith of this plant was formerly much used in the wicks of candles or 'rush lights'. Rare in chalk and limestone. May–July.

Field Woodrush, *Luzula campestris* (Good Friday Grass). Also known as Chimney Sweeps, Black Caps, Smuts, God's Grace, Hair Beard and other names. This tufted creeping plant, 3–8 in. high, has dark-green hairy leaves and dark chestnut-brown flowers, with bright yellow anthers that are longer than their stalks. Widespread on heaths and dry pasture up to 3,000 ft. April–May.

BIBLIOGRAPHY

Clapham, A. R., Tutin, T. G. and Warburg, E. F. *Flora of the British Isles*. Cambridge University Press. (This is the standard reference book on the subject), 1952.

Martin, W. Keble. *The Concise British Flora in Colour*. Ebury Press and Michael Joseph, London. (A remarkable work with paintings of 1,400 plants), 1965.

McClintock, David and Fitter, R. S. R. *Collins Pocket Guide to Wild Flowers*. Collins, London. 1955.

McClintock, David. *Companion to Flowers*. Bell, 1966. An admirable bedside book.

Nicholson, B. E., Ary, S. and Gregory, M. *The Oxford Book of Wild Flowers*. Oxford University Press, London, 1962.

Perring, F. H. and Walters, S. M. *The Atlas of the British Flora*. Nelson, London, 1962.

Trees

The Value of Trees – Their History in Britain –
Windbreaks Around the House and Garden – Shelterbelts
on the Farm – Planting for Amenity – Tree Management –
Tree Families – Trees and Sites

THE VALUE OF TREES

It is hard to exaggerate the importance of the part played by
trees in protecting man, beast and soil from the wind and con-
tributing to the fertility of the land. Their roots serve as a
sponge, draining the ground of surplus water in times of flood
and helping to preserve moisture during periods of drought.
Their deep tap-roots may extract mineral nutrients from the
sub-soil and their shadows help to retain the dew in the grass
in times of great heat. Trees, with green grass and water, are
surely the prime factor in shaping a beautiful landscape.

Trees are also a crop, a point that the preservationists sometimes forget. They should not generally be protected beyond
their proper life span, except when their contribution to the
beauty of the landscape is exceptionally important, or when
they are trees of unusual historic interest. It may also be reasonable in nature reserves to preserve dead trees, or the dead
branches of trees, where these are vital for the welfare of certain fauna. Wood-dwelling beetles of the *Platystomidae* family,
for example, will only thrive where there is dead wood, and
woodpeckers may flourish most where they have access to
some decaying timber.

Normally the enlightened countryman will remove the
sickly and dying trees, or the trees in their prime that were

planted for timber, while constantly planting for tomorrow. Unfortunately, many private landowners, farmers and local authorities find it beyond their means to do this, though the Forestry Commission's Small Woods grants (£22 4s. an acre) and more generous grants under the Agriculture Act, 1947, offer some help. Tax relief under the Capital Expenditure Claim may prove valuable, too. See page 229 for addresses of Conservancy offices of the Forestry Commission.

Local Authorities. The environment in both town and country is enormously improved where trees are generously planted, as the Russians have realised. More than 50,000 mature or semi-mature trees are transplanted in Moscow each year. In Britain, too, 10,000 semi-mature trees were transplanted in towns and on derelict industrial sites during the five years up to 1965, more than twenty times as many as in the previous five years. This is an important new development. The Government's White Paper on *Leisure in the Countryside* (HMSO 1s. 6d.), issued in February, 1966, promised Exchequer grants for the lavish planting of small woods, clumps and rows of trees by local authorities throughout Britain. It is vital that the right trees are planted in the proper places. The species selected must be suitable for the soil and situation. See page 139 for a list of trees and sites.

A HISTORY OF TREES IN BRITAIN

Our forest trees are generally pollinated by the wind. Showers of pollen, drifting in the breeze and falling into fens, bogs and mud at the bottom of lakes, may survive for long periods. Indeed, while the living cell-contents of the grains, deprived of oyxgen, eventually decay, the fatty outer membranes endure in peat bogs for thousands of years. This phenomenon has resulted in the fascinating new study of *palynology* or *pollen-analysis*.

Methods of Pollen Analysis. Under the microscope pollen

grains prove to be objects of great beauty and immense diversity, the oval grains of elm contrasting with the triangular grains of hazel, and those of beech or pine may be several times larger than the grains of birch and alder. Professor H. Godwin, FRS, and others, have developed systems of identifying the hundreds of pollen grains which chemical or mechanical treatment in the laboratory may release from fragments of ancient peat no larger than an ear of wheat. If pollen removed from different layers of the soil profile is examined, it may be possible to establish the nature of the vegetation on the site over successive periods of thousands of years. Each pollen type in every sample of 150 grains is listed and its percentage of the total is recorded.

What has been revealed. Research has shown that in the Late Glacial Period between about 18,000 B.C. and 8500 B.C., the vegetation of this country was dominated by sedges and grasses, with much arctic willow, dwarf birch and the arctic-alpine flora of the kind that has survived in parts of Teesdale. As temperatures increased, the birches, aspen and pines seem to have spread for a time, but they soon retreated again before the ice, at least in the north.

The Post-Glacial Period, following the swift dispersal of the ice sheets which had penetrated as far south as the Thames Valley, saw a big advance of birch, and many districts of the south contained pine and some elm, oak and hazel. These trees may have invaded from the Continent across the dry bed of the North Sea, but it is possible—though this is only speculation—that they spread north from a reservoir of tree species that survived the Ice Age on land now hidden by the English Channel.

Mesolithic times. Round about 7000 B.C. pine appears to have displaced birch as the dominant species, and hazel became more abundant than at any time before or since. Elm and then the oak became more abundant too. Lime, though absent from

Ireland—where elm was the dominant species after hazel, also became a surprisingly common forest tree in Britain, and alder increased in the ill-drained areas.

Boreal Period. The climate improved again towards the end of this Period around 6500 B.C., and pine retreated before the advance of the mixed oak forests and a dramatic spread of alder. These oak-alder forests were to dominate the landscape and the lives of its late Mesolithic and Neolithic peoples for many centuries.

Iron Age. As this began around 500 B.C., our climate seems to have deteriorated, becoming 'a source of constant merriment to successive generations,' and producing a marked decline in the lime and a big advance of the birches. Beech and hornbeam invaded many areas. Their pollen has proved particularly abundant in deposits of peat from this period taken in south-east England. Small quantities of beech pollen have also been found in many other parts of England and Wales, proving that the tree was not uncommon at least in the Iron Age.

Historical times. For centuries the forests, largely shaped by climatic influences, had controlled the lives of primitive men. Now man began by degrees to control the forest. Professor J. Iversen, in Denmark, has shown how clearings may be cut in the forests with the stone axes used by Neolithic Man. Fire, too, proved a powerful weapon. Through successive centuries the woods were hacked and slashed and burned until, by 1544, any further unauthorised felling of timber was prohibited by the King.

WINDBREAKS FOR HOUSE AND GARDEN

Benefits. Cold winds bring higher fuel bills, and a stout hedge of beech or hawthorn, cypress or hornbeam planted around the house and garden can appreciably reduce costs, though hedge-cutting can be a heavy item. Strangely little research into these problems has been carried out in Britain, but a good hedge around a greenhouse has been found to reduce the expense of heating by 10 or even 15 per cent. Experiments in the United States have shown that well planned shelterbelts on three sides of the house will reduce coal consumption by two or three tons a year.

This fact is not surprising. A 20 miles per hour increase in wind force may more or less double fuel consumption. A well-planned shelterbelt or wind-break may reduce wind pressure by half to three-quarters for a distance twice as long as the height of the trees or hedge. Many householders and gardeners in England, Scotland and the Scilly Isles, taking their cue from the Elizabethan gardeners, have proved the value of the sheltered plot.

Sunlight and shadow. Care must be taken to ensure that trees do not unduly darken rooms or deny precious sunshine to the garden. A small seedling is sometimes planted without a thought for what height it may reach in fifty years time. Wind-breaks against the prevailing south-west wind do produce some shadow at the end of a winter's day. But the gain in temperature should be ample compensation.

Frost pockets. Cold air behaves like flood water, flowing downhill or accumulating before any obstruction. Care must be taken not to create frost pockets by ill-advised planting. Tall windbreaks on sites where cold air may be trapped should be open at the base so that the frosted air may flow freely. Many Kent and Sussex orchards are skilfully protected by stout hedgerows and shelterbelts which divert the cold air down hill along the sides of the escarpment. So, too, are many Scottish estates that would suffer heavy losses in yields without them.

Atmospheric humidity may rise 2–3 per cent in the vicinity of windbreaks, a big advantage during dry spells, but some funguses and insect pests may profit, too. Hedges and trees which keep out the cold air and break the force of the wind are thought to increase the abundance and activity of insect pollinators, parasites and predators, and to raise heavily the yield of Conference pears, Cox's Orange Pippin apples and other crops. The subject is discussed in detail in J. M. Caborn's valuable *Shelterbelts and Windbreaks* (Faber, 50s.).

SHELTERBELTS ON THE FARM

The landscape of tomorrow is bound to differ greatly from that of today. Farms and fields will be larger and hedgerows fewer. This fact enormously increases the importance of shelterbelts. Nowhere does this apply more strongly than in those few districts such as Breckland, the Fens or the fields of east Fife where wind erosion is a serious and costly problem. The advantages of mixed shelterbelts on exposed sites in the Cotswolds, the chalk downlands, and other areas are also well known, protected acres carrying cattle for two or three weeks longer than fields where trees are few. Particularly valuable are the crops of rich green grass which flourish in sheltered fields a couple of weeks before the spring growth occurs on exposed sites.

Facts and figures. It is beyond the scope of this book to go into detail about this subject, but it should be pointed out that much research into the effects of shelterbelts on farm crops has been carried out in Europe. Yields of oats in Russia have increased by as much as 25 per cent, and similar figures have been obtained for grass in Denmark and potatoes in Germany. Protection from westerly winds in Jutland, where weather conditions are somewhat similar to our own, produced increased yields of 23.2 per cent for beet, 24.1 per cent for grass and clover, 21.5 per cent for lucerne, and 16.9 per cent for potatoes.

Problems. A dense, high barrier of trees which the wind cannot easily penetrate can produce lodging, the wind rebounding upwards before crashing down on to the crops on the far side of the trees. This problem can easily be avoided by ensuring that the shelterbelt is broader at the base than at the crown and not too thick, so that it breaks rather than blocks, the flow of the wind. Shrubs and trees forming the shelterbelt should be of different species, ages and sizes, reducing wind pressure by 50 per cent to 75 per cent, but allowing some currents of air to flow freely between the twigs.

Where shelter produces cool, damp and shady conditions, viruses and fungi may prove more troublesome to potato crops. It is also a fact that poorer crops are frequently produced in the immediate vicinity of the shelterbelts; but the compensating increase some distance away more than makes up for this failing, as a mass of facts and figures from many countries prove. German agriculturalists consider that if 1 per cent of good arable land is devoted to shelterbelts, one can reasonably hope for increased yields of about 10 per cent. But it is hard to lay down hard and fast rules when conditions obviously vary from farm to farm and from field to field. Every farmer must plan his shelterbelts in the light of local conditions, including the nature of the soil and situation.

What type of shelterbelt? Swift-growing trees like poplars and willows will soon ensure an adequate height. Pioneers like silver birch—which will grow 4 to 5 feet in a wet summer—quickly produces a useful screen at a lower level. Alder, too, is useful on wet sites. Beeches and sycamore, sometimes mixed with conifers, have proved themselves on chalk downland, and hazel is always valuable, since it is adaptable to a wide variety of sites and situations, and is well liked by game and other wild life. Oak, hornbeam, cherry and larch are all strongly recommended for many sites, and maple, lime, ash, sycamore, aspen, spruce, silver fir and blackthorn have been most successful in the lower canopy of shelterbelts at home and on the Continent. The pines—including Scots, Corsican and maritime pines—have proved effective, with sitka spruce, in warding off coastal gales.

It should be added that pheasants and partridges are quick

to welcome shelterbelts, and the partridge has proved to be an important predator of the potato beetle, *Leptinotarsa decemlineata*.

Useful information can be obtained from the publications of the Forestry Commission and the Ministry of Agriculture, Fisheries and Food. Particularly valuable are the *Report of the Committee on Hedgerow and Farm Timber* (the Merthyr Report), (HMSO, 4s. 5d.), *Shelterbelts and Microclimate*, Forestry Commission Bulletin No. 29, (20s. 8d.) and the Ministry of Agriculture's *Shelterbelts For Farm Lands* (HMSO, 1961). Other recommended literature includes J. M. Caborn's *Shelterbelts and Windbreaks* already mentioned (page 103) and J. D. Ovington's *Woodlands* (English Universities Press), 1965.

PLANTING FOR AMENITY

Many of our country towns and villages owe much of their beauty to the wise planting of trees by past generations of landowners. Too often little replanting is being done nowadays, and some of these places may be almost bare of trees in a hundred years time.

Role of Civic Societies. It is a hopeful sign that more than 500 towns and villages now have civic or amenity societies, and more are being formed at the rate of two a month. The most enlightened of them are much concerned with this matter, and they generally favour not the fussy little exotic shrubs and flowering trees but the true native broad-leaved trees, or useful introduced species like the sycamore, the sweet chestnut or Japanese larch.

Where to plant. Lay-bys, picnic sites and derelict industrial sites often need trees, and many an eyesore may be hidden by them. But it is always wise to obtain advice from an experienced forester with knowledge of amenity planting. Trees need enough space to develop properly. They generally prefer company, growing towards the light in groups that can be thinned.

What to plant. It is useless to plant oak, ash or elm in shallow, hungry soils, though silver birch, Scots pine and even beech may fare well, and so will sycamore.

Poplar, ash and willow prefer damp sites, but drainage must be satisfactory if trees are to prosper. Our countryside contains many dead trees that have perished because of repeated flooding.

Wind is important. Scots and Austrian pine thrive in it, but no other conifer will do so. You can hardly beat the London plane for areas where the air is heavily polluted. Sycamore is robust, standing up well to strong winds, but it needs company in its early days, and ample room to develop when mature.

Straight rows of trees and square-cut corners are not often desirable, whereas groups of Scots pine beside a road or clumps of limes, oaks or silver birches are most attractive. But it is no use planting trees without giving some thought to their management in the years that follow.

TREE MANAGEMENT

The key to sound management lies in adopting clear-cut aims. Timber production demands techniques quite different from those required for trees primarily planted to screen cars in a lay-by or to provide shade for picnickers. The prime object of the conservationist managing a woodland nature reserve may well be the maximum diversity of trees species, and he will desire trees of different ages in every group to ensure a rich variety of plant and animal communities. To some extent, this is true also of the forester in our state woodlands now that the original monocultures are giving way to a natural diversity of structure and species aimed at maintaining sustained yield.

Fire precautions, weed control, and the thinning of trees when the occasion demands it are essential duties wherever they are grown. It is often better for a man with a pruning hook to do too little rather than too much. A prime example here concerns the lopping of trees too often carried out by local authorities. Reducing roadside trees to bare stumps, thereby opening the way to disease and fungal infection, is senseless. A little light pruning may be all that is needed.

The publications of the Forestry Commission offer abundant advice. Books worth consulting include:

Graham, E. H. *Natural Principles of Land Management*. Oxford University Press, 1944.

James, N. D. G. *The Forester's Companion*. Blackwells, Oxford, 1955.

Kostler, J. *Silviculture*. Oliver and Boyd, Edinburgh, 1956.

Ministry of Housing and Local Government, *Trees in Town and Country*. HMSO, London, 1961. New ed.

Morling, R. J. *Trees* (for landscapes). *Estates Gazette*, London, rev. ed. 1963.

Neal, E. G. *Woodland Ecology*. Heinemann, London, 1958.

Ovington, J. D. *Woodlands*, English Universities Press, 1965.

Troup, R. S. *Silvicultural Systems*. Clarendon Press, Oxford, 1952.

TREE FAMILIES

While most flowering plants are *Angiosperms*, producing seeds enclosed in some form of case, as with the familiar oak, elm and ash, *Gymnosperms* bear seeds which are naked and exposed. The most prominent members of this class are the conifers, named after the cones bearing the seed, and usually possessing evergreen needle-shaped leaves.

Tree Trunks. The thickened main stem of the tree below the branches is termed the bole. The dry heart-wood in the centre of the trunk is darker in shade than the sapwood which surrounds it. This sapwood will carry moisture containing nutrients up to the branches and twigs even when the main trunk is hollow.

New layers of sapwood, forming a sequence of tiny tubes through which water can ascend, are wrapped round the branches and trunk each year between spring and early autumn. These annual rings reveal the age of the tree; they also shed interesting light on the weather in past years. A broad ring represents a wet, warm summer when growing conditions

SAPWOOD
PITH
HEARTWOOD
BARK

Flowers, fruit and heart of a tree. Each ring represents a year of growth.

were good, while a slender ring may denote drought. Tree-rings for 1921 and 1959, for example, are thin, for these were years of much heat and little rain. One American authority has shown, through the study of felled redwoods, that his country endured a severe drought which continued from 1276 to 1299.

THE GYMNOSPERMS

Ginkgo Family *Ginkgoaceae*

Maidenhair tree, *Ginkgo biloba.* Darwin hailed this tree as 'a living fossil', the only surviving member of the Ginkgoaceae, which has apparently flourished in China for 10 million years, though whether it exists in the wild today is open to doubt. Introduced to the Botanic Gardens at Utrecht in 1730, it was soon brought to England, a famous specimen more than 70 feet tall thriving in the Royal Botanic Gardens, Kew, and others can be seen at Windsor, Oxford, and in the grounds of the Bishop's Palace at Wells. Easily recognised by the leaves which are strangely similar to the fronds of maidenhair fern. The tree prospers in towns.

PINE FAMILY *Pinaceae*

Monkey Puzzle, *Araucaria araucana.* A South American tree, discovered by the Spaniards in 1780 and introduced to Britain in 1796. Early examples were introduced to Kew and Piltdown, Sussex, and Victorian gentry found it a useful status symbol, which is why it is always planted in the *front* garden and not out of sight at the back, despite its ugliness. It thrives in well drained sunny ground away from frost pockets. Chile pine.

Scots Pine, *Pinus sylvestris.* One of our three native conifers and a splendid choice, planted in clumps, for poor sandy soils. On deeper soils in southern England where it has been reintroduced since prehistoric times, it will grow 100 feet, and its trunks flushed red in the late evening form a wonderful sight. The smaller male flowers, with their pale yellow pollen, are on the same tree as the female flowers. Natural regeneration may turn some heaths into pinewoods. The fallen needles, however, do help to prevent erosion of these light sands. Turpentine, resin and tar are among the tree's products.

Corsican Pine, *Pinus nigra. Var. corsicana.* Hardier than the Scots pine from which it can be distinguished by the twisted nature of the pair of bright green needles with faintly toothed margins, which are commonly 3 inches long. The terminal bud is pointed, whereas those of Scots and Lodgepole pines are blunt; and the cones and seeds are larger. The bark is grey and never bears the distinctive red flush of the last species. Its roots are long and thin, and young trees are best transplanted in winter when the ground is moist—though the tree is tolerant of drought, and yields good timber in E. England as well as in the S. Midlands and S. Wales.

Austrian Pine, *P. nigra, Var. austriaca.* Bushy appearance and long dark green needles distinguish from Scots pine. The

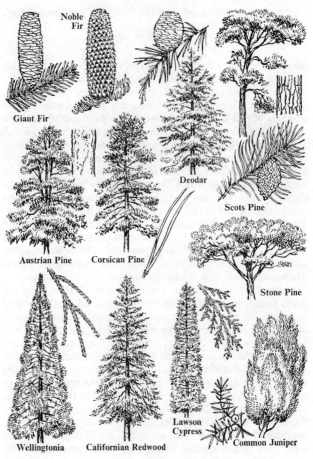

Noble Fir

Giant Fir

Deodar

Scots Pine

Austrian Pine

Corsican Pine

Stone Pine

Wellingtonia

Californian Redwood

Lawson Cypress

Common Juniper

cones are lighter. Admirable for coastal areas. It flourishes in the New Forest and on Brownsea Island, Dorset.

Stone Pine, *P. pinea* (Umbrella Pine). This last name gives a clue to its somewhat ungainly appearance. A native of the Mediterranean where it will grow 100 feet, this ornamental tree will seldom exceed half that height in Britain. Short single leaves are produced at first, but clusters of them 5–6 in. long are produced later. The seeds are edible, which may explain why this tree was possibly introduced to Britain in Tudor times.

Lodgepole Pine, *Pinus contorta. Var. latifolia.* Introduced from the western states of North America in 1853 or 1854. True green or yellowish green needles—rather than blue-green ones—distinguish it from the Scots pine. Dull brownish black bark. Most useful on poorer soils of Wales, western Scotland, northwest England and Ireland, and the Forestry Commission plant large quantities.

CEDARS *Abietaceae*

Cedar of Lebanon, *Cedrus libani.* 'Where an interruption is desirable to break the view, . . . I plant a cedar', said Capability Brown, hence the comparative abundance of this mountain tree of the eastern Mediterranean. Possibly introduced here in the 17th century, but few are planted today. The best examples are often on the lawns of country houses where, on good soil and faced with competition, they may grow 50 to 80 feet or even more; though in most gardens they stand alone, sending out extensive lower branches at a height of 6–10 feet, and casting up twin or triple boles to a height of 40–50 ft. The inch long needles survive on the tree for 3–5 years. Some specimens fail to produce flowers until over 100 years old.

Atlas Cedar, *C. atlantica* (Algerian Cedar). Another attractive member of the family, a native of the Atlas Mountains in Morocco, and so similar to the Cedar of Lebanon that some botanists fail to distinguish if from *C. libani*.

Deodar or **Indian Cedar,** *Cedrus deodara.* Shorter branches and a more pyramidal form, with a spire-like crown, distinguish this tree from its relatives. A native of the Himalayas, it was introduced in 1831 and hailed as a profitable source of timber; but these early hopes were not fulfilled, the variable British climate proving less congenial than Indian weather. However, this handsome ornamental tree frequently attains a height of 50 feet in England, and sometimes a little more.

LARCHES *Abietaceae*

European Larch, *Larix decidua.* Our only deciduous conifer, producing fresh green foliage each spring, larches are a most attractive addition to our landscape, though some two hundred years after the introduction to Britain of *L. decidua*, William Wordsworth (1770–1850) was condemning it as 'less pleasing' than any other tree. The bunches of needles or 'short shoots' make recognition easy, though the solitary first year needles at the tip of the twig cause a little confusion as they often behave like evergreens, remaining on the tree while all the other leaves wither and fall. A native of the European mountains, the larch will grow 80–140 ft. tall and develop a bole six to twelve feet in diameter when conditions are favourable, though it may be felled for timber when only 40 years old, for it is a rapid grower. It needs sunlight and space, and produces timber stronger than most and ideal for gates, fences and boats.

Japanese Larch, *L. leptolepis.* This native of the Japanese mountains was brought to Britain in 1861, and has grown increasingly popular, by virtue of its rapid growth, in the past half century. The russet or rust-red twigs distinguish it from the European larch which it is tending to displace. It is shorter than the European larch, and the needles are a less vivid green.

Hybrid Larch, *L. eurolepis.* Successive Dukes of Atholl played a prominent part in making known the virtues of the European larch, and the fourth Duke planted no less than 27 million larches on 15,000 acres. Years later, at Dunkeld, Perthshire, in 1904, the female flowers of a Japanese larch chanced to be cross-pollinated from male flowers of one of the Duke's European larches. The hybrids grew so much faster than either parent, and fared so well on poor land judged unsuitable for both species, that the Forestry Commission now have seed orchards in which the two parent trees are planted in alternate rows to promote cross fertilisation. The characters of the hybrid are variable and intermediate between their forebears.

FIRS *Abietaceae*

Silver Fir, *Abies alba.* A native of Central and Southern Europe. Introduced to Harefield Park, Uxbridge, in 1603. Specimens 200 feet high have been grown in Germany, but 80 ft. is nearer the average height for Britain, though it has been known to reach 150 ft. A slow grower at first, it begins after some 12 years to grow steadily for about 200 years, producing seedless cones after only 20 years and fertile seed when twice that age. The grey-brown trunk is smooth and erect, though older specimens—and it may live 400 years—may appear silver-grey and marked by cracks. The yellow-white timber is useful for indoor or under-water work.

Giant Fir, Grand Fir, *A. grandis.* A native of North America, reaching 250 ft. in its home territories and over 100 ft. in Britain. Long and short leaves—the former lengthier than the inch long leaves of the silver fir—lie flat on its branches. The buds, unlike those of the last species, are resinous. Useful timber is produced from this ornamental tree.

Noble Fir, *A. nobilis.* Another North American tree often preferred nowadays to the silver fir, with recurved tips to the upper leaves and big globular cones. The foliage is light green and silvery beneath.

Common or **Norway Spruce,** *Picea abies.* The Christmas tree,

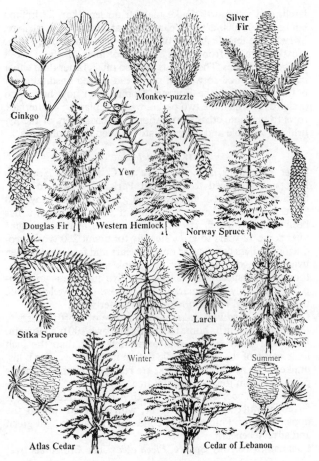

Silver Fir

Ginkgo

Monkey-puzzle

Yew

Douglas Fir   Western Hemlock   Norway Spruce

Sitka Spruce

Larch

Winter   Summer

Atlas Cedar   Cedar of Lebanon

114

native to most of Europe apart from Denmark and the Netherlands, and introduced to Britain some time before 1548. Its fossil remains have been found in Tertiary formations in Britain. Prince Albert introduced one to Windsor Castle as a Christmas tree in 1841, and Princess Lieven, according to Greville's *Diary*, adopted them at earlier Christmas seasons. It grows 18 in. a year or more on good sites, and 80 ft. trees are produced in 50 years. Continental specimens will grow 200 ft., but 120–150 ft. is good for Britain. It is a graceful tree, assuming an erect pyramidal form, with a tapering trunk—often 10 ft. in circumference—and a prominent leading shoot at the crown. The smooth light brown bark gradually becomes scaly and bits and pieces may fall off. The branchlets, almost opposite, are thickly clad with rich-green pointed needles half to three-quarters of an inch long, which endure for six years or so. It does well in deep shade, but may need light, moist soil for really rapid growth. The roots remain near the surface and it often fares badly in gales. Light, durable timber is much used.

Sitka spruce, *P. sitchensis.* A native of Alaska and the Pacific coast of N. America which arrived in Britain early in the last century. A quick grower, reaching nearly 200 ft. in America, and a few individuals in Britain exceed half that figure. Stiff, pointed needles tinged with blue distinguish it from the Norway spruce. Short, pale-brown cones with a rugged edge to each of the slender scales are distinctive. The grey-brown bark looks smooth and feels rough. It thrives so well on the poor, peaty soils of Wales, Scotland and North and west England, where the rainfall is high, that the Forestry Commission annually sow some 3,000 lbs of seed, most of it imported from British Columbia. It does less well on the drier ground of south and east England, but over the whole country, it is planted more than any other tree. Paper mills claim much timber.

Douglas Fir, *Pseudotsuga menziesii* (Douglas spruce, Red fir). In its native Washington, D.C., U.S.A., this remarkable tree has been known to grow over 300 ft. and to survive for 750 years. One at West Dean, Sussex, is 160 ft. high, and the specimen at Powis Castle, near Welshpool, Montgomeryshire, is 181 ft. tall. Its potential height in Britain is a matter for conjecture. Its name commemorates David Douglas (1798–1834) who introduced the seed to Britain. While tolerant of drought, it fares best where there is a good rainfall, growing 30 in. a year on well drained soil in the West Country. The solitary bright green needles an inch or so long leave a smooth round scar on the twig if torn off. Long pointed buds on the shoot—rather similar to those of beech—are distinctive.

CYPRESS FAMILY *Cupressaceae*

Juniper, *Juniperus communis*. An attractive grey-green shrub, indigenous to Britain and much of Europe, which may sometimes grow into a 12 ft. miniature tree. The gin-like scent of the sharp blue-green needles in whorls of three is often noticeable. The greenish female flowers grow at the axils of the leaves, and the yellow-green male flowers or catkins are on separate plants. The green berries ripen to silvery-purple in autumn, becoming blue-black in their second year. In recent years this widespread species has much declined, especially on its favourite chalk downs of S.E. England, mainly owing to more intensive farming. The plant also thrives on the limestone hills, heaths, moors and birch woods of the north and in the Highlands.

Lawson Cypress, *Chamaecyparis lawsoniana*. A native of Oregon and California that was discovered in 1852, this neat and hardy evergreen is widely grown in English gardens, though it does not reach the vast heights—120–200 ft.— achieved in its native haunts. The scaly dark-green leaves, in rows of four, survive for several years. Crimson male flowers appear at the tips of the branchlets, and small globular cones are produced. Its strong, light timber is valued in America, but the main stem too often forks in our own climate for it to be acceptable to foresters.

Western Hemlock, *Tsuga heterophylla* (Prince Albert's Fir). A valuable—and beautiful—conifer from North America that is now popular with British foresters, for it grows well in the moderate shade of other trees and yields a profitable timber crop. The scent of its crushed leaves is said to resemble that of the hemlock of roadside verges, though the two species are in no way related. The tree is easily recognised by the haphazard manner in which the needles of varying length grow out from the stem, with no kind of order about it. It will grow 100 ft. in Britain, and twice as much across the Atlantic. Numbers of egg-shaped cones are produced.

Wellingtonia, The Big Tree, Mammoth Tree, *Sequoia gigantea*. A tree that will live for 3,000 years and grow to 320 ft. in its native North America. Specimens planted in England 70 years ago now stand 150 ft. high, and the tallest of all, at Endsleigh, on the Devon–Cornwall border, is 165 ft. tall. The conical form and spiral arrangement of the leaves are distinctive. Tree-creepers frequently roost in it.

Californian Redwood, *S. sempervirens*. Another gigantic tree, growing 350 ft. in N. America where it was discovered in 1795. Its value as timber is considerable. The motor road through Yosemite National Park, California, cuts through the bole of one tree. It is less resistant to frost than the last species, but sometimes does well in Britain if planted in sheltered gardens where it may grow rapidly to 150 ft. The trunk is brown, with thick soft bark, and the needles may be likened to yew.

YEW FAMILY *Taxaceae*

Yew, *Taxus baccata*. Venerated in Britain in prehistoric times, this tree may owe its prominent position in churchyards to its status as a symbol of triumph over death. It is most common in the south and west of England, where Christian influence was powerful, and less common in districts of Eastern England that were long under pagan rule. The famous Crowhurst yew, now largely hollow, is 33 ft in diameter and it is thought to be well over 1,000 years old. The dark, glossy-green and pointed leaves, like the rusty-red bark and seeds, are poisonous to humans and animals, and dead clippings of yew are particularly dangerous. Yet wild deer which begin sampling the leaves at an early age appear to be safe, for they frequently eat large quantities without harm. The innocuous red fruit protecting the poisonous seed is much liked by nuthatches, marsh and coal tits, as well as mistle thrushes. The finest yew wood in Europe is the Kingley Vale National Nature Reserve, four miles from Chichester, Sussex.

THE ANGIOSPERMS

MAGNOLIA FAMILY *Magnoliaceae*

Tulip Tree, *Liriodendron tulipifera* (Yellow Poplar, Whitewood). An attractive tree from Ohio and Florida, U.S.A., where it will grow 200 ft. Specimens grown in Britain since the 17th century, often to a height of 80 ft. The large lobed leaf which appears to be cut off in the middle and which grows on a stalk 3 in. long is distinctive. Long, pointed winter buds, sheltered by twin scales, grow on short stalks, and the grooved bark is grey. The magnificent greenish-white flowers—yellow inside— bloom June–August. The fruits rarely ripen in Britain.

LAURACEAE FAMILY *Lauraceae*

Sweet Bay-tree, *Laurus nobilis*. Introduced to Britain from the Mediterranean in the early 16th century, this standard tree or shrub fares best in warmer parts of south and south-west England, though nowhere does it attain a height of 80 ft. as in S. Europe and Africa. The smooth, lean evergreen leaves are much in demand for flavouring fish dishes and soups. Male and female flowers grow on different plants.

LIME FAMILY *Tiliaceae*

Common Lime, *Tilia europaea.* A familiar hybrid between the small and large-leaved limes, this pleasant tree is often planted around country houses and sometimes occurs in hedges and small woods. Heart-shaped leaves, dark-green above and paler below, with tiny teeth round the edge, and a straight, tall trunk are typical. A height of 80–90 ft. is not unusual in good light soil. The yellowish clusters of flowers, with a strong scent comparable to honeysuckle, are attractive to many useful insects. Many specimens are 500 years old. The light wood is much used in musical instruments.

Small-Leaved Lime, *T. cordata* (Red Lime). Smaller leaves with tiny reddish hairs, and erect flowers distinguish this tree from the last species. It favours limestone woods.

Large-Leaved Lime, *T. platyphyllos.* Larger pointed leaves and flowers usually restricted to about three to a cluster. Widespread but not often found in woods.

THE ROSE FAMILY *Rosaceae*

Sloe or **Blackthorn,** *Prunus spinosa.* Abundant short spikes of the tiny white flowers of this small tree or shrub make a pleasing sight in early spring, especially as they stand out sharply against the dark twigs. There are five white petals and 15–20 stamens surrounding the solitary carpel in the flower, which is generally fertilised by bees. The twigs are densely massed in hedgerows, and a small black plumlike fruit is produced. Common almost everywhere. March–May.

Almond, *P. amygdalus.* A native of western Asia that has gained immense popularity for suburban streets and gardens. The leaves tend to be narrower than those of other Prunus. The pink flowers—or white ones of the Bitter Almond—appear in March–May, and the edible seeds sometimes ripen even in S. England.

Wild Cherry, Gean, *P. avium*. Probably a native of Britain, though the Romans may have added to our stocks, and cultivated cherries of Kentish orchards are said to have come from Flanders in the time of Henry VIII. Yet hawkers were selling them in London in 1415. Gean is the most widespread and tallest species, 80–100 ft. with shining light brown bole, drooping, toothed and oval leaves, shaded bronze in spring before turning pale green. White flowers have 5 heart-shaped petals, faintly notched. Fruit red or black. Common in woods, hedges, especially in southern beechwoods.

Wild or **Dwarf Cherry,** *P. cerasus*. Named after Cerasus-Kerasund—a town in western Asia where Lucullus obtained the cherries that were cultivated in Italy. A suckering shrub, 3–10 ft. tall, from which the rare Morello cherry of acid soils is derived. Cup-like flowers with notched oval petals help to distinguish it. It is never found north of Cumberland.

Bird Cherry, *P. padus*. A shrub or small tree up to 30 ft. high easily distinguished from the other cherries by the small fragrant flowers springing from long loose spikes—not clustered in umbels—and by the black, bitter fruit, small and with a wrinkled stone. Common only in Wales and N. England. The strong red wood of all the cherries is useful for furniture.

Crab Apple, *Malus sylvestris*. A small woodland and hedgerow tree, 20–50 ft. high, with rounded form, reddish-brown twigs and toothed, pointed oval leaves, sometimes downy underneath, but varying a good deal in shape. Pink tinted and streaked white flowers in umbel-like clusters with yellow anthers. The small yellow-green or scarlet apple contains so much malic acid that it is best not eaten raw.

Wild Pear, *Pyrus communis*. The cultivated pear probably came to Britain from southern Europe or Asia and the wild form may be considered an escape. A small, long-lived tree 20–60 ft. high, the species may be identified by its pyramidal form, dark-yellowish twigs, toothed and pointed oval leaves, downy underneath, and clusters of white flowers with purple anthers. The small fruit is green until late autumn, when it turns a brownish yellow. It is too gritty and sour for eating. Uncommon; and very rare outside S. England.

Medlar, *Mespilus germanica.* Another escape from cultivation. Indigenous to Greece and the Middle East, and probably introduced here late in the 16th century. The true Medlar is a multi-branched and thorny shrub or tree that may be 10–20 ft. high, but many of our specimens lack thorns and may be from seed derived from gardens and sown by birds. Large oblong and undivided leaves, downy beneath and generally untoothed, go yellow in autumn. The single short-stalked flowers, white or pale pink with red anthers, have long leaf-like sepals which survive on the brown fruits. Both flowers and fruit measure about an inch across. Uncommon in south-country hedgerows. It blooms in May–June and the fruit ripens October–November.

Quince, *Cydonia vulgaris.* A native of Iran and the Middle East which flourishes on sheltered sites in S. England. Large single pink or white flowers with long leaf-like sepals and smooth leaves. The fruit looks like a distorted pear and has a strong scent and acid flavour, but it is much in demand for jam-making.

White Beam, *Sorbus aria.* A delightful but little known 'beam' —derived from the Saxon word for 'tree'—which in exposed places may be a mere shrub 4–5 ft. tall. On good chalk or limestone soil it will grow rapidly for ten years, then slowly mature into a tree 40 ft. tall. Smooth bark, becoming slightly fissured with age, broad, oval leaves, with much variation in the toothing, and white cottony down beneath. The heads of white flowers and red berries comparable to Rowan, with which it hybridises. Widespread but local in woods and scrub-edges on calcareous soil. Known in the north as the Chess Apple.

Wild Service, *S. torminalis*. Maple-like green leaves, with hairs on the under-surface when young. Larger flowers and slightly smaller fruit distinguish it from the last species. These brown, egg-shaped fruits can be eaten when frosted. Never in Scotland and rare in North. Clay and limestone soils preferred.

Mountain Ash, Rowan, *S. aucuparia* (Witch Wood, Fowler's Service, Wiggin, Wicken, Cock-drunks). This native of Britain and most of Europe has come much into favour in recent years, for it will thrive almost anywhere, producing a straight smooth bole, large alternate pinnate leaves superficially resembling those of ash—to which it bears no relationship—thick clusters of creamy-white flowers, and vivid red berries. It flourishes on mountains up to 2,600 ft. Bird-catchers used the fruits for bait. Formerly used as a charm against witches.

Hawthorn, *Crataegus monogyna*. A common thorny shrub whose 3–5 lobed leaves and white or pinkish strongly-scented flowers must be as familiar as any in the land. It blooms in May–June, about a month after Blackthorn. The round dark-red berries are much in demand by birds. Also known as May, Whitethorn, and Quickthorn.

PEA FAMILY *Leguminosae*

Common Laburnum, *Laburnum anagyroides*. Springtime in suburbia owes much to this attractive tree from Central and Southern Europe, which Gerard grew in his English garden in 1597, when it was known as Beane Trefoyle. It prospers on most soils, but seldom grows more than 20–30 ft. The seeds, in long downy pods, are poisonous. The timber is well liked by wood turners and makers of musical instruments.

Locust, or **False Acacia,** *Robinia pseudacacia*. One of the first American trees to be introduced to Britain early in the 17th century. It owes its name to American missionaries who associated the fruits with 'locusts and wild honey' eaten in the wilderness by John the Baptist. William Cobbett, on returning from America in 1820, extolled the tree's virtues for timber and demand exceeded supplies, though the tough wood is inclined to crack. A light elegant tree that is an asset to any large garden, it has a heavily lined bole and graceful, lean leaves in seven to ten pairs. White, fragrant laburnum-like flowers appear in May, and there are slender dark brown seed pods.

BOX FAMILY *Buxaceae*

Box, *Buxus sempervirens.* This evergreen shrub or small tree, with grey, faintly fissured bark, drooping branches and small oblong, oval leaves in pairs, may be indigenous to the North and South Downs, the Cotswolds and Chilterns. The small whitish-green flowers are clustered near the base of the leaves, with the female flower being the uppermost one in the middle of each cluster. March–May. This tree will grow 20–30 ft.

THE PLANE FAMILY *Platanaceae*

The London Plane, *Platanus acerifolia.* What would London be without its planes? No other tree thrives so well in the face of fog, fumes, asphalt and flagstones, growing 70–90 ft. in conditions that might discourage the hardiest of species. Yet this hybrid did not appear before 1670, and nowhere does it grow wild. Its leaves, resembling those of sycamore to which it is not related, soon lose any coating of grime when it rains; and the outer bark, cast off by the soft bark beneath, carries away any harmful coating.

WILLOW FAMILY *Salicaceae*

White or **Huntingdon Willow,** *Salix alba.* A common species, probably a native of Britain, recognisable by rather upright branches and silvery white foliage due to the hairy nature of the leaves. These are 2–4 in. long, faintly toothed, and narrow and pointed at the tips. If not lopped, it will grow 60–80 ft., whereas all too many of the lopped specimens fall a prey to disease.

Crack Willow, *S. fragilis* (Withy). The name of this most common willow of damp sites—which also grows 1,300 ft. up on the Northumbrian hills—results from the brittleness of the branches and hairless twigs which break off easily at the base. The long narrow and faintly toothed leaves may extend to 6 in. The male catkins, some two inches long, and the thinner female catkins grow on different trees.

Pussy Willow, Goat Willow or **Sallow,** *S. caprea*. This sallow, 6–15 ft. tall, thrives in drier places, and its bright pollen-covered male catkins are most attractive in April and May. The variable leaves are broader than those of other willows, and extend to 2–4 in. The catkins or 'palms' are more or less unstalked and appear before the leaves. Widespread and common **Cricket Bat Willow,** *S. coerulea*. A hybrid between the white and goat willow, mainly found in E. England. It grows rapidly and will attain 100 ft. Its pyramidal form and thin, almost hairless leaves distinguish it from other species.

Weeping Willow, *S. babylonica*. The most beautiful of the willows, probably introduced into Britain from China in the 17th century, and now a familiar sight in riverside gardens.

Dwarf Willow, *S. herbacea*. Our smallest willow, only a foot or two high, and restricted to mountains and hills. Least Willow.

Creeping Willow, *S. repens*. A variable bush ranging in height from a few inches to 6 ft., and the only lowland willow with creeping roots. Small silky leaves and slender catkins. Locally common on damp heaths, fens and dunes. April–May.

Almond-Leaved or **French Willow,** *S. triandra*. The specific name of this small tree—rarely over 20 ft.—is derived from the three stamens in the male flower. The bark often flakes off. The slender lance-shaped leaves are 2–4 in. in length, and the tree's habit of producing straight, pliant shoots used in basket-work makes it a common pollarded tree on river banks.

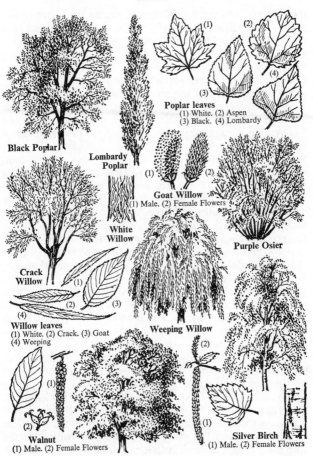

Black Poplar

Lombardy Poplar

Poplar leaves
(1) White. (2) Aspen
(3) Black. (4) Lombardy

Goat Willow
(1) Male. (2) Female Flowers

White Willow

Crack Willow

Purple Osier

Willow leaves
(1) White. (2) Crack. (3) Goat
(4) Weeping

Weeping Willow

Walnut
(1) Male. (2) Female Flowers

Silver Birch
(1) Male. (2) Female Flowers

Bay Willow or **Sweet Bay Willow,** *S. pentandra*. A tree of wet places, with hairless shiny twigs, thick, dark green leaves that smell like the bay tree, and catkins that are often later than those of other willows. The only willow with 5 stamens or more in the flower. Mainly in the N. and N. Ireland. May–June.

Osier or **Withy,** *S. viminalis*. Much used for basket work, this shrub or small tree of wet sites is widespread and common. Young flexible branches are clothed with short hairs, but these are soon discarded. Long, narrow lance-shaped leaves may be 8–9 in. long. Catkins appear in March–April before the leaves open.

Purple Osier, *S. purpurea*. An attractive osier, 6–10 ft. tall, with purple bark and thin, tough branches. The broad, long leaves have serrated edges. The male catkins make a fine sight in spring when covered with golden pollen. This is our only willow with the stalks or filaments of the two stamens in the male flower joined. Widespread and locally common.

Common Sallow, *S. atrocinerea*. Downy twigs, ridges beneath the bark, and small, narrowing leaves, generally with brownish-shaded hairs distinguish this species. Widespread and abundant in damp ground. March–April.

Round-Eared Sallow, *S. aurita*. A small bush of moist woods and damp heaths, particularly in the N. and W., with small, oblong and wrinkled leaves, and growing to 2–4 ft. The leaves are usually downy underneath, and the large stipules echo the shape of ears, hence the name.

White Poplar, *Populus alba* (Abele). Dark gashes on the smooth grey bark—less smooth at the base—and cottony white down on the young twigs and buds distinguish this short poplar which rarely exceeds 50 ft. The lobed and triangular leaves on long vigorous shoots are covered underneath with white down; leaves on short stalks are not so lobed and more oval. The vertically flattened leaf stalk ensures that the leaves tremble with every breath of wind. Inch long cylindrical catkins can be seen in March and April. Male white poplars are uncommon in Britain. The tree may well have been introduced here from the Netherlands.

Aspen, *P. tremula.* Whereas the last species will reach its prime in 50 years and survive for the best part of two centuries, this graceful tree with the fluttering leaves tends to decay after about half a century, especially if insects penetrate the bark. Yet it grows 40–80 ft., and suckers freely. The thin, bluntly toothed leaves more or less heart-shaped, are on long, slender, flattened stalks, hence their quivering. Common in damp woods and on heaths, particularly in the N. and W.

Black Italian Poplar, *P. x. canadensis, P. serotina.* A tall tree which appeared in Britain in the 18th century as a hybrid of the black poplar with an American species, *P. deltoidea.* It is the last of the poplars to come into leaf, and the stem lacks the swellings and burrs of *P. nigra.*

Black Poplar, *P. nigra.* While reaching 50–60 ft., it is less lofty than the last species, with branches that spread more and arch earthwards. Swellings and nodules occur on the bole. It is indigenous to the eastern counties where it thrives in rich wet soils.

Lombardy Poplar, *P. pyramidalis, P. Italica.* Some botanists consider this familiar tree to be a variety of the black poplar. Others regard it as a separate species, a native of Iran and northern India, which long ago became abundant in Lombardy and other areas of Europe. The almost vertical branches which give the tree a slender cypress-like shape are unmistakable. It is a rapid grower, reaching 60 feet in its first 20 years if planted in good, damp—but well drained—soil, and 100 ft. in 30 years.

BIRCH FAMILY *Betulaceae*

Silver Birch, *Betula verrucosa.* Perhaps our most graceful tree, a pioneer that is quick to colonise heaths and hillsides up to

2,500 ft. above sea level, providing shelter for other species. Untroubled by extreme heat or intense cold, it flourishes from Lapland to Siberia. It will grow 4–5 ft. in a wet year on the acid heaths and peats of Surrey and Sussex, though 1–2 ft. a season is a more normal rate of growth. After about 60 years it decays, though I know 50 ft. specimens that have survived 80 years. The peeling black and white bark, glossy brown twigs, and variable oval, pointed, toothed leaves make it easily recognisable. The male catkins are longer than the female ones. This species was formerly *B. alba*, then *B. pendula*.

Downy Birch, *B. pubescens*. Differs from the last species in not being rugged at the base of the trunk or having warty outgrowths on the duller twigs, which are covered with down. The leaves are darker green and downy, and the bark may be whiter. It favours wetter conditions and is most common in Scotland and N. England, hybridising with the last species.

Dwarf Birch, *B. nana*. A low downy undershrub found in the high moorland bogs of Scotland. Uncommon.

Alder, *Alnus glutinosa*. **Aller.** A common tree of riversides and low-lying damp ground where it normally grows 30–40 ft. high, though specimens on good moist soil and in a humid microclimate may be two or three times as tall. Rough, black bark, glossy 3 in. leaves, rounder than those of birch, and sticky when young, are distinguishing features. Conspicuous red scales mark the male catkins and red-brown bracts cover the fleshy scales of the erect female spikes. The fruit, produced when the tree is 20 years old, contains air bubbles that aid distribution by stream and river.

HAZEL FAMILY *Corylaceae*

Hornbeam, *Carpinus betulus* (Yoke Elm). A native of the English Midlands and south-east where it has long been coppiced. Smooth grey bark dotted with white, and leaves that are rougher than those of beech and narrower than the leaves of hazel. They are hairy beneath and doubly toothed, arranged alternately on the stem, and extending to 1–3 in. They become a brilliant yellow or golden in autumn. The unisexual flowers are on the same tree, the male catkins hanging down while the smaller female ones are erect until the fruit has formed. These small nutlike fruit remain on the tree for months. Abundant only in S.E. England.

Hazel, *Corylus avellana.* The undeveloped 'Lamb's Tails' appear in autumn, gradually lengthening throughout the winter, and by February these male catkins are bright with yellow pollen. The female flowers are strangely inconspicuous, though they comprise vivid red styles and stigmas springing from a two-chambered ovary protected by small bracts. These cells, when fertilised, develop into the kernel of the hazel nut, so attractive to the squirrels and birds that ensure the distribution of the species. The pointed, oval leaves are toothed and sometimes have a purplish tint. Widespread and abundant in woods, hedgerows and gardens, preferring good well drained soil.

BEECH FAMILY *Fagaceae*

Beech, *Fagus sylvatica.* Surely the most beautiful of forest trees, growing slowly on the poorer soils, or more quickly on good calcareous soils, to a height of 100 ft., and developing a smooth round trunk that may be 20 ft. in girth. The long, pointed buds are borne alternately and protected by overlapping brown scales. The silky oval leaves are a most attractive light green when young, and a brilliant russet and copper shade in autumn; the shrivelled leaves sometimes remain on the tree until forced off by the next crop of leaves. Female flowers, unlike the male flowers on the same tree, are unstalked. The beech mast—3-sided nuts, in a bristly husk—contain 17–20 per cent oil that can be used in cooking. It is a valuable nurse for other forest trees, though eventually it will dominate

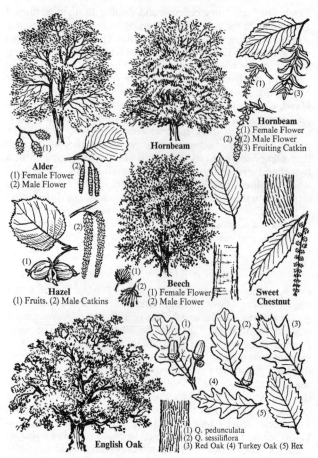

Hornbeam

Hornbeam
(1) Female Flower
(2) Male Flower
(3) Fruiting Catkin

Alder
(1) Female Flower
(2) Male Flower

Hazel
(1) Fruits. (2) Male Catkins

Beech
(1) Female Flower
(2) Male Flower

Sweet Chestnut

English Oak

(1) Q. pedunculata
(2) Q. sessiliflora
(3) Red Oak (4) Turkey Oak (5) Hex

competing species through the heavy shade of its foliage. The timber is useful for furniture.

Copper Beech, *F. sylvatica var. purpurea.* This popular ornamental tree is not a separate species. It suddenly developed in Hanleiter Forest, Germany, some two centuries ago. Photosynthesis occurs quite normally, ample chlorophyll lying with the purple colouring substance in the outer sections of the leaves.

Oak, *Quercus robur.* Our largest and most familiar tree, with rough, furrowed, grey-brown bark, crooked branches and broad crown. The lobed, oblong leaves have short stalks, and turn a rich brown in the autumn. The male flowers hang in loose catkins a couple of inches long or more and are easily unnoticed amid the leaves; the female flowers on the same tree are usually on short erect stalks a little higher than the male catkins. Acorns are produced when the tree is 60–70 years old. The timber is usable at 150 years, but trees should not be felled so early, and they will continue growing for 500 years. Common in woods and hedges especially on clay, but the finest specimens may be on sandy loams. The tallest oak is 128 ft. at Berwick. The greatest girth 39 ft. 9 in. at Bowthorp, Lincs.

Durmast Oak or **Sessile Oak,** *Q. petrae.* This native oak is most common on the acid soils of the N. and W., and in S. and W. Ireland, though it can also be seen on the light acid sands of the S. and E. It lacks the two lobes at the base of the leaves found in the last species. There is little or no stalk to the acorn, a longer stalk on the leaf.

Turkey Oak, *Q. cerris.* A Balkan tree that reached Britain in the first years of the 18th century. It does well on the light soils of S. England, but is less common northwards. Thick, greyer bark, longer and much more deeply jagged leaves, faintly downy beneath, and acorns with little or no stalk are aids to recognition. It is more pyramidal in form than our native oaks.

Holm Oak, *Q. ilex.* An evergreen oak from the Mediterranean, brought into Britain in the 16th century, and now common in parks and gardens. The oval leaves, pointed at the tip, endure for two years. The bark is black.

American Red Oak, *Q. rubra.* The brilliant red leaves, about eight inches long, have made this a popular ornamental tree in Britain. Other species have been introduced here, including *Q. coccinea,* with more pointed leaf lobes.

Sweet Chestnut, *Castanea sativa.* A native of the Mediterranean, probably introduced to Britain by the Romans. The spirally twisted bark, rich green lance-shaped and jagged leaves 10 in. long, and the stiff, sweet-smelling catkins are notable features. The pale yellow male catkins, like the less conspicuous female flowers, are borne on the same tree in May–July. The annual October harvest of nuts is not dropped before the age of 25 years. Five centuries probably forms the average life span in England, but many specimens are much older. Most reach a height of 60–80 ft.; a few have passed 100 ft.

ELM FAMILY *Ulmaceae*

Common Elm, *Ulmus procera.* The English Elm, as it is often called, is a most beautiful hedgerow tree, common in the S., but less so in Scotland, and rapidly becoming less abundant as the fields grow in size and fashions change. Dutch elm disease killed many specimens, and its shallow rooting habits, large size and susceptibility to pests and diseases make it unsuitable for urban planting. It is no longer easy to buy young elm trees. Yet this handsome species deserves to be encouraged in the countryside. The bole is deeply furrowed downwards, and the twigs clothed with corky bark. Broad oval, and pointed leaves are borne alternately on the stem. Their hairs can sting—mildly—like a nettle's. The tree grows 80–100 ft., lives for 500 years or more, and suckers freely.

Wych Elm, *U. glabra.* A tall dome-crowned tree of open woodland, with leaves that are larger and rougher than those of the

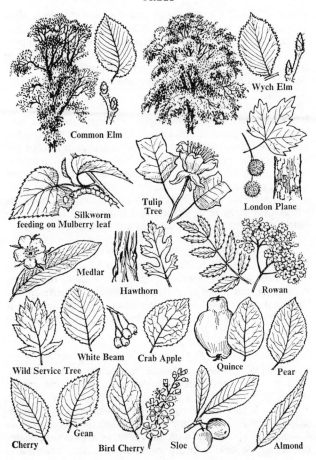

Common Elm

Wych Elm

Silkworm feeding on Mulberry leaf

Tulip Tree

London Plane

Medlar

Hawthorn

Rowan

Wild Service Tree

White Beam

Crab Apple

Quince

Pear

Cherry

Gean

Bird Cherry

Sloe

Almond

133

English Elm—3–6 inches long—and the shorter stalk is often almost hidden by the rounded base of one side of the leaf. Suckers are seldom produced. Dark red-brown flowers appear in February–March, though seed cannot be expected before the age of about 30 years. Most common in N. and W., particularly in limestone woods. Hybridises with other elms.

MULBERRY FAMILY *Moraceae*

Black Mulberry Tree, *Morus nigra.* Mulberry trees have been cultivated in China as food for silkworms for at least 4,600 years, and these Asiatic trees were being grown in Europe 900 years ago. The species may not have been introduced to Britain until after the 15th century, but James I insisted on the lavish planting of St James's Park and Greenwich Park in 1609. They grow slowly, the rough, heavy trunk producing low branches which bear large heart-shaped and three-lobed leaves alternately on the stem. Few specimens are planted today.

HOLLY FAMILY *Aquifoliaceae*

Holly, *Ilex aquifolium.* The glossy green leaves of this evergreen need no description. It is odd that some of the leaves, particularly the higher ones, lack the normal prickles or spines. The small 4-petalled white flowers develop red berries only if a male tree is near at hand. It grows slowly, but some British specimens are 50 or 60 ft. high.

SPINDLE TREE FAMILY *Celastraceae*

Spindle Tree, *Euonymus europaeus.* A most attractive tall shrub, 6–12 ft. high, notable for the rich red, yellow and mauve shades of the leaves in autumn and the bright pink berries. The greyish bark is smooth, the pale green leaves are lance-shaped, slightly toothed and opposite; and the greenish-white flowers with 4 petals and 4 stamens lie at the axils of the poisonous leaves. Spindle is locally common in woods, hedges and scrub on chalk and limestone, but it also thrives at times on clay and other soils. Uncommon in Scotland. May–June.

Horse Chestnut Family *Sapindaceae*

Horse Chestnut, *Aesculus hippocastanum*. A native of the Balkans, the Middle East and Northern India which was probably introduced to Britain in the 16th century. Much planted in parks and shelterbelts, it likes dry or moist base-rich soils, but fares quite well in heavy marls and clays or even shallow chalk, especially in a warm micro-climate. The heavily protected brown buds thick with resin are a familiar sight as they gradually unfurl in early spring. The leaves may be as much as 18 in. across, each one being divided into five or seven leaflets that broaden before suddenly tapering to a point. The flowers comprise a bell-shaped calyx with 5 lobes and 4–5 petals of unequal size splashed with yellow and pink dots that guide visiting insects to the hoard of nectar. Every schoolboy is familiar with the 'conkers', produced almost annually from the age of 20 years. It is a rapid grower, but seldom reaches 80 ft., or survives more than 200 years.

Red-Flowered Horse Chestnut, *A. carnea*. A smaller hybrid of the last species with *A. pavia* which appeared about 1820.

Maple Family *Aceraceae*

Sycamore, *Acer pseudoplatanus* (Great Maple). A handsome tree from Central Europe, probably introduced to Britain in the 15th century. Growing 18 ft. in 10 years, and 40 ft. in 25 years on good deep soil, it makes a useful addition to parks and farm shelterbelts, and it even fares well on light acid sands and in exposed sites open to winds from the sea. It lives for 150–250 years and may reach a height of 80 ft. The leaves, divided into 5 lobes, are larger than those of field maple, and frequently sticky with sugar from the sap. The separate male and female flowers hang in long yellow-green clusters in May and June.

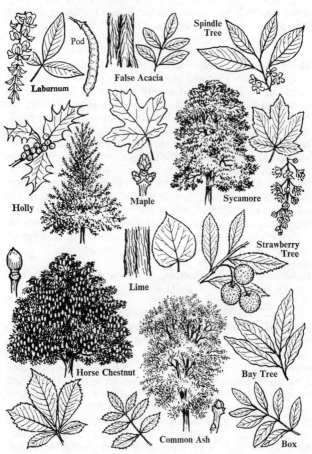

Laburnum   Pod   False Acacia   Spindle Tree

Holly   Maple   Sycamore

Lime   Strawberry Tree

Horse Chestnut   Bay Tree

Common Ash   Box

Common in woods, hedges, parks and gardens. There is some demand for the wood for turnery and household uses.

Field or **English Maple,** *A. campestre.* This small tree or shrub is probably indigenous to England south of Northumberland, and its has been introduced to Scotland and Ireland. Although sometimes growing 20–40 ft., it is more often found as a shrub in hedgerows and thickets, with light grey rough bark, pairs of opposite kidney-shaped leaves divided into five lobes which are a glossy light green in springtime, darkening with age and turning rich red and yellow in autumn. Greenish-yellow flowers appear in May and June, and the downy fruits are akin to those of sycamore. Most common on chalk and limestone.

WALNUT FAMILY *Juglandaceae*

Walnut, *Juglans regia.* A native of the Himalayas, the Middle East and S. Europe, probably introduced to Britain in the 15th century. With rugged grey bark, and large green ash-like leaves comprising two, three or four pairs of leaflets and a terminal one, all producing a pleasant aromatic scent, it makes a handsome tree which grows to a height of 40–100 ft. with a trunk that may be 18 ft. in girth. The tough wood is much in demand for gun stocks and furniture.

OLIVE FAMILY

Ash, *Fraxinus excelsior.* An exacting tree, demanding fertile, moist and fairly deep soil, and the damp, cool northern and eastern slopes if good timber is to be produced; though it will grow in most soils if protected from frost and granted ample light. Apart from the elder, it is our only native tree with opposite pinnate leaves. These are 6–10 in. long, with toothed lance-shaped leaflets produced from black buds. The inch-long keys or fruits are borne almost annually after the fortieth year. It attains a height of 80–100 ft. The tough timber is in demand for estate work and secures good prices.

HONEYSUCKLE FAMILY *Caprifoliaceae*

Elder, *Sambucus nigra.* Our only native shrub with opposite leaflets on each side of the leaf-stalk. Quickly grows 10–20 ft. in woods. Large umbel-like clusters of small creamy-white flowers and ripe black berries a familiar sight in hedgerows, thickets and other sites, especially on chalk downs and around rabbit warrens and badger setts.

Wayfaring Tree, *Viburnum lantana.* A downy shrub with opposite faintly toothed oval leaves, umbel-like creamy white flowers, and red berries that ripen to black. Locally common on chalk and limestone in S. Not in Ireland.

Guelder Rose, *V. opulus.* A tall shrub or small tree, 6–12 ft. high like the last species, with maple-like leaves, clusters of white flowers, and brilliant red berries. Frequent in fens, damp woods, heathland borders and other sites.

Honeysuckle, *Lonicera periclymenum.* Much disliked by foresters for the damage it does to young tree-stems, this woody climber with opposite oval, pale leaves twines in a clockwise direction, producing the familiar beautiful 2-lipped flowers with a long thin tube and a strong, sweet scent. The red berries are relished by coal and marsh tits and many other birds. Common in woods and hedgerows.

HEATH FAMILY *Ericaceae*

Strawberry Tree, *Arbutus unedo.* A small evergreen tree or shrub, a native of south-west Ireland and the Mediterranean countries, with alternate lance-shaped, leathery leaves, creamy-white clusters of flowers, and red berries. Local to Counties Cork and Kerry; rare.

TREES AND SITES

It is foolish to spend time and trouble planting trees on the wrong sites. Foresters have learned to look for certain 'indicator' plants that offer a clue to the nature of the soil and the kind of tree that could flourish there.

Wet low-lying areas rich in silts deposited by rivers and flood waters, and bearing alder, reeds and tussocks of purple moor grass.	Hybrid poplars, alder, crack, common and cricket bat willows.
Wet fertile clay with well grown sedges.	Alder, willow, western red cedar and Norway spruce.
Moist and fertile valley land.	Ash, elms, sycamore, hornbeam, alder, walnut lime, maple, western red cedar.
Good heavy clays, loams, and marls in the English midlands.	Oak, Turkey oak, lime, maple, hornbeam, Norway and Sitka spruce, Japanese larch, Scots or Corsican pine.
Poor acid sandy heathland invaded by fourth-rate oak scrub and slow-growing ash.	Silver birch and Scots pine.
Ill-drained heathland bearing little but crossed-leaved heath.	Lodgepole pine.
Black north country peat, wet and bearing purple moor grass.	Norway and Sitka spruce.

A much more detailed key to the selection of tree species for particular sites will be found in J. M. Caborn's *Shelterbelts and Windbreaks*, Faber, 1966.

Other recommended books are:

Brimble, L. J. F. *Trees in Britain*. Macmillan, London, 1948.

Edlin, H. L. *Know Your Conifers*. Forestry Commission Booklet No. 15, HMSO, London, 1965.

Edlin, H. L. *Trees, Woods and Man.* Collins, London, 1955.

Holbrook, A. W. *The Country Life Pocket Guide to Trees in Britain.* London, 1966

Stokoe, W. J. *The Observer's Book of Trees.* Frederick Warne, London.

Butterflies and Moths

Introduction – Life Cycle – Migration – Conservation –
What to Look For: 1, Butterflies; 2, Moths

INTRODUCTION

There are well over 200,000 species of butterflies and moths in the world, and species new to science are constantly being discovered. They are among the most recently evolved of the insects, and no fossil remains are older than the Tertiary Era of the past 75 million years. The butterflies on the British List number 68 species, of which eleven are migrants, and there are more than 2,000 species of moths in this country.

Butterflies and moths can be distinguished from each other by the nature of their antennae. In the butterfly, these organs of smell and balance are thin at the base, thickening to knob-like tips. The antennae of moths are generally thick at the base, tapering to a slender point; or they may be fringed or toothed. It should be added that the red and black burnet moths which fly by day like butterflies have club-like antennae, and the skipper butterflies, close relatives of the moths, have antennae that are only faintly thickened at the tip. Incidentally, if cabbage white butterflies lose their antennae, their sense of smell declines by less than half.

Many moths lay eggs that produce caterpillars harmful to the forester, farmer and gardener, though many more do not. The clothes moth's caterpillars have aroused the wrath of housewives since Old Testament times. Apart from the large and small cabbage whites, no British butterflies are harmful to man.

141

LIFE CYCLE

Butterflies and moths never grow. All increase in size occurs at the caterpillar stage.

Eggs. Most butterflies lay their eggs singly, each one on a separate plant or leaf, to which it becomes attached by a sticky secretion. The ringlet and marbled white butterflies dispense with this method, scattering their eggs as they fly over pastures, meadows and roadside verges. Nine species, including large and small tortoishells and large cabbage whites, lay their eggs in dense groups of over 100 or more. The top of the egg is seen under the microscope to dip faintly, and in the middle are minute openings or micropyles—'little doors'—through which the spermatozoa of the male penetrates to the interior of the egg and fertilises it. Some species, such as the small tortoishell, lay eggs in the autumn which hatch out in the following spring.

Larva. On emerging from the egg, most young caterpillars may promptly eat the shell. Speckled wood caterpillars die if denied this early meal of chitin. Marbled white and small skipper caterpillars eat nothing else before retiring into hibernation for the winter. Most caterpillars may be caught feeding at any hour of the day or night, munching their way through many times their own weight in food. The caterpillars of the familiar meadow brown, ringlet and wall butterflies feed only at night, while those of the rare swallow-tail, marbled white and dark green fritillary confine their meals to daytime. The Scotch argus caterpillar will eat at any hour of the day or night while it is young, but only during darkness as it approaches the chrysalis stage. The larvae of the skippers, using a comb-like flap at the anus, expel their excreta up to three feet, thus keeping their immediate surroundings clean. (Ford, E. B., 1945.)

Moulting. Periodically the business of eating and growing is interrupted by a short interval during which the caterpillar sheds its skin. Following much twisting and turning by the caterpillar, a slit develops in the skin of the back, and the head and then the thirteen segments are thrust through this opening. The new soft skin quickly hardens, and feeding is resumed—until the moulting process is repeated a number of times.

The Chrysalis. The larvae of some species spend their days in a silken shelter of their own construction, or in a tiny tent of grass neatly bound firm with silk—for all larvae have silk glands and a liquid is produced from two spinnerets on the head which, when dry, forms silk. On approaching the chrysalis stage, some species like the orange-tip or the whites make themselves firm by spinning a silken girdle around the waist. The blues and coppers may tie themselves to a leaf by a slender network of silk above and below, while the fritillaries and tortoishells hang head downwards from a blanket or pad of silk fixed to a hook in the tail. The thick outer cocoon and inner bed of silk protecting pupae are proof against rain and frost.

The Perfect Insect. Eventually the shell of the chrysalis splits along the thorax, between head and abdomen, and at the lower section of the wing cases, permitting the adult or imago to crawl out to freedom. The cramped, wet wings are extended; fluids from the body flow into them and within an hour or so the insect is ready for flight. These wings will be flapped 8–12 times a second, compared with 20–30 times a second for the dragonflies, and 50–70 times by some of the larger moths.

Feeding. The butterfly's appetite is modest. Lacking jaws, and possessing only a proboscis or tongue—and one family of moths lack even that and do not eat at all—the butterfly is content to suck nectar from the flowers, juice from the rotting fruit, or dew from the grass. Yet this is a creature that may migrate vast distances, crossing oceans and deserts with all the energy and the purposeful flight of powerful birds.

MIGRATION

Insect migration is a phenomenon that deserves increased attention, for it is as complex as it is fascinating. The impulse to migrate is so strong in some butterflies and moths at certain times that they will fly for hundreds of miles without changing course, granted the right weather conditions. Migrating butterflies travelling low above the ground and finding the way obstructed by tall oaks have been observed to ascend to the crowns of the trees before descending on the other side. They will sweep through railway tunnels and in and out of buildings which stand in their path, sometimes attaining a speed of 15 miles an hour or more.

Not all butterflies migrate in large swarms. Clouded yellows usually reach our shores in parties of two or three. If trapped and released many hours later when its companions have hurried on, a butterfly will return to the same course and rapidly fly off as if in pursuit of them.

Sometimes vast flocks may be seen. People in the streets of Barcelona, one day in 1870, could hardly see where they were going as flocks of painted lady butterflies estimated to number 40,000 drifted by. Few experts suspected that these creatures ever attempted a return passage later in the year, but in 1952, when insects of the same species left the Atlas Mountains in Morocco in vast numbers, hosts of them surging through Kent and Sussex and on to the Midlands, Wales and Scotland, there were signs that some of the migrants or their offspring attempted a return journey. Other invasions of painted lady butterflies from the Mediterranean occurred in Britain during 1964 and, on a smaller scale, in 1966.

Our native red admirals, too, are frequently reinforced by some migration from the Continent and Africa, and there is evidence that some of them fly south on a return journey in September and October. There is no evidence, however, of any return of the cabbage white butterflies which sometimes invade our east coasts. In the hot weeks of July, immense flocks of these insects numbering several millions make their way from Scandinavia into Central Europe, and some of them may be drifted to these shores.

Clouded yellow butterflies usually arrive here in small numbers during June, laying eggs which produce more individuals in August or even as late as October. In 1947, however, no fewer than 36,000 were recorded in Britain. Again, the Bath white, though quite common in France, is extremely rare in this country. Yet in 1945, more than 500 specimens were caught here, compared with about a hundred for the whole of the previous century.

It is probable that most or all of the thousand Camberwell beauties from Scandinavia recorded in Britain in the last century arrived aboard ships. It is significant that few were seen in England during the war; yet after trade with Scandinavia was resumed in 1945 and 1946, 59 of these handsome creatures were counted here. It is possible that they had been seeking hibernation quarters among timber loaded on to ships when the vessels put to sea.

The Cause of Migration. No one really knows why butterflies and moths migrate. Overcrowding in the insects' home quarters and a consequent shortage of food could be powerful factors in producing the phenomenon.

CONSERVATION

No aspects of conservation offer more difficult problems than those concerning the lepidoptera. The undoubted decline in many species of butterflies in recent years may be attributed to various causes. More intensive farming and forestry, the destruction of woods and hedgerows, the ploughing of headlands, the use of herbicides and insecticides, the displacement of downland turf by arable crops, the growing tidiness of roadside verges and of some churchyards, all these developments and more may have exercised a harmful influence. A sequence of mild winters, bringing a premature release from hibernation followed by cool, wet summers may also prove damaging.

Much research is needed if we are to understand all the factors influencing butterfly populations. Already there are signs that the sharp decline of the chalkhill blue butterfly is connected with modern changes in grazing pressure. The provision of piped water to the fields and the erection of electric fencing have opened some stretches of downland to grazing throughout the year, with harmful results on the butterflies; whereas on some downland grazed only in winter, the chalkhill blues still thrive. That may not be the whole story. On some sites the decline of the rabbit and the absence of sheep has enabled coarser grasses to smother the vetches on which the butterflies feed.

Again, a colony of the uncommon Duke of Burgundy fritillary butterflies was recently saved from destruction by raising by an inch or two the cutting blade of the roto-scythe. For the close-cut mowing was reducing the stock of cowslips on whose leaves the insect's larvae feed. By raising the cutting blade, more cowslip leaves were made available for the caterpillars. It is often small, subtle touches of this kind that make all the difference between life and death for our lepidoptera.

WHAT TO LOOK FOR (1)

BUTTERFLIES *RHOPALOCERA*
Danaidae

Monarch, Milkweed, *Danaus plexippus.* This most handsome resident of America was discovered in England in 1876. Since then about 160 specimens have been reported here and more than 60 of them have been captured. The insect is a warm orange shade, with thick black veins and dense black margins to the wings. These margins are spotted with white dots. There is controversy over how it arrives here. It does not necessarily tend to turn up near the western coasts amd there is strong evidence that it is brought to Britain by shipping. Yet it is also a fact that in mid-June, 1941, H.M.S. Abelia was on convoy duty 800 miles out in the Atlantic when a solitary monarch butterfly alighted on her rail, and other specimens have landed on ships making for our shores while they were far out to sea. The caterpillars are dependent upon milkweeds of America and the insect could not survive long in Britain.

Satyridae

Speckled Wood, *Pararge aegeria.* Plentiful throughout England and Wales, particularly the S. and W., abundant in Ireland, but very local in S. Scotland. Dark brown with yellowish spots, it is a species of the woodland rides and margins, and the boundaries of sunny, well-wooded lanes. The first generation flies in May and June, the second in August and September. The green, white striped caterpillars feed on couch, cocksfoot and other grasses.

Wall Butterfly, *Pararge megera.* Bright tawny in colour, with dark veins and margins and a black spot with white centre on each fore wing. Four smaller spots occur on the hind wings, though there is much variation. Common in S., E. and W. England, local in N. A keen lover of sunshine, hence its habit of resting on sunny walls, open cliffs of gravel pits etc. Whitish green and white spotted caterpillars feed on couch, cocksfoot and other grasses. Flies May–June. Second batch July–August. Most common near coasts.

Small Mountain Ringlet, *Erebia epiphron.* Our only Alpine butterfly. Restricted to the mountains of Scotland down to 1,500 ft., and the Lake District of England. Dark velvety brown and flies low only in the sunshine, though it is confined to some of the least sunny regions. Mat grass is the staple food of the green-yellow larva.

Scotch Argus, *Erebia aethiops.* A small brown or black butterfly restricted to damp hillsides and borders of moist woods in Scotland and, possibly, odd moorlands in N. England. The larva feeds at night on moor grass.

Marbled White, *Melanargia galathea.* Midlands and S., particularly Oxfordshire–Berkshire chalk and limestone country. Creamy white with black markings. Much inclined to favour grassy slopes and roadside verges which it may seldom leave. The white-brown caterpillar, with brown lines, prefers sheep's fescue, cocksfoot, cat's tail and other grasses. No cocoon is made, and the pupa hides amid moss and grass.

Grayling, *Eumenis semele.* Throughout most of Britain on heaths, sandhills, downs, flying short distances, when disturbed, to thyme, heather or pine trees, where it drinks the sap. The only butterfly to construct a cocoon underground amid roots of grass. Brown mottled caterpillar feeds on several grasses. This species cannot endure damp sites.

Hedge Brown, Gatekeeper, *Maniola tithonus.* Throughout England, particularly the S. Brownish-orange with brown margins and black spot on fore wings. Flies in July–August when sunny, visiting wood sage, marjoram or bramble flowers, though the pale hairy caterpillar feeds on grass.

Meadow Brown, *Maniola jurtina.* A most common butterfly throughout Britain. Open woods and rides, country lanes and verges, gardens and meadows all attract it. Dark brown, marked with dull orange and white-centred black spot on the fore wing, larger in the female. The rich-green caterpillar feeds at night on grass.

Small Heath, *Coenonympha pamphilus.* Abundant on commons and downs, meadows and pastures. This small butterfly is light tawny with a brown margin to the wings and a black spot near the tip of the fore wings. The green caterpillar has a dark green dorsal stripe, feeds on grasses, and grows to maturity in little more than a month. Thus eggs laid in May and June produce butterflies that are on the wing in August. Perhaps our most abundant butterfly.

Large Heath, *C. tullia.* Common on the Yorkshire and Lancashire moors. Absent from all counties south of Staffordshire. Variable brownish shades, with spots on fore and, particularly, hind wings. Caterpillar feeds on beak sedge—very rare in the S.—and several meadow grasses. Eggs are laid in July, caterpillars appear in the same month or in August and, after hibernating through the winter, pupate in May and June. The butterfly is on the wing in late June and July.

Ringlet, *Aphantopus hyperantus.* A dark grey-brown species— sometimes almost black—found all over England, Wales and S. Scotland. Black spots ringed by pale lines on wings. Pale brown caterpillar with grey-black line on back, white stripe on underparts, and 3 dark stripes on cheek, eats couch and other grasses in damp shady places. Eggs hatch August, caterpillar hibernates October, feeds again March, and the butterfly emerges in July. It favours woodland rides and lush meadows, and flies in dull weather.

Nymphalidae Family

Small Pearl-Bordered Fritillary, *Argynnis selene.* Common in some districts throughout England and Wales, particularly around mixed woods, heaths and marshy land bordering brooks in some southern counties. The eggs are laid in the middle of summer on the dog violet, and the pale caterpillar, with brownish warts beneath the bristles and a black head, loses no time in eating the shell. Later on it becomes a pinkish shade. The butterfly is a rich tawny shade, heavily marked in black and silver and a newly hatched colony make a beautiful sight as they alight on the stems of purple moor grass and stretch their wings in the sun.

Queen of Spain Fritillary, *A. lathonia.* One of our rarest migrants, rather similar to the silver-washed fritillary. Occasionally found Kent-Norfolk.

Pearl-Bordered Fritillary, *A. euphrosyne.* Not uncommon in the woods of many English and Welsh counties, this attractive butterfly is similar in shade—perhaps a little lighter—than the small kind, though there is much variation in colouring and markings. The caterpillar is black and hairy, feeding on dog violet, primroses and pansies after emerging from hibernation in March. The perfect insect appears in May and June, or even in late April.

Dark Green Fritillary, *Mesoacidalia charlotta.* A strong flier, locally common in July and August in coastal areas and on some moorlands, downs and grassy slopes. Prominent black spots, with much variation of the typically 'fritillary' shading and markings. Purplish-grey—white caterpillar feeds on the dog violet.

High Brown Fritillary, *Fabriciana cydippe.* Local in the more extensive woods of the south and Midlands. Not north of Cumberland. The black caterpillar, with pinkish-brown head, feeds on sweet and dog violets. The butterfly roosts in trees.

Silver-washed Fritillary, *Argynnis paphia.* This beautiful butterfly is common in some areas of the S. and W. of England, where it is associated with mature woodland, such as the New Forest and the mixed oak woods of the Weald, where it flies in July and August. The white-greenish eggs are laid on the trunks of trees, and the velvet-dark caterpillar with a pair of yellow lines on the back follows a meal of egg shell with the leaves of dog violet, before hibernating. It begins feeding again on violet leaves in April. The wing span of the butterfly is 31–39 mm.

Marsh Fritillary, *Euphydryas aurinia.* An attractive small

TYPICAL BUTTERFLY

antenna
eye
foreleg
midleg
hindleg

labial palpus · proboscis
veins · cell
costa
FOREWING
inner margin
thorax
HINDWING
termen
veins
abdomen

UNDERSIDE · UPPERSIDE

Small Tortoiseshell caterpillars and cast skins

Chrysalis

Peacock caterpillar

Speckled Wood and caterpillar

Peacock

Camberwell Beauty

Small Tortoise-shell

White Admiral

Purple Emperor

Silver-washed Fritillary and caterpillar

151

butterfly of marshy ground, much declining and decidedly un-common in many counties especially in the eastern half of England. Devil's bit scabious and, in captivity, honeysuckle are the food plants of the small black caterpillars, which hibernate in August–March within a silken web that can with-stand many weeks of submergence in winter floods.

Glanville Fritillary, *Melitaea cinxia.* A small bright orange-brown insect confined to the S. shores of the Isle of Wight, where it appears in May and June. The black larva with white dots feeds on the narrow-leaved and sea plantains.

Heath Fritillary, *M. athalia.* A woodland species, now decidedly rare outside N. Kent. Larva feeds on cow-wheat or, occasionally, plantain and wood-sage.

Red Admiral, *Vanessa atalanta.* A favourite butterfly through-out Britain. Black with brilliant scarlet bands across the fore wings and round the margins of the hind wings, relieved by white dots and touches of blue. On the wing May–October or even November. Buddlaea, over-ripe orchard fruit, or the flowers of ivy, thistle and hops attract it. The black cater-pillars edged with white—sometimes grey fringed with greenish-yellow—eat the leaves of stinging nettles, which they bind with bands of fine silk into a green tent. A migrant.

Painted Lady, *Vanessa cardui.* Some years large numbers in-vade Britain from France and North Africa in May and June, flying at all times of day and well into the evening. They are usually alone, occasionally in big flocks, and their dark green eggs are laid singly on the leaves of thistle, though the grey-green—blackish larva touched with pale yellow will also sample burdock, mallow and stinging nettle.

Small Tortoise-shell, *Aglais urticae.* A beautiful species, with vivid orange-red wings heavily marked with broad yellow and black patches and touches of blue near their edges. Wing span 25–27 mm. Eggs are laid in May and July beneath terminal leaf of stinging nettle. Yellowish caterpillars have a black line down the back and a black hairy head dotted with yellow. Numbers usually together. The butterfly often hibernates in churches and garages.

Large Tortoise-shell, *Nymphalis polychloros.* Common in S. England until around 1903, this beautiful butterfly suddenly became unaccountably rare. Some increase began to be noticed around 1945. The black caterpillars, very hairy and with a yellow-brown band on the back, dwell together near the top of tall elms, though they may also be found on sallows, willows, poplars, whitebeam and cherries. The butterfly is on the wing in July–August and again in spring after hibernation.

Peacock Butterfly, *Nymphalis io.* Unmistakable with its 'peacock eyes' and brownish red wings touched with a little blue. A common species in S. England, though it became oddly scarce in the north before increasing again in the past 30 years. The wing span is 27–31 mm. Winters in old tree trunks, outhouses, or in the interiors of churches where they flutter against the windows as the sun shines. The hairy black caterpillars, dotted with white spots, feed on stinging nettles.

Camberwell Beauty, *Nymphalis antiopa.* (See page 145.) Chocolate brown wings with yellow margins and blue spots on a dark border make this rare Scandinavian visitor unmistakable. The caterpillars are black, speckled with white warts beneath the hair. They feed on birch, elm, sallow and willow. Wing span 30–38 mm.

Comma, *Polygonia c-album.* The deeply cut or jagged wings, and a white 'comma' on the undersides, distinguish this common species. Yet until the mid-1920s it had largely vanished from all but a few parishes in the Midlands. The food plants of the black, yellowish ringed caterpillars are nettles, hops and currants, though elm and gooseberry are also eaten. The butterfly takes to the woods in autumn and hibernates on the underside of a branch where it is usually missed by birds. They seek nectar from willow and sallow catkins in springtime.

Purple Emperor, *Apatura iris.* This handsome butterfly, with a wing span of 31–38 mm., is one of the most splendid of the rarities, with its purple gloss and white markings against a dark brown background. The New Forest used to be a key stronghold of the species, but it vanished after 1947, and today it is most numerous in the woods of West Sussex, where it may be attracted to the rotting rat or squirrel on the gibbets of gamekeepers. It can be seen in powerful flight in July, and the green, yellowish caterpillar is dependent upon the leaves of sallow, to which it binds itself by stout bands of silk.

White Admiral, *Limenitis camilla.* Dark wings with white markings not unlike the last species, though lacking its purple sheen, are the dominating feature of this butterfly. Half a century ago it was almost restricted to Hampshire and West Sussex, then it advanced far afield over the southern half of England. Today it is an uncommon resident of damp woods in many counties of the south and east, where its strong, graceful flight can be seen in July. The greenish yellow larva feeds on honeysuckle. In autumn it bends a leaf round itself, attaches it firmly to a twig by silken strands, and spends the winter in it.

Riodinidae

Duke of Burgundy Fritillary, *Hamearis lucina.* A local, not very common species of woodland rides and clearing in the south and Midlands. Rare in the north. It is a small blackish butterfly with bright tawny spots. The caterpillar is brown and covered with white hairs. It feeds mainly on the leaves of cowslip, and also primrose between June and August. Some butterflies emerge then, but the majority remain as pupae until the following May or June.

Lycaenidae

Long-Tailed Blue Butterfly, *Lampides boeticus.* A rare migrant, recorded fewer than thirty times since it was discovered more

Chalkhill Blue

Common Blue

Adonis Blue

Large Blue

Holly Blue (Female) and caterpillar

Small White

Meadow Brown (Female)

Hedge Brown

Large White (Female)

Pale Clouded Yellow

Ichneumon Flies on caterpillar

Clouded Yellow

155

than a century ago. Common in Africa and S. Europe. It is a powerful flier, easily mistaken for the common blue. The green-olive caterpillars graze upon the green seeds of the pea family, including garden peas.

Small Blue, Little Blue, Bedford Blue, *Cupido minimus.* A midget, sooty-brown or bluish-black butterfly, with grey-white undersides tinged with blue at the base of each wing. The brown-pinkish caterpillars, which feed on the flower buds of kidney vetch, live for ten months or more before assuming the chrysalis state in May or June. This species is most common on the chalk grasslands of S. England, and rare in East Anglia and the north, though it does occur here and there on sandstone as well as chalk and limestone.

Short-Tailed Blue, *Everes argiades.* The rarest of our migrants, discovered in Somerset in 1874 and on Bloxworth Heath, Dorset in 1885, since when only three more specimens have been seen, though it thrives in Brittany. Velvet blue in shade, with green caterpillars that feed on bird's-foot trefoil.

Silver-Studded Blue, *Plebejus argus.* Dry open heather moors form the typical habitat of this small purplish-blue butterfly with a black border round the wings of the male. The female is sooty-brown with orange-shaded marks on the outer margins of the wings. The light brown caterpillars, dotted with white, feed on bird's-foot vetch and hatch out in April, the eggs having been laid on the tips of gorse in the previous late summer. The insect flies in June–August.

Brown Argus, *Aricia agestis.* A small brown butterfly of the chalk downs and limestone where the rock rose grows. Widespread but local, it is scattered about many counties from Yorkshire to Cornwall and Kent, and various areas of Wales, but remains absent from large parts of Britain. There are vivid red markings on the outer margins of the wings, which are fringed with white. The caterpillar has a black head, and green body with white hairs. The butterfly is on the wing May–June and August.

Common Blue, *Polyommatus icarus.* This blue-mauve butterfly—the female is smoky-brown tinged with blue—is familiar in almost all parts of the British Isles, particularly chalk grasslands of the south and sandy heaths. The insect is on the wing from May to September, and a first brood of caterpillars—green with brown hairs and a black head—will be found in April feeding on bird's-foot trefoil or on restharrow. A second brood may be found in June and July, when they may sample the leaves of red clover, yarrow, plantain or other plants.

Chalkhill Blue, *Lysandra coridon.* This silvery-blue butterfly of the chalk downs, with a black border to the wings, has sadly declined since the war. But it can still be seen on the wing in July and August in many places, when eggs are laid singly—the female is sooty brown—amid the vetches. The caterpillars hatch out the following spring. They are rich green and hairy and graze on the horseshoe vetch.

Adonis Blue, *Adonis bellargus.* This vivid blue insect is another species of the south country chalklands, but it is even more local, being largely confined to a few counties south of the Thames including the Isle of Wight. The female is dull brown or almost black, with orange spots bordering the wings, though there is much variation. The green bristly larva shares the horseshoe vetch with the last species and they are guarded and 'milked' for their honey-dew by certain species of ants. The ants have been seen to seize the larvae and carry them to the right food plants.

Mazarine Blue, *Cyaniris semiargus.* This purplish-blue butterfly is mentioned here only because it is on the British List, having been recorded in Kent and Berkshire in this century. But it has long been extinct here, though it can be found far across Europe.

Large Blue, *Maculinea arion.* Worth a chapter in itself this rich blue butterfly with blackish borders is now confined to certain corners of Devon and Gloucestershire where much research is being undertaken into its conservation. Briefly the eggs are laid on the flower buds of thyme. Sometimes after the third moult, the caterpillar drops to the ground and sets off through the grass. It can survive only if found by certain species of small red ants who will caress and milk the honey gland on the tenth segment, before eventually carrying the caterpillar to their nest where it is fed on ant larvae for the next six weeks. Feeding begins again after the long winter hibernation in the nest. It turns into a chrysalis, suspended by a strand of silk to the roof of the ant's nest, and some three weeks later the perfect insect emerges and slowly makes its way along ant corridors to the outside world where the whole fantastic process begins again.

Holly Blue, *Celastrina argiolis.* An attractive species, common in the south and much of Wales and the Midlands, with wings of lilac-blue and a narrow dark border to the fore wing, and a broader black edge to the wings of the female. It is on the wing in April and May when eggs are laid in the flower buds of holly, buckthorn or dogwood. During June and July the larvae eat mainly holly and a little buckthorn, broom or gorse; but larvae from the second brood—and the butterflies are on the wing again in July and August—rely almost entirely on ivy, plus some bramble. Numbers fluctuate widely from time to time.

Small Copper, *Heodes phlaeas.* Common over most of the British Isles other than the Scottish Isles. The orange coloured butterfly heavily spotted with black, and with a dark margin to the fore wings, and light grey hind wings, may be found in playful flight after any other butterflies over heathland, meadows, railway cuttings and almost any other type of habitat. It often rests on the daisies though the green caterpillars eat the leaves of dock and sorrel before and after hibernation. There are at least two broods a year and sometimes four. Wing span 12–16 mm.

Lycaena phlaeas

Large Copper, *Lycaena dispar.* A splendid species with vivid orange coppery wings and green caterpillars that feed on the leaves of the great water dock. Formerly abundant in the fens of Cambridgeshire, Huntingdonshire and in East Anglia, it became extinct in Britain in 1848. After unsuccessful attempts had been made to re-introduce it from the Continent, the Continental sub-species, *batavus* was established in 1927 at Woodwalton Fen, now a National Nature Reserve, where it continues to thrive.

Green Hairstreak, *Callophrys rubi.* Widely distributed about the wet heathlands, tall hedgerows and woodland boundaries of Britain, this small butterfly is easily missed as it folds its brown wings and allows the green underparts to merge it with the background. The pale green caterpillar with yellow stripes on the sides and a black line down the back feeds on needle whin, broom, dyer's greenweed, dogwood, bramble, rock rose and other species, and the greenish eggs are often laid on gorse petals, bird's-foot trefoil buds and other plants. The insect remains in the chrysalis state from July until the following May.

Brown Hairstreak, *Thecla betulae.* This blackish-brown butterfly with a large orange patch on the wings, and tawny-orange undersides, is somewhat local in the southern half of England and Wales and very rare in the north. It favours open borders of woods, alighting on the oaks or bramble blossom, while the pale green larva feeds on sloe.

Purple Hairstreak, *Thelca quercus.* Widespread and frequent amid the larger oak woods, but often overlooked as the purplish-blue butterfly spends much time amid the higher branches of oaks and ash on which it sometimes perches. The eggs are laid on the twigs of oak beside the leaves that form the food of the caterpillars, and to which the chrysalis is fastened.

White-Letter Hairstreak *Strymonidia w-album*. Two white lines on the underside explain the name of this widespread if local species. Blackish wings with brown underparts edged on the hind wings by a black-bordered orange band are easily overlooked as the butterfly flits around the elms or brambles where it often alights. The yellowish green hairy larva feeds on the leaves of wych elm, oak, lime and other trees.

Black Hairstreak, *Strymonidia pruni*. A dark brown or brownish black butterfly with orange markings on the hind wings, which is perhaps the rarest of our native butterflies, being confined to odd sites in Huntingdonshire, Northamptonshire and western Buckinghamshire. The caterpillars feed on blackthorn.

Pieridae

Wood White, *Leptidea sinapis*. An uncommon species of woodland, mainly in the S. and W. of England and Wales, and fairly widespread in S. Ireland. It is creamy-white, with a prominent black mark on the tips of the fore wings of the male. The green caterpillar, dotted with black in the front, and lined with yellowish-green, feeds on the tuberous pea. The insect can be seen in weak flight across woodland glades and rides in May and again in July–August, and it often favours shade.

Black-Veined White, *Aporia crataegi*. Round white wings and prominent black veins must have made this insect conspicuous to Kentish and New Forest entomologists a century ago, but it vanished from its last strongholds—in Kent—during the 1920s.

Large White, *Pieris brassicae*. A familiar migrant, sometimes reaching our south coast in vast numbers, with broad black markings on the tips of the white wings. The caterpillars, feeding on any members of the cabbage family, protect themselves

160

Black-veined White

Monarch

Brimstone

Painted Lady eggs

Comma

Marbled White

Red Admiral

Orange Tip

Painted Lady

Wall (Female)

Small Copper and caterpillar

Grayling (Female)

with an offensive smell; but this does not prevent heavy destruction from the ichneumon fly. Eggs laid in clusters, whereas the small white lays them singly.

Small White, *Pieris rapae.* This pest species is also reinforced by heavy migration, though it often appears early in the year after pupating in greenhouses and garages. Those on the wing at that time have only small black markings on the tips of the fore wings; butterflies reared later in the year have more prominent black spots. The green caterpillar with a brownish head feeds on nasturtiums and mignonette as well as cabbages.

Green-Veined White, *Pieris napi.* Dark ribs on the underside of the wings distinguish this common species of damp woods and fields from the last species. The first brood appears on the wing from late April or May–June, and the second batch in late July–August. The larva eats charlock, garlic mustard and water cress, not cabbages.

Bath White, *Pontia daplidice.* (See page 145.) Some 60 specimens had been observed in Britain in the hundred years up to 1944; then 500 were counted in 1945, as already related. The black markings comprise five round spots or more on the fore wings. The larvae eat wild and garden mignonette.

Orange-Tip, *Anthocaris cardamines.* A most attractive butterfly, seen on the wing in May and June when the orange patch covering half the fore wing of the male, and the greyish-green hind wings of both sexes are conspicuous. Eggs are laid on the stalks of lady's smock and hedge mustard. The hairy larva is bluish-green, and easily missed as it munches away through June and July.

Brimstone, *Gonepteryx rhamni.* This bright yellow butterfly, with reddish spots on the pointed wings that are 27–30 mm wide, is perhaps the longest living of all our butterflies, with the possible exception of the tortoishells. Emerging from hibernation in March, it can be seen on the wing until June. The green caterpillar feeds through June and July on buckthorn, and the perfect insect emerges in August. The scent of the greenish-yellow female attracts a courting male a full hundred yards.

Clouded Yellow, *Colias croceus.* Beautiful orange coloured wings with black borders, a large dark spot on each fore wing and an orange spot on the hind wings distinguish this migrant. It is liable to appear anywhere, especially in fields of clover and lucerne during the late summer, for it is here that the eggs are laid. The green, black-specked caterpillar can be found on these plants and trefoil in June and September–October. In August, 1941 and 1947, some West country fields were yellow with these butterflies.

Pale Clouded Yellow, *Colias hyale.* A rare migrant, with primrose yellow wings in the male and very pale wings in the female. The borders of the fore wings are shaded black. The pale green caterpillars feed on clovers and lucerne.

New Clouded Yellow, *Colias australis.* Distinguished as a separate species as recently as 1947, this butterfly lacks the black border on the hind wings of the last species, and the males are a richer yellow above and orange-shaded beneath. The orange blotches are bigger. The larvae feed on horseshoe vetch. Found in S. England.

Papilionidae

Swallow-Tail, *Papilio machaon.* This beautiful butterfly has large yellow wings surrounded by bands of black, blue and more yellow, and a round patch of red on the hind wings. On the Continent it may be seen in the woods and meadows, but our British swallow-tails, on the edge of their range, are restricted to Wicken Fen and the Norfolk Broads. The green and orange spotted larvae feed on milk parsley, angelica, wild carrots and fennel. Recommended: *The Swallowtail Story*, a colour film, sound, 29 minutes; distributor, Saffron Films, Saffron Lawn, Berkhamsted, Hertfordshire.

Hesperiidae

Dingy Skipper, *Erynnis tages.* Extremely widespread on open land, especially on the Downs, this small mouse-coloured insect flies in May and June, laying eggs on the bird's-foot trefoil. The white-green caterpillar is fully grown by August, when it makes a tent of grass bound by silk and hibernates until April when it promptly pupates without feeding again. The butterfly folds its wings over the body like a moth.

Grizzled Skipper, *Pyrgus malvae.* White spots on the black wings distinguish this small insect which is widely distributed south of Yorkshire, favouring heaths, downland valleys, small woods and meadows, where the pale green larvae eat wild strawberry, brambles and cinquefoil.

Chequered Skipper, *Carterocephalus palaemon.* This blackish-brown insect with orange or yellow spots is largely confined to the woods of Lincolnshire, Northamptonshire and Buckinghamshire where it may be seen from late May to early July on flowers of ground ivy, bugle, or the brome grass on which eggs are laid.

Small Skipper, *Thymelicus sylvestris.* A small fawn-coloured insect with dark outer margins to the wings and a black mark on wings of the male. Common in damp ground where the light green caterpillars with a bluish-green stripe on the back and a white stripe below, feed on various grasses.

Essex Skipper, *Adopaea lineola.* The wide head, and black undersides of the knob of the antennae distinguish this small butterfly—wing span 11–13 mm.—from the Small Skipper. It occurs on embankments overlooking salt marshes and in rough ground bordering woods in S. E. England, particularly Essex, where it was first identified at the end of the last century. It flies in July–August, and the larvae feed on various coarse grasses, such as couch.

Lulworth Skipper, *Thymelicus acteon.* A coastal species, olive in hue, with orange spots on the fore wings, and found only within a mile or two of the sea from Swanage to Weymouth and on the Old Red Sandstone of South Devon. The yellowish-green larva, lined with pale yellow, feeds on couch and false brome grasses. Flies July–August.

Silver-Spotted Skipper, *Hesperia comma.* A resident of the chalk in S. England, where the butterfly may be seen in swift flight during August. Eggs are laid on the hair grass. The insect is like a large skipper, but with greenish under-parts spotted a silvery shade.

Large Skipper, *Augiades sylvanus.* A common resident of most English counties and of Scotland south of the Forth, where it may be seen flying about woodland rides, coastal cliffs, rough pastures and meadows during June–July. It is a yellowish tawny shade, with a black patch on the male's fore wings. The greenish white eggs hatch in twelve days or so, and the pale green larva attaches itself by five or six strands of silk to a blade of cocksfoot grass. Wing span 12–15 mm.

BIBLIOGRAPHY

Ford, E. B. *Butterflies.* Collins New Naturalist Series, London, 1945.

South, R. *The Butterflies of the British Isles.* Warne, London, 1941, new ed.

Stokoe, W. J. *Butterflies.* Observer Series, Warne, London, 1962, new ed.

Southwood, T. R. E. *Life of the Wayside and Woodland.* Warne, London, 1963.

Temple, Vere. *Butterflies and Moths in Britain.* B. T. Batsford, London, 1946.

Williams, C. B. *Insect Migration.* Collins New Naturalist Series, London, 1958.

WHAT TO LOOK FOR (2)

Moths *HETEROCERA*

If a man speaks of his rosy footman, small tabby, spring usher, satin carpet or pretty pug, he is clearly a student of the lepidoptera, for all these are the names of moths. There is a green carpet moth, a dog's tooth, a small blood vein, and even a doubtful rustic, all of them moths on the British List.

The first part of this section has described every butterfly in Britain. Only a few pages can be spared for our 2,000 species of moths, and one must turn to Richard South's *Moths of the British Isles*, in two volumes, for an adequate treatment of them. Patience and zeal are the prime requirements of the skilled observer, and there is no better way of gaining first hand knowledge about these fascinating and very various creatures than by rearing them. The eggs can be found on appropriate leaves, singly or in pairs or clusters.

In time the eye becomes accustomed, as a bird's must be, to spotting moths in every sort of habitat. The Noctuids will be found lurking in the long grass, a yellow underwing may be discovered beneath the strawberries, the pugs and carpet moths may be detected on brick and stone walls, the pupa of the privet hawk moth may be hidden in the soil of the rose bed; and approaching rain or thunder may prompt a magpie or light emerald moth or a host of other colourful insects to seek refuge in the house, for light possesses a deep fascination for them. Moths in flight steer themselves by the moon, and a caterpillar, confronted with a light on the left and its staple diet of leaves on the right, will turn left to the lamp and starve to death.

How does one begin? It is wise policy to seek familiarity with particular groups, and none is more fascinating than the hawk moths.

Hawk Moths, *Sphingidae*, Ten of the seventeen species in

Britain are residents and seven are migrants, some of them visitors from the Atlas Mountains in Morocco and other distant places. Dusk rather than night is the time when they prefer to fly—apart from the death's head—and in the half light their large eyes and long antennae, thick in the centre and slender at the base and tip, look strangely menacing. All are fast, powerful fliers, beating their broad wings 70 times a minute, and hovering with the skill of some miniature kestrel.

Privet Hawk Moth, *Sphinx ligustri.* Our largest hawk moth, this resident of S. England is a light brown shade, often mottled with white, and has rounded, toothed antennae folded along its back and 'a face like a squirrel', to quote Miss Vere Temple, who has raised them. No other hawk moth is so frequently brought to me. The caterpillar, with the curved horn or spine characteristic of all but the small elephant hawk moth, is three inches long and of a bright apple-green with seven white stripes, touched in front with violet and in the rear with yellow. It burrows four inches into the soil before pupating and should not be disturbed for examination until its new skin has hardened, or it will perish. The perfect insect emerges and crawls up through the soil in the following June or July, drying itself in the sunlight before setting off in search of its favourite privet.

Lime Hawk, *Mimas tilia.* With a wing span of 27–35 mm., and a variable red-brown or green shade, this attractive creature is often found in village and suburban gardens in southern England where limes abound. The green caterpillar, with yellow points and yellow lines on the sides bordered with red or purple, spends July and August feeding high up in the limes, or sometimes in elm or birch. The moth emerges from the ground—usually near the trunk of a lime or elm—on a May or June afternoon.

Humming Bird Hawk Moth, *Macroglossum stellatarum.* Bird or insect? The question is frequently asked as this little insect,

Elephant Hawk
moth and
caterpillar

Death's Head
Hawk moth

Privet Hawk moth
and caterpillar

Poplar Hawk moth

Peppered moth of
industrial areas

Peppered moth

Humming Bird Hawk moth

Puss moth caterpillar

Garden
Tiger moth

Wood
Leopard
moth

Emperor
moth (Female)

168

with a wing span of 20–22 mm., leaves its native Mediterranean haunts and migrates to Britain, where it may be seen at any hour of the day and in sunshine or rain, flitting from flower to flower and hovering on faintly buzzing wings. One was seen to visit 194 flowers in seven minutes, and it shows a decided preference for blue or yellow petals. At night a lighted room may attract it into the house, where it may fall to the floor if the light is switched off, though late in the season it will seek dark corners in which to rest. In a good migration year its greenish eggs may be found on bedstraw, and the green or brownish caterpillars, with white dots, may be seen at night during July and August eating the leaves of hedge or lady's bedstraw or even wild madder.

Elephant Hawk, *Deilephila elpenor*. This olive brown moth is common among the rosebay willow herb in cleared woodland, and it can sometimes be observed at dusk in June hovering before the flowers of honeysuckle. The plump, dark caterpillar—it is yellowish-white at first—measures three inches, and grazes on willow herb or bedstraw.

Poplar Hawk, *Laothoe populi*. A common species, sometimes found in urban parks and recreation grounds as well as in the countryside. It has a wing span of 35–45 mm., and varies in colour from ash-grey to brown and reddish-yellow. It spends the day on the trunks of poplar, willow or other trees, flying at night.

Death's Head Hawk Moth, *Acherontia atropos*. Our most remarkable moth, measuring 4½ to 5 in. from wing-tip to wing-tip, and bearing the skull mark on the back of the thorax. It squeaks like a mouse when touched. The yellowish-green caterpillar is almost 5 in. long and is usually found on the leaves of potato, woody nightshade or snowberry, to which the moth is attracted by scent. Not uncommon in S. England, to which it migrates from S. Europe and Africa.

Pine Hawk, *Hyloicus pinastri*. Once a rarity confined to Essex and Suffolk and odd corners of the New Forest, this species, with a wing span of 35–40 mm., has now colonised many pine-woods in S. England where its brown form on the boles of the trees may easily be mistaken for a knot in the trunk. At dusk it flies in search of the nectar of honeysuckle. The young cater-pillar is striped green and yellow from end to end, so that it is hard to distinguish from the pine needles on which it feeds, though it eventually changes to a reddish-brown shade that matches the pine boles. Flies May–September.

Eyed Hawk, *Smerinthus ocellata.* A common insect in S. England, with 'eye' markings on the hind wings. It flies by night from late May–July, often laying eggs on apple trees, and spending the days on the boles of trees.

Convolvulus Hawk, *Herse convolvuli*, **Unicorn** or **Bindweed Hawk.** Fastest and most powerful of our moths, with pale grey pointed wings, mottled brown, and red and black and slender white bands meeting a broad grey central stripe on the body. It comes in June and July from southern France or Germany and feeds on the tobacco plant, into whose flower it stretches a tongue 3 to 4 in. long. The green variously marked caterpillar feeds on bindweed.

Broad-bordered Bee Hawk, *Hemaris fuciformis.* No larger than the Humming-bird hawk moth which they somewhat re-semble, this species and *H. tityus* have transparent wings rather like those of a bumble bee, but with reddish-brown borders to them. They are not uncommon in the southern half of Britain, flying to bugle and rhododendron in the sunshine of a May and June morning. The pale green larva of the Broad-bordered bee hawk feeds on honeysuckle; that of the Narrow-bordered bee hawk prefers wild scabious.

PROMINENTS *Notodontidae* Family (Back-toothed)

The 25 British resident species are large or medium-sized night-fliers, wintering as pupae—apart from the plumed prominent which remains in the egg stage—and spending the summer days on tree trunks, their brown wings folded over the back like a tent.

Puss Moth, *Cerura vinula.* The leaf-green caterpillar—black when young—resembles the curled poplar leaf on which it lies with the double prongs of the tail held together like a leaf stalk. When attacked it arches its front segments, displaying two red-rimmed 'eye spots', the forked tail expands and red whip-like threads lash to and fro. If this fails to alarm the attacker, a burning colourless liquid containing 40 per cent formic acid is ejected from the prothoracic gland, and this can prove most painful to the human eye. The larvae also eat the leaves of willow and sallow through July and August. By the time they dismount down the trunk, the caterpillars have turned a chocolate brown tint to match the boles.

TUSSOCKS *Lymantriidae* Family (Destroyers)

The eight large British species are often brightly coloured, with flat tufts of hair, constantly likened to shaving brushes, on the backs of the caterpillars.

Pale Tussock, Hop Dog, *Dasychira pudibunda.* A common species with greyish white wings, often resting on young bracken in the woods during late May and June, and much attracted to light. The beautiful green or yellow hairy caterpillar feeds on birch, hazel, oak and hops from July to September.

EGGARS AND LACKEYS *Lasiocampidae* (Hairy caterpillars)

Oak Eggar, *Lasiocampa quercus.* A common moth—one of eleven large hairy and nocturnal species in Britain—unique in northern districts for its two year cycle. The first winter is spent in the caterpillar stage, the second as a pupa. The name is prompted by the insect's colour. The gregarious larvae feed on blackthorn, sallow, fruit trees and other plants, but not normally on oak.

Assembling. Like the Kentish Glory, the Emperor and other moths, the mature female Oak Eggar can attract hosts of male suitors from as far afield as four kilometres distance; and they will fly up or down wind in response to this remarkable faculty that is not yet properly understood. Flies July–August.

Endromidae Family (Shaggy coats)

Kentish Glory, *Endromis versicolora.* The only member of this family in Europe, the Kentish glory is fairly common in Scotland, and the brown and white males, with bright red hind wings, assemble in huge numbers around the pale furry female. If alarmed they rapidly soar out of sight. The males, emerging in March or April, fly fast through the sunshine, while the females spend their days on twigs of birch or on heather, emerging at night. The gregarious caterpillars feed on birch, alder, sallow and lime.

Saturnidae Family

The Emperor Moth, *Saturnia pavonia.* A relative of the great Atlas moth, and our only member of a family largely associated with China, Japan and India, and including the Chinese silkworm moth. Soft chocolate and white fore wings and orange hind wings, and the prominent large 'eyes' on the wings distinguish this handsome British moth. The beautiful pale grey female flies mainly at night, but the male can often be seen in the day over the north country moorlands, the East Anglian heaths or Ashdown Forest and the New Forest. Neither insect possesses a tongue and they cannot eat. The large green and black caterpillar feeds on heather, bramble, sloe and other plants.

HOOK TIPS *Drepanidae* (Sickles)

Pebble Hook Tip, *Drepana falcataria.* A common species on damp ground. It is a slender greyish moth with a wing span

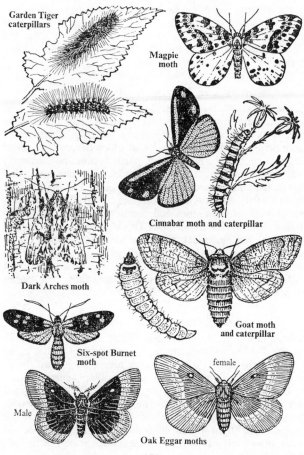

Garden Tiger
caterpillars

Magpie
moth

Cinnabar moth and caterpillar

Dark Arches moth

Goat moth
and caterpillar

Six-spot Burnet
moth

Male

female

Oak Eggar moths

of 15–19 mm., and appears in May and June. A second browner generation emerges in July and August. The green and brown larva spins a web on the underside of alder and birch leaves. Like all six British species of the family, it has a pointed or spiked tail and 14 legs.

TIGERS AND FOOTMEN *Arctiidae* Family

Garden Tiger, *Arctia caia*. Brilliant red hind wings and body, and white and brown fore wings cause this day and evening flyer to be constantly mistaken for a butterfly. There are 31 large British species in the family, of which the garden tiger or 'burning bear' is the best known, partly because of the woolly bear caterpillar which feeds on docks, plantains and other plants, including hawthorn and hollyhocks. The markings of the moth vary widely. Gaudy colouring and the highly poisonous content of the tissues and prothoracic glands have persuaded birds to beware of them. This is generally true, too, of the bright red and black **Cinnabar Moth,** *Callimorpha jacobaeae*, whose orange and black ringed caterpillars eat the poisonous ragwort. Yet the cuckoo has become a specialist at feeding on caterpillars with poisonous hairs that other species cannot abide.

OWLETS *Agrotidae* (Rustics)

A large family of more than 300 British species, of which 25 are small. Most of them are brown or grey moths that blend well with the trunks of trees. They are usually night flyers, much attracted to lights, and their caterpillars generally graze on broad-leaved trees, herbs or grasses. Four species spend two to four years as pupae. The **Large Yellow Underwing,** *Tryphaena pronuba*, is a common fast-flying member of the family, with bright yellow hind wings which are concealed under the mottled brown fore wings when it comes to rest.

174

Wing span 23–27 mm. If disturbed this garden moth may run for shelter rather than fly away.

LOOPERS *Geometridae* Family (Waves, Carpets, Pugs etc.)

The caterpillars of most members of this family—and there are some 270 British species—have only ten legs. In the absence of legs in the middle of the body, they move along a twig or leaf by 'looping'. While four hind legs seize the leaf, the caterpillar stretches forward and clutches the twig ahead. Then the hold of the hind legs is relaxed and the body loops forward. Most of them are night-feeders, with a habit of remaining motionless for long periods at an angle which makes them strangely like a twig—hence the term 'stick caterpillars'. The colourful **Magpie Moth**, *Abraxas grossulariata*, with black and yellow markings on the white wing, is a common member of the family familiar to gardeners, for the creamy white caterpillars marked by black dots and a broad reddish line do much damage to gooseberries and red currant bushes.

The **Peppered Moth**, *Biston betularia*, was once regarded as a white moth 'peppered' with black. Then it was found that black or Melanic forms stood a better chance of survival in industrial areas where trees and buildings are coated with grime. Today the black specimens outnumber the white ones, and no fewer than 70 species of large moths in our industrial areas are developing dark or black coloration.

BURNETS AND FORESTERS *Zygaenidae* Family (Sharks)

The **Six-spot Burnet**, *Zygaena filipendulae*, is the most common member of this family, of which there are ten British species, all brilliantly coloured lovers of the sunshine, with long fore wings, short, round hind wings and long tongues. The six-spot burnet flies in July and August, but it is sluggish early in the day and country folk used to call it the 'Ten o' Clock Sleeper'. It can usually be found on chalk grassland,

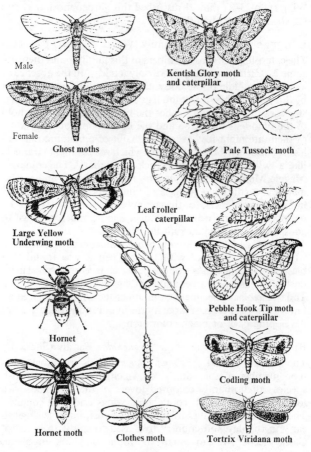

Male

Kentish Glory moth
and caterpillar

Female

Ghost moths

Pale Tussock moth

Large Yellow
Underwing moth

Leaf roller
caterpillar

Pebble Hook Tip moth
and caterpillar

Hornet

Codling moth

Hornet moth

Clothes moth

Tortrix Viridana moth

176

damp meadows and on cliffs. The second most common moth of the family—with only five red spots on the blue-black wings—flies in May and June.

GOAT MOTHS *Cossidae* Family

The **Goat Moth**, *Cossus*, is the largest and most common of the three British species of this family, all of which eat their way into the bark of trees, leaving behind a passage thick with saw-dust. Like its cousins, *Cossus*, so named because it stinks like a billy goat, must chew huge quantities of wood in order to extract adequate nutriment from the timber-cells, and it generally continues boring through the tree and out again during a period of three years. Bred in captivity on a diet of beetroot it will become mature within twelve months. Many trees, including oak, ash, willow and poplar are attacked by this pest, and one can often hear the large bald salmon-pink caterpillar at work making a noise like gnawing mice. The brown moth emerges in July and, lacking a mouth or tongue, fails to eat and soon dies.

Leopard Moth, *Zeuzera pyrina*. A white moth with blue-black spots which has often been associated with the London area, where it may visit street lights and surrounding trees. The dull white caterpillar spends two or three years burrowing into the stems and branches of trees and shrubs.

CLEARWINGS *Sesiidae*

The fifteen British members of this family are strangely like hornets or wasps. The **Hornet Moth**, *Sesia apiformis*, with yellow head and bands of yellow round the shoulders and abdomen, contrasting with brown, could well be mistaken at first sight for a hornet. These moths tend to emerge on bright mornings, and like to sunbathe on tree trunks.

GHOSTS AND SWIFTS *Hepialidae* (Fevers)

The larvae of these large British moths—five species—feed underground on the roots of bracken, grasses and other plants. The **Ghost Moth,** *Hepialus humuli*, is unusual in that the male displays before the female, hovering and dancing with quick-beating white wings, and the larger yellow-brown female responds by flying straight to him.

LEAF ROLLERS *Tortricoidea* (Twisters)

Many agricultural pests are to be found among the 347 British species in this family; and though all but ten of them are small, the damage they cause can often be large. *Tortrix viridana* is the moth which will strip oaks of their leaves, though the trees are generally quick to respond with fresh growth. The **Codling Moth,** *Ernarmonia pomonella*, produces caterpillars that bore their way into apples and pears. 'This family,' said an entomologist, 'gives moths a very bad name.'

CLOTHES MOTHS, LEAF BORERS *Tinaeoidea*

The study of these small moths is a life's work, for there are 735 British species, many of them valuable scavengers. One species dwells in the nests of ants, which it keeps clear of rubbish; others devour fungi, dead wood, rotting refuse or scale insects. Three species earn the distinction of being a *Clothes Moth*—each one confined to a different region. *Tinaea pellionella*, the *Skin Moth*, produces a small white larva with a brown head which dwells on clothing or in fur or feather from August to May. The moth is on the wing between July and October. She never lays eggs in sunlight or fresh air, and neither eggs nor caterpillars can survive long in sunshine. Nor can the parent moth penetrate paper or polythene bags.

BIBLIOGRAPHY

Ford, E. B. *Moths*. Collins New Naturalist Series, London, 1955.

Sandars, Edmund. *An Insect Book for the Pocket*. Oxford University Press, London, 1946.

South, R. *The Moth of the British Isles*. rev. ed. 2 vols, 1961.

Wigglesworth, V. B. *The Life of Insects*. Weidenfeld and Nicolson, London, 1964.

More Insects

Grasshoppers – Dragonflies – Beetles – Ants, Wasps and Bees

The study of insects is still a strangely neglected field of natural history, compared with botany or ornithology. It is worth mentioning that the rare Glanville Fritillary butterfly in the Isle of Wight owes its name to one Lady Glanville whose will was disputed, during the 17th century, on the grounds that she was 'interested in butterflies and other insects'. Anyone who concerned themselves with the strange world of these small creatures was long considered eccentric, and even today a hundred people know their birds to every one who can identify the beetles.

Yet few fields of knowledge offer more fascination, or more scope for original research, than the study of insects. Any young naturalist or photographer who is uncertain where to apply his talents might be well advised to explore these areas of biological study of which we know so little. There is space here only to glance at one or two groups.

GRASSHOPPERS AND CRICKETS *Orthoptera*

The grasshoppers of the British Isles are divided into the four-teen Short-horned species of the *Acrididae* family, and the Long-horned species, or Bush Crickets of the *Tettigonidae* family, and their classification is based on the length of the antennae.

The short-horned species are vegetarians, and themselves provide food for game birds, domestic fowls and other creatures. Their loud song or stridulation is produced from eighty

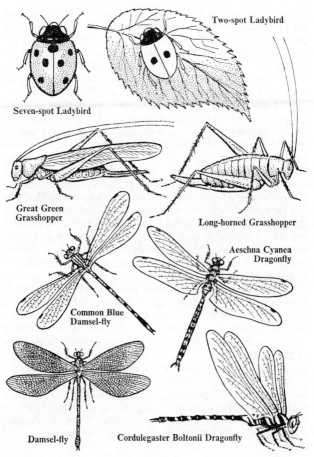

Two-spot Ladybird

Seven-spot Ladybird

Great Green
Grasshopper

Long-horned Grasshopper

Aeschna Cyanea
Dragonfly

Common Blue
Damsel-fly

Damsel-fly

Cordulegaster Boltonii Dragonfly

or ninety tiny points on the hind legs which are rubbed against the forewings when the sun shines—and there is a close link between the temperature and the hours of sunshine and the volume of grasshopper song. The female digs a hole in the ground with her tail before laying eggs. These remain underground through the winter and hatch in spring, and the larvae spend five to eight months maturing into adults.

Whereas short-horned grasshoppers have their ears or tympana in the first segment of the body, the long-horned species have ears in the fore legs, and their song is produced by rubbing sections of the wings together. The **Great Green Grasshopper**, *Tettigona viridissima*, with a length of 32–35 mm. for the female, who is slightly larger than the male, is a carnivore which does most of its feeding at night. About 60 eggs are laid in the ground in the late summer, after a courtship that may last for several days and which involves much caressing with the long antennae before the male throws himself on his back behind the female, grips her firmly and produces a gelatinous red pouch containing the sperms which binds itself to the sword of her ovipositor. This done, he hurriedly escapes before the mate can eat him.

Crickets have longer tails than the grasshoppers, and their hardened fore wings lie upon the abdomen, with the right fore wing across the left. The **House Cricket**, *Gryllulus domesticus*, also known as the Cricket on the Hearth, ventures out of doors in summer, but soon retreats to any warm corner of a building at the approach of winter. The attractive **Field Cricket**, *G. campestris*, is a vegetarian, living on grass, which digs itself a winter burrow. The cheerful chirping song of the male carries for a good hundred yards. Our only **Mole Cricket**, *Gryllotalpa*, is a rarity, which spends most of its time underground preying on other insects. Gilbert White, in Letter 48 of the *Natural History of Selborne*, describes his discovery of its 'nest'.

DRAGONFLIES, DEMOISELLE-FLIES *Odonata*

There are five thousand species of dragonflies, and 42 of them can be found in Britain, where they must be among our oldest inhabitants. Fossilised remains of dragonflies like those seen today appear to date from Permian times, some 200 million years ago.

Life Cycle. The eggs are laid in water, often inside the stems of aquatic plants. A legless, wingless pro-nymph emerges which moults within a few minutes into the larva or nymph, a robust, stout carnivore preying on other aquatic creatures. The larvae of the delicate and graceful Demoiselle-flies (*Zygoptera*) forsakes the water after a year, while the large Dragonfly nymphs do so after two years.

A stem of reedmace or iris is climbed and the final transformation occurs, the imago crawling out of the nymphal skin through a hole behind the head and neck. The wings are expanded and dried in the sun and the insect is soon displaying its superb, swift flight. Country people sometimes call these beautiful creatures 'Horse stingers' or 'the Devil's darning needle,' but they have no sting and never bite humans. With their ability to twist and turn in flight and even to reverse, they are too powerful for most other winged insects, but they themselves are often victims of the hobby and some other birds.

It is remarkable how quickly dragonflies colonise new ponds, and the countryman who desires to enrich our fauna can perform no better service than to encourage the creation and wise management of more ponds in gardens and on heaths and village greens. Ponds dug at Woodwalton Fen National Nature Reserve in 1962 had been adopted by no fewer than twelve species of dragonflies, or roughly a quarter of the British List, within four years. Other ponds known to me had attracted two or three species of demoiselle-flies in the course of a single year. The **Golden-ringed Dragonfly,** *Cordulegaster boltonii,* is a beautiful and very large species, with black and yellow banding along the abdomen. Eggs are laid in mud in many ponds in the West Country, on the Surrey heaths and elsewhere in the south and west. It also thrives in South Scotland.

Common over most of Britain is the *Aeschna juncea*, which emerges from ponds fringed with vegetation in late July. It can often be seen in August some distance from its breeding haunts. *Aeschna cyanea*, which is 48 mm. in length, also flies in late summer from still waters. It is most common in the south. From early June to September, larger waters in southern England often attract the lovely **Emperor Dragonfly**, *Anax imperator*, the male a brilliant blue, the female a green shade, and reaching a length of 54 mm., or two and a half inches. Unfortunately, they are most hostile to other species of dragonfly. They are common in S.E. England, rare in the north.

The graceful Damsel-flies, like *Agrion virgo* and *Agrion splendens*, are less inclined than the larger dragonflies to wander far from their breeding waters. The former is common in the south, flying in June and July and clearly preferring running water, though it also occurs around ponds. The latter species, *A. splendens*, flourishes in the Midlands, Wales and Ireland as well as the south. There is much variation in their colouring.

BEETLES   *Coleoptera* (Case Wings)

More than a quarter of a million beetles are known to science and 3,600 of them are British species. If many of them are seldom seen, it is because they find it wise in an often hostile world to keep out of sight. Every type of habitat has its different beetles, each with a structure so well adapted to its environment that the human observer must often marvel. Consider the fascinating case of the species discussed in the next paragraph.

Oil Beetles, *Meloe proscarabaeus* and *M. volaceus*. These common, slow, cumbersome creatures are purplish-black in colour and about an inch long. They can often be found in springtime on roadside verges or in fields where the female lays about ten thousand eggs—no mean feat—in holes in the ground. Beetle eggs usually hatch within one or two weeks and these are no exception. Soon hosts of small six-legged larvae are clambering

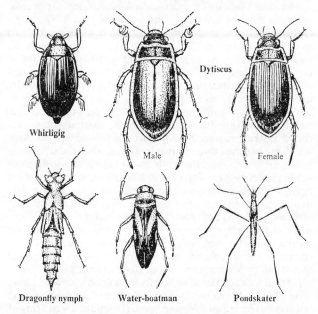

Whirligig

Dytiscus

Male

Female

Dragonfly nymph

Water-boatman

Pondskater

up the stems of wild flowers where they wait until a hairy leg appears. They cling to the first one that comes along. If it happens to be that of a bumble bee of the *Anthophora* family, the larva will be carried back into the bee's nest where it promptly devours its host's egg which is mounted on a cell of honey. Then

185

after a quick change of skin, the larva settles down to eat the honey which sustains it until it becomes an adult. All this is hard lines on the bee, but on average only two out of the parent beetle's ten thousand eggs succeed in producing another generation.

The **Tiger Beetles**—the green *Cicindela campestris* is our most common species—are no less curious in their ways. The larva, on hatching from the egg, extends the hole in which it is born to a depth of a foot or so. Then it clambers up, blocks the entrance with its flat head, hangs in an upright position by means of hooks on its back, and looks around for prey. As any small creature approaches, the larva opens the trap-door formed by its head and swallows the passerby.

Whirligigs are small round beetles, gregarious by nature, which float about the surface of ponds, swirling round and round in their eagerness to pounce on minute animal prey, which are watched through two half-eyes, while the remaining halves are focussed on the world above. The 110 British carnivorous water beetles of the *Dytiscidae* (Divers) family produce equally aggressive larvae which flourish on a diet of tiny fish, mollusca and insects. The **Great Diving Beetle,** *Dystiscus marginalis*, which I once found in a well used for drinking water, will live for years by preying on every other sort of aquatic creature including goldfish, and many an unsuspecting young naturalist has brought one home in triumph—only to discover that it will empty his aquarium of all other insect life.

The **Devil's Coach Horse** or **Smelly Parsnip,** *Staphylinus olens*, is best known for its habit when in danger of raising head and tail and producing an offensive smell. It is one of a vast army of beetles that are invaluable to man as devourers of harmful insects.

The **Greater Stag Beetle,** *Lucanus cervus*, is our largest beetle— four inches long—and though we know far too little of its distribution, it does seem to be least uncommon, though possibly

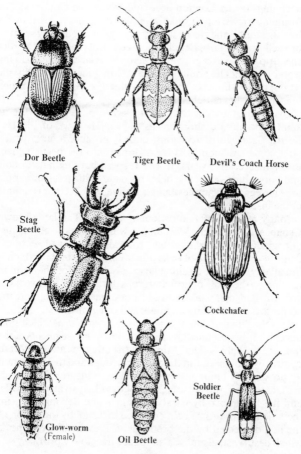

Dor Beetle

Tiger Beetle

Devil's Coach Horse

Stag
Beetle

Cockchafer

Glow-worm
(Female)

Oil Beetle

Soldier
Beetle

declining, in the London area and the Home Counties. The formidable jaws, looking like miniature deer antlers, are thought by some authorities to be largely ornamental, but they seem to be used in the course of fights between rival males. The beetles spend up to five years growing to maturity as larva in the decaying wood of oak. The adults emerge late in June and usually die within a month or so, though pet stag beetles will live much longer on a diet enriched by honey.

By contrast the British **Dung Beetles** have a long life as adults and quite a short one as pupae. The eggs of the **Dor Beetle,** *Geotrupes stercorarius,* quickly produce a larva which after some few months is transformed into the beetle which, through successive years, works at speed burying pats of cow and horse dung. The male helps his mate to dig a separate hole for each egg, an example of paternal intervention that is unique in the insect world.

Many of the chafers must count as pests. The large brown **Common Cockchafer,** *Melolontha,* which bangs itself against our windows in May as it flies towards the light, does much damage to the foliage of oaks and other forest trees in which it lies all day. The soil-dwelling larvae are much more harmful in feeding on the roots of growing crops during their four years of growth. Badgers, rooks and gulls take many larvae, and the adults are well liked by nightjars and other birds.

It is the female **Glow-Worm,** *Lampyris noctiluca,* which produces the brightest blue-green glow from the last segments of the tail, and the light is clearly aimed at the other sex and subject to control by the insect. But the egg, larva, pupa and the male adult all possess this luminous quality in a lesser degree. Their eggs are laid in damp ditches and other places likely to attract snails, and the larvae live by paralysing snails and devouring them, their victims meantime being reduced to 'soup' by the action of the liquid injected by the beetle larva. Presumably, chemicals which destroy snails must also reduce the glow-worms.

There are 45 small species of Ladybirds in Britain, and their good work in eating greenflies and other aphids is too well known to need detailed description. The **Seven-Spot Ladybird,** *Coccinella septempunctata,* is the most common species, and after hibernating in fencing, beneath bark or leaves or in sheds, it appears in early spring and lays clutches of eggs which rapidly produce lively black larvae that consume huge quantities of aphids, like their parents. Unfortunately, experiments to assemble large quantities of ladybirds to destroy aphids in a garden were only partially successful, too many of the predators dispersing.

ANTS, BEES AND WASPS *Hymenoptera*

This Order contains at least 100,000 species, and several times that number probably await discovery. They include insects notable for the large size of their brains and the almost incredible nature of their instincts. Bees, wasps and ants fall within the *Aculeata* group. Most bees and wasps are solitary, but all find food for their own larvae, and some species, like all our 36 British ants, have developed a highly intricate social life that is dependent upon the distinctive duties performed by particular sections of the community.

The **Wood Ant,** *Formica rufa*—our largest ant—is an interesting example, and one that is widespread in the coniferous woodlands of Britain. Their nests are sometimes as much as five or six feet high and ten or twelve feet in diameter—though ant heaps of that size are probably the best part of a century old. They are usually built around the stump of an old tree or a living shrub, and are thatched with pine needles and fragments of oak leaf or twigs that are proof against frost and rain. A colony may contain 100,000 ants or more and a number of Queens always remain active in the warm heart of the nest where they lay eggs at an average rate of one every ten minutes for some years. There is a record of one Queen living for sixteen years.

It is normally on sultry days in high summer when new nests are established. For it is then that the winged females and the male ants take off on their nuptial flight. The sexes pair while in the air or immediately on landing. If the flight is short the female may fly straight home again, rubbing off her wings against a stone and entering the old nest where she is warmly received by the worker ants who are undeveloped females. The males, their task done, soon die. If the nuptial flight is of long duration, the female may find herself alone and in strange territory where she must found an entirely new colony.

First she finds a hole, or digs a fresh one, with a nesting chamber for her eggs, and she now carries sperm from the male to fertilise each one. Soon she is feeding her larvae from her mouth, drawing all the time upon reserves of fat, for she may not eat for months on end after setting off on the nuptial flight. After pupating—and it is these pupae that are the so-called 'ant eggs'—worker ants will eventually supply the female with food and also go out foraging for the larvae, and they will add new chambers to the nest. Some worker ants have the duty of closing the entrances to the nest during heavy rain and cold and opening them again in dry, warm weather. No ants of this species possess stings, but they carry a receptacle in the venom gland containing 50 to 70 per cent formic acid, an amount equal to nearly a quarter of the whole body weight of the insect. These ants are protected in many Continental forests on account of their immense destruction of insect pests.

WASPS AND BEES

The seven British species of wasps of the *Vespidae* family form a fascinating subject for study. They range from the **Spider-hunting Wasp**, *Pompilus fuscus*, which digs a nest for itself in woodland paths and lies in wait for the spiders that are fed to its larvae, to the **Potter Wasp**, whose nest of clay and small pebbles made firm by the insect's own saliva is grafted on to the

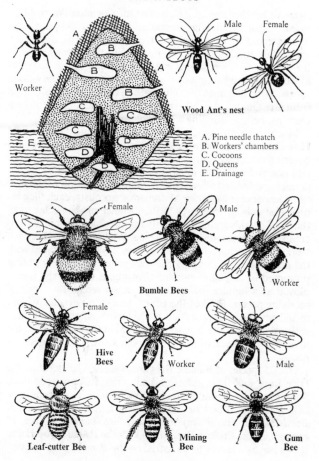

Worker

Male   Female

Wood Ant's nest

A. Pine needle thatch
B. Workers' chambers
C. Cocoons
D. Queens
E. Drainage

Female   Male

Worker

Bumble Bees

Female

Hive Bees   Worker   Male

Leaf-cutter Bee   **Mining Bee**   **Gum Bee**

191

stems of heather and other plants. Our **Common Wasp,** *Vespa vulgaris,* usually build their remarkable nest of wood-pulp paper underground or in a decayed tree or bush. The adults are vegetarian, relishing jams and nectar, but the larvae are fed in the nest—which may be as big as a football—on insect prey killed and chewed at first by the Queen; and then by the worker wasps. With the onset of cold weather, the wasps perish, apart from the Queen who hibernates in some shed or on house-curtains, before founding a new colony in spring.

Much has been written about the remarkable dances of the **Hive Bee,** *Apis mellifera.* A bee returning to the hive after discovering nectar will dance with greater vigour if the hoard is a rich one and excite the interest of other bees. A figure-of-eight dance is performed which is slanted in the direction of the nectar. The dancers wag their abdomens vigorously, each flick representing about 75 metres in the distance of the nectar from the hive. All this sounds so wildly improbable that it is hard to credit, but it just happens to be true. We know, too, that each worker bee, during a life of some thirty days, will be faced with the menial task of cleaning the cells of the hive, before being promoted to a spell of nursing. For about a week she is employed as a builder, before being transferred to the work of receiving nectar, food of the adults, and storing pollen which, mixed with honey, is the food of the larvae. After almost three weeks the worker bee is placed on guard at the approach to the hive. The last week of her life is spent visiting the flowers for nectar.

Our 25 species of **Bumble Bees** are fatter and hairier than the Hive Bees, and their habits and colouring differ a good deal. Some are underground nesters, others prefer to nest in the bark of a tree, a bird-box or the nest of a mouse. Six species of *Bombidae,* of the *Psithyrus* genus, are parasites, like *P. campestris,* the **Cuckoo Bee,** which kills the *Bombus* Queen and leaves her own larvae to be reared by the *Bombus* worker-bees.

The 28 British **Leaf-cutter Bees**—*Megachilidae* Family—nest in decayed wood, the nail holes of posts and other sites, constructing cells out of fragments of leaf cut from specific plants. All are solitary bees, working only for themselves and their own children—though some die after laying their eggs and never see their own families. Our 101 **Mining Bees** too, are usually solitary creatures, sometimes digging deep burrows—as much as two feet—for their nests. Many of them remain faithful to the ground where they were born, and large 'villages' containing up to 2,000 nests may be found in close proximity, their occupants 'keeping themselves to themselves'. The **Gum Bee** (*Colletidae*), with a short, forked tail, lives in large colonies nearly a foot beneath the soil.

BIBLIOGRAPHY

Butler, C. G. *The World of the Honeybee*. Collins, London, 1954.

Clegg, John. *Freshwater Life of the British Isles*. Warne, 1966.

Clegg, John. *The Observer's Book of Pond Life*. Warne, London, 1956.

Corbett, P. S., Longfield, C. and Moore, N. W. *Dragonflies*. Collins, London, 1960.

Linsenn, E. F. and Newman, L. Hugh. *The Observer's Book of Common Insects and Spiders*. Frederick Warne, London, 1964, revised ed.

Longfield, C. *The Dragonflies of the British Isles*. Wayside and Woodland Series, Warne, London, 1937.

Ragge, D. R. *Grasshoppers, Crickets and Cockroaches of the British Isles*. Warne, 1966.

Taylor, Geoffrey. *Some British Beetles*. Penguin, London, 1948.

Wigglesworth, V. B. *The Life of Insects*. Weidenfeld and Nicolson, London, 1964.

Mammals

*The Origin of Mammals – Scope for Research – How
to Watch Them – Insectivores – Bats – Rabbits and
Hares – Rodents – Carnivores – Ungulates*

THE ORIGIN OF MAMMALS

Mammals, so-called from the mammary glands which supply
the young with milk, are of fairly recent origin, if their development from reptilian ancestors is measured in geological terms.
Yet some of our beasts of prey, such as the badger, fox and
otter may well be counted among our oldest inhabitants.

Animal Remains. Badger remains have been found in Pleistocene deposits dating from about 250,000 years ago. Our carnivores or beasts of prey, like the wolf that disappeared from England and Wales in the 16th century, and from Scotland and
Ireland early in the 18th century, may have survived from the
inter-glacial period 120,000 years ago. That might be said, too,
of the beavers that could still be found in Cardiganshire late in
the 12th century. During the fourth and final inter-glacial period,
extending over 100,000 years to about 18,000 B.C., shrews, bats,
the stoat and the polecat, the long-tailed field-mouse or wood-
mouse, and possibly red squirrels existed in Britain.

Colonisation. Judging from its distribution, which extends to
Ireland and the Outer Isles, the pygmy shrew has been here as
long as any mammal. The mole, which could hardly have bur-
rowed for earthworms during the Ice Age, may be one of our
more recent acquisitions, though it arrived before the Straits
of Dover parted these Islands from the Continent some 7,000
years ago. It is not known when Ireland and the Outer Islands
were separated from the mainland, but it was probably within

the last 20,000 years. The pygmy shrew penetrated to Ireland, but not the common shrew, the mole or the weasel. Most mammals are good swimmers and deer are among those which have used this means to colonise fresh sites.

SCOPE FOR RESEARCH

Strangely little research into British mammals had been carried out until recent years, but the formation in 1954 of the Mammal Society of the British Isles (c/o The Institute of Biology, 41 Queen's Gate, London, S.W.7) gave a marked impetus to interest in the subject. The publication of the Society's *Field Guide to British Deer* (1957), followed by the *Handbook of British Mammals* (1964) did much to stimulate scientific studies in the field, including the National Badger Survey. In 1965 the Nature Conservancy offered grant-aid to the Mammal Society for a survey of mammal distribution, past and present, on a national scale. Meantime the British Deer Society (43 Brunswick Square, Hove, Sussex), which developed out of the former Deer Group of the Mammal Society, has built up a comprehensive picture of deer distribution in these Islands.

We know so little of the fox, most common of our carnivores, that it has long been necessary to rely largely on American sources when describing its breeding biology. No one really knows whether woodmice make their own burrows, or what seasonal pattern of activities dominates the secretive lives of otters, though it is thought that they breed in every month of the year. The scope for research into mammals is enormous.

HOW TO WATCH THEM

A naturalist with many prize-winning films to his credit confesses that he does not begin filming until he has become familiar with the scene and its wild life over a period of many months. Those who embark on deer or badger watching are wise to make a preliminary survey of the country—and to ensure that their presence on private property is authorised. It is vital, too, that every effort is made to avoid disturbing the creatures to be studied. This means *never* following deer into their lair or sanctuary where they lie up in the day. It is also wise not to trample too near the entrance to the setts of badgers, for human scent may linger there for eight hours or more. A fresh sett may soon be deserted if there is human disturbance. An old-established one will probably not be, but the animals may emerge later in the evening.

Wind. Whether watching deer, badgers or foxes, it is important to station oneself down-wind. Allowance has to be made for sudden changes of wind direction—and local air currents do not always match the movements of the clouds.

Clothing. This must blend with the background as well as being comfortable. When watching deer, vivid red pullovers and even white handkerchiefs are best left at home. Light brown, khaki or olive-green clothing makes the observer most inconspicuous. All movements must be cautious and quiet, and creaking shoes or a rustling mackintosh can ruin a night's work.

Positioning. More may be seen of mammals by sitting still or standing motionless than by hours of persistent searching. Deer stalkers are normally advised not to approach nearer than fifty to eighty yards to the deer. Badger-watchers may well be advised to take up a watching position against a tree trunk or bush—or in a tree—some ten yards or more from the sett.

The stalker of deer—or the student of foxes—will try to ensure that all his noiseless movements into the wind lie against a background of trees, and he will pause, look and listen before silently crossing any open space. Yet the crack of a twig beneath the feet may not alarm deer or badgers if one remains silent and still for several minutes. When within sight of deer, no movement should be made unless all the animals are grazing.

Animals at close quarters. An effective way of watching deer, badgers and foxes is to erect a simple hide five or six yards from a well-used track or a favourite drinking place, or near a wallowing scrape of deer, where the animal rolls in the mud. *High seats.* This is a ladder with a seat near the top, fixed to a tree by strong rope, and generally 12–15 ft. high. Or it may rest on wooden supports, hidden from the deer but independent of any one tree.

Feeding wild mammals. The simple habit of putting out suitable food and lying in wait may present excellent opportunities to watch hedgehogs, woodmice and other animals. Most mammals other than the bank vole and possibly the squirrels seem to be colour-blind, and an observer with a torch wrapped in red cellophane may obtain fascinating insight into the private lives of many nocturnal creatures. I know of several wild badgers which regularly take sweet foods from the hand.

The observation of otters is more difficult. One may watch their holts, follow their tracks, inspect the 'altars' where they eat their prey—often a rock or tree-trunk on the banks of a stream—and never catch a glimpse of them. Many naturalists have never seen one. Anglers and river bailiffs stand the best chance—which is a way of saying that the more time you spend sitting quiet and still near a stream, the better your chance of encountering otters. The late Oliver Pike discovered that an otter was in the habit of visiting a wet sand quarry at the end of his garden. He put out food for it and the day came when the animal regularly took fish from his hand.

Equipment. If the ability to keep silent and still is a prime need for the naturalist, keen eyes, ears—and a nose for the smell of fox and stoat—are more valuable than any amount of costly equipment. But a notebook and pencil is always important, for observations should be recorded without delay. Field glasses with a magnification of 7×50 or 8×30 are highly desirable for deer stalking, and the photographer will need telephoto-lens with a broad aperture, and mounted on a tripod. Tele-lens are also essential for cine-cameras. Animals are highly sensitive to sound as well as to scent and movement.

Longworth traps (Longworth Scientific Instrument Co., Radley Road, Abingdon, Berkshire) for the live trapping of small mammals have been used to glean much new knowledge of animal populations. Shrews and woodmice, probably our most abundant mammals, readily visit these traps when baited with cat foods and other meat, and so do voles. A nesting compartment lined with grass and well-stocked with food will sustain and shelter the animals during their few hours in the trap.

Animal Tracks. Much may be discovered from a study of animal tracks, especially in the morning after a fall of snow. A fox leaves behind a single line of dog-like tracks, with only the

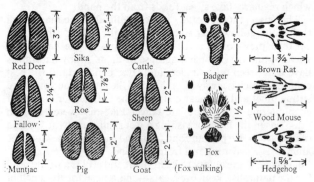

Tracks (showing hind print with approximate size).

faintest impression of the claws or hairs impressed in the snow between the four toes. The badger deposits an impression of five toes and sharp claws between, and the broad pad of the foot behind. Weasel tracks often wind in and out of vole and mice runs under the snow, with 7–12 in. between each bound, whereas the male stoat will leap roughly twice as far—19 to 23 in. in my experience—with the hind feet falling into the marks made by the fore feet. The seals or tracks of otters show five toes and the interdigital webbing between.

An experienced observer can often identify the sex and age of deer by their slots or tracks. Briefly, the slots of red deer are roughly three fingers wide at heel and if the animal is walking they may be two feet or so apart. Fallow deer slots—and it is these which are most frequently found in English gardens—are a little over two fingers wide at heel and the step may be 1¾ ft. Roe slots are some 1¼ ft. apart and barely one and a half fingers broad at heel. The little muntjac, now steadily increasing its range, has a pace of less than a foot and the slot is extremely narrow—barely a finger broad.

Other signs. Most countrymen are familiar with the sight of pine cones, gnawed down to the core by squirrels, or hazel nuts containing the broad round hole made by woodmice, the several holes of dormice, the tiny round hole of the nut weevil, *Belaninus nucum*, the ragged incisions made by the nuthatch, or the half or three-quarter shell ripped away by squirrels. There is scope for more study here, and the day may yet come when naturalists can catalogue the key features distinguishing food half-eaten by one species from that left by its relatives.

Patterns of behaviour. The lives of many small mammals both by day and night follow a regular rhythm of activity alternating with periods of rest lasting for one to three hours. Common and pygmy shrews, voles and harvest mice, as well as foxes, deer and otters may be watched in daylight; but I have fewer than a dozen records of badgers being abroad in full daylight. Animal actions such as preening, washing and displaying normally conform to a distinctive pattern. Badgers and otters may follow the same paths through successive decades—though it is unlikely that individual badgers survive beyond their early teens, and too many are killed much earlier. Rabbits regularly place their feet on exactly the same inch of ground when travelling along well-used tracks within their territory.

INSECTIVORES *Insectivora*

Hedgehog (Urchin), *Erinaceous europaeus*. One of our few hibernating mammals—and even the hedgehog will sometimes stir during unseasonal warmth in winter. Widespread throughout the British Isles, but probably decreasing. Common in fields, gardens, scrub, open woodland and heathland, but rare in marsh or high moorland or dense woodland. Most active at dusk and dawn, moving slowly and noisily in search of food, with frequent pauses to taste the scent. Moves quickly at times, as when crossing a close-cropped lawn between woodland. Rolls up into a prickly ball at hint of danger, and many are run-over. Eaten by badgers and some foxes—for both these animals will penetrate their defences. Good climber and swimmer. Food: earthworms, snails, slugs, insect larvae, including many beetles. Quick to welcome a saucer of milk if put out regularly. Breeding: 3–7 young reared May–June. Some hedgehogs have a second brood August–October. Gestation period 30–35 days. Hibernates November–December to March.

Mole, *Talpa europaea*. Originally an animal of broad-leaved woodland, moles have successfully invaded almost all types of habitat other than bleak mountains and acid sand where the earthworm population is small or non-existent. Found at almost 3,000 ft. in Lake District, but retreats from low-lying water meadows as floods rise, only to swim back and reoccupy runs within a day or two of water subsiding. Not completely blind; keen sense of touch and sensitive to vibration, but capable of tracing beetle or worm by scent only at range of one or two inches. Solitary, avoiding contact with its own kind except in breeding season which is February–June, with most families born in April and early May. Most females have only one litter

Hedgehog with young

Mole

Common Shrew with young

Bechstein Bat

Pigmy Shrew

Noctule Bat

Water Shrew

Hares boxing

Pipistrelle Bat

Mountain Hare

Rabbit

Long-eared Bat

a year. Gestation period probably about a month. Food: earth-worms and other soil fauna, including many larvae of beetles and flies and also slugs. Life span 3 years, sometimes longer. A few moles on pastures with a small earthworm population may make many molehills, while many moles on good land may pro-duce few.

Common Shrew, *Sorex araneus*. Abundant almost everywhere, especially in thick low grass and scrub, and its soft whimpering cries may often be heard. Breeds May–September, most litters being reared June and July. 5–8 young. Carnivorous, eating many insects and larvae and often storing them. Earthworms, spiders and harvestmen feature prominently in diet. Solitary in their habits.

Pygmy Shrew, *S. minutus*. Distribution ranges from 4,400 ft. high on Ben Nevis down to lowland meadows with good cover. Absent from Channel Islands and Shetland. The only shrew in Ireland. Rare in mature woodland, where common shrew is plentiful. 4–6 young. Breeding season April–October.

Water Shrew, *Neomys fodiens*. Largest and darkest of the shrews, and much heavier than its relatives, with noticeable white hairs beside the eyes and ears. A resident of clear water streams which has sometimes been found a mile or two from water. Little is known about its food and only in recent years has much been discovered about its breeding. Diet includes insects, snails, frogs and small fish. Two litters between mid-April and September.

BATS *Chiroptera*

The only mammals that fly have been oddly neglected by naturalists, other than a few pioneers like Michael Blackmore; though an increasing volume of research is now being carried out into their ways, and the remarkable discoveries of recent years confirming that bats in flight are guided by echo-location have added impetus to these studies. Today even amateur naturalists may be found listening to echo-locating squeaks of bats on ultrasonic receivers, or marking with small metal bands bats caught in Japanese mist nets. It is important, as exponents of these new methods would agree, that this growing spate of research should be carried out with a minimum of disturbance—or discomfort—for the bats. The indiscriminate ringing or banding of these mammals is most undesirable.

Pet bats are quickly tamed and they fare well on a diet of moths, beetles, spiders and mealworms, augmented by hard-boiled egg and biscuit meal. Blackmore reports that they like cream cheese, and need to have access to water.

Pipistrelle, *Pipistrellus pipistrellus.* Our most familiar bat, emerging from buildings, trees and rocks almost anywhere in Britain as the temperature exceeds 40° F. It is dark brown or reddish, and the smallest of our bats. Hibernates late October to early March. The solitary young is born in late June or early July after a gestation period of 44 days. Gnats form the staple diet, but larger prey is sometimes eaten. I have watched a pipistrelle hunting in warm sunlight in the late June afternoon, repeatedly returning to its roost and flying out again.

Long-eared Bat, *Plecotus auritus.* Widespread and common in the British Isles around trees and buildings. Ears 34–37 mm. long. It is not yet known whether it hibernates in trees, but it does so in buildings and caves, sometimes emerging for brief flights in mild winter weather. Some evidence of migration over North Sea. Solitary young born June or July; food includes moths, butterflies, craneflies and beetles, often snatched from boles or leaves of trees.

Noctule, *Nyctalus noctula.* Widespread and common in England and Wales, seemingly rare in Scotland. A large brown bat with a forearm of 49 mm. or more, and a wing span of about 370 mm. Often emerges well before sunset, with strong, sustained flight at up to 80 ft., with frequent sharp dives. Gregarious. Known to be migratory on the Continent.

Bechstein's Bat, *Myotis bechsteini.* Our rarest bat, recorded only in a few southern counties and in Shropshire. Greyish brown with white underparts. Known to utter a low 'buzz' and high-pitched squeaks. Preys on moths.

Mouse-eared Bat, *Myotis myotis.* Our largest bat and also our youngest—in the sense that it was discovered here in 1956, the first time for more than 2,000 years that a Continental mammal has begun to colonise these Islands through natural migration and without aid from man. It is confined at present to Dorset. Wing span well over 400 mm. Shrieks loudly when alarmed. Can fly for long distances.

RABBITS AND HARES *Lagomorpha*

Rabbit, *Oryctolagus cuniculus.* A native of Spain, probably introduced to Britain as a delicacy by the Normans. Fetched high prices in Tudor times—which implies a low population—but common in 17th century and a major pest of farms and woodlands in past century or more, thriving in almost any habitat, including salt marshes, dunes, and mountains. Most active at dusk and at night, but readily feeds by day if undisturbed. Eats grass, herbs, cereals, and will prevent growth of scrub, but tends to leave elder, ragwort, thistles, bracken, nettles, black nightshade, daffodils and birch. An adult rabbit will eat 2 lbs. of carrots a day. Average loss of winter wheat to rabbits, 1951–54 estimated at 1½ cwt per acre, or over 6 per cent of national yield. Litters averaging 4–5 may be born any month, mainly January–June. Pre-natal mortality rate sometimes as much as 64 per cent. Gestation period 28 days. Young in nesting burrow 3 weeks; doe ready to mate again straight after birth of young. Strict peck order among the several bucks and does in each warren. Most rabbits live in burrows, but some lie up in scrub.

Myxomatosis. This disease, largely spread in Britain by the rabbit flea—with some illegal aid from humans—reached the Edenbridge area of Kent in 1953 and rapidly spread during 1954 to most of Britain, destroying all but a tiny proportion of the population. Attenuated strains of the disease, some of them most virulent, occurred in most English and Welsh counties in 1965 and 1966 when the rabbit population was undoubtedly increasing in many districts. Many rabbits now recover from milder strains of the disease and remain immune for life. Young born to these 'innoculated' rabbits may inherit some antibodies and are likely to recover from the disease in their early days, but they soon lose immunity unless 'innoculated' by infection in their first weeks. In short, rabbits are likely to be with us for ever, but foxes and other predators, Rabbit Clearance Societies and myxomatosis all take an annual cull.

Brown Hare, *Lepus europaeus.* Long hind legs and loping gait, long black-tipped ears, black top to tail, and large flat droppings all distinguish these beautiful animals from the smaller rabbit. Unlike the smaller blue mountain hare, this species does not dig shallow burrows, but lies in a 'form' in lush vegetation. Most abundant in the open arable farmland of Cambridgeshire, Huntingdonshire, and East Anglia. Also numerous on open downland, and frequently found in open woodland where it can cause much damage to growing timber. Less common in most westerly counties. Spring antics of the 'mad March hares' are delightful to watch, but strangely little written about them, nor about their feeding habits.

Blue Hare (Mountain Hare), *Lepus timidus.* A native of the Scottish Highlands, and Ireland—where the race is believed to be sturdier—and also found now in Scottish Lowlands, Pennines, North Derbyshire. Rare in N. Wales. Numbers fluctuate even more than those of the larger Brown Hare. Heather and cotton grass form the staple winter diet, with rushes, gorse, and perhaps lichens.

RODENTS *Rodentia*

Red Squirrel, *Sciurus vulgaris.* Sadly scarce nowadays in much of Britain, but flourishing in Norfolk and in most northern and western counties, Wales and Scotland. It also occurs in the Isle of Wight and Anglesey. It tends to become rare or absent when area is occupied by grey squirrels, for reasons not fully understood, but has also dwindled in some places free from the greys. Thrives in coniferous woodland. No real hibernation by either of our squirrels, but said to be less active in snow, wind or rain. Nest (drey) of bark and twigs, lined with leaves, grass and moss at joint of branch with trunk. Breeds January–April and May–August. Gestation 46 days. Feeds on seeds of forest trees, particularly Scots pine; insects, fungi, berries, roots, some eggs and young of birds. Sometimes guilty of stripping bark near crowns of conifers and can cause much damage on occasions. Readily tamed.

Grey Squirrel, *S. carolinensis.* Larger and heavier than last species and without the long ear tufts. Brown or rufous patches on summer coats may cause confusion with native species. Abundant in mixed woodland in much of Britain, including London's parks, and still spreading north and westwards. A native of eastern Canada and the United States, these animals were introduced to Britain on numerous occasions between 1876 and 1929, and now occupy some 40,000 square miles at a density which, in richly varied mixed woodland, may be as high as 5 per acre, though numbers fluctuate according to the autumn seed harvest and winter weather. Breeds late winter and early spring and again in the late summer. Average number of young 4, born in drey of leafy twigs with side entrance, often 30–40 ft. up in large fork of tree or near crown. Acorns, beech mast and other woodland fruit forms staple diet, with shoots of oak in spring, bulbs, fungi, insects, grain, orchard fruit and much else, including occasional eggs and young of birds. Easily tamed, but illegal to keep them without licence from Ministry of Agriculture. Nuts are stored singly and traced by scent.

Bank Vole, *Clethrionomys glareolis.* Hedgerow banks, scrub and woodland form the habitats of this buff or light grey mam-

Red Squirrel

Grey Squirrel

Water Vole

Short-tailed Vole

Bank Vole

Wood Mouse

Harvest Mouse

Brown Rat

Harvest Mouse

Black Rat

Edible Dormouse

Common Dormouse

mal, which feeds on fungi, insects, berries, etc. Breeds April–September in nest of grass and moss in tree stump or below ground. Common.

Short-tailed Vole, *Microtus agrestis.* More numerous than the last species, and more inclined to fluctuate dramatically from plague dimensions to modest populations. This is most noticeable in young plantations where much damage may be done to trees. Main food is the stems of grass. Breeds March–September or later.

Water Vole, *Arvicola amphibius.* The misnamed Water Rat, with a brown or black coat can often be found on the banks of ponds and streams, where its grazing activities may leave a 'mown' strip of grass. Also eats much other vegetable food and a little animal food such as water snails and fresh-water mussels. Nests in burrows or in reed-beds. I watched one take much reedmace down its burrow. Litters average about 4. April–October.

Wood Mouse (Long-tailed Field Mouse), *Apodemus sylvaticus.* Brown back, white underparts, large ears and long tail distinguish this species of open woodland with light cover, hedgerows, gardens and fields. Nest of shredded grass is under ground, but sometimes in sheds or even houses. Less active in moonlight. Food stored in bulk. Breeds April–October, especially July–August, building up woodland population of 5 to 40 per acre. Food includes seeds, fruits, corn, buds, snails, roots.

Yellow-necked Mouse, *Apodemus flavicollis.* Bigger than the last species, and a brighter colour, with a yellow-buff collar between fore legs. Little known of distribution, but found in stores, garden sheds, churches and beehives. S. England.

Harvest Mouse, *Micromys minutus.* Smaller than a house mouse, with long prehensile tail with which it clings to stems of corn. May be less rare than is supposed, for it is often overlooked. Animal of the herb layer, dwelling in marshland, cornfields and adjoining hedges, heaths, reed beds and other open land. Nest of grass, like a cricket ball, found in a variety of sites from long grass 6–10 in. above ground to the exceptional one 4 ft. high in a gorse bush. Breeds May–September, litters of 5–9 recorded. Gestation period 21 days. Young independent 14–16 days. Feeds on grain, leaves, berries, insects.

House Mouse, *Mus musculus*. Smaller size, less prominent eyes and ears, musky smell and greyer shade distinguish from wood-mouse. Buildings, walls and hedgerows and open fields form habitat. Squeaks heard far more often than with other mice. Makes nests of paper, cloth and other materials and will rear up to ten families a year in suitable surroundings. 5–6 families more usual in buildings, with 5 or so young in average litter. Females protect small territories.

Black Rat, *Rattus rattus*. A native of Malaya and surrounding countries, which penetrated to Britain in Middle Ages, climbing to top storeys of buildings. Formerly abundant in town and country, but much declined since 18th century as brown rat spread. Now restricted to a few ports where it may still outnumber the larger brown rat in and around the docks. Much declined in London docks since the second World War.

Brown Rat (Norway Rat), *Rattus norvegicus*. A pest of town and country buildings, often spending the summer in woods, hedgerows, and old rabbit warrens, migrating back to buildings in autumn. Frequently abundant along river banks. Likes to burrow in sheltered south-facing slope where food is plentiful. Eats almost anything, including house mice, grain, fruit, frozen meat stores, etc. Probably 91–97 per cent of adults die annually, but 3–5 litters reared each year, young leaving nest after 3 weeks. Gestation period 24 days. These pests serve as a reservoir of Salmonella food poisoning and leptospiral jaundice.

Edible Dormouse, *Glis glis*. Introduced to Tring, Hertfordshire, in 1902, these large squirrel-like creatures, grey above and white below and smaller than a grey squirrel, are confined to the Luton–Beaconsfield–Aylesbury area. A native of broad-leaved woodland in Central Europe and the Middle East, they have a habit of entering houses in autumn to hibernate. Fruit, nuts, the bark of willow and plum trees, and insects are eaten.

Dormouse, *Muscardinus avellanarius.* A silent and nocturnal inhabitant of mixed woodland, often coppiced, with oak, beech, hazel, sweet chestnut and honeysuckle. About 4 young are raised in the two annual litters, and a typical life span may be 4 years. But the population appears to be declining, probably owing to the destruction of habitats, and they have long been far from common in many areas. Forest seeds, berries, shoots and bark form staple diet. Hibernates alone in October and winter nest is sometimes dug out by foxes, badgers and magpies.

Coypu, *Myocastor coypus.* A South American rodent, reared in England for its fur, which escaped and during 1950s reached pest proportions in East Anglia. Particularly numerous in the reed beds and on river banks and marshes of the Norfolk Broads. Most active at dusk and dawn and in the night. At first its clearance of reeds and reedmace was welcomed, but the animals soon seriously damaged farm crops and disturbed habitats of interesting birds. By winter of 1962, 100,000 killed in East Suffolk and Norfolk River Board area. Hard weather, 1962–63 reduced them near to extinction, but some recovery since then.

BEASTS OF PREY *Carnivora*

Red Fox, *Vulpes vulpes.* More than 50,000 foxes are probably killed in Britain annually by shooting and hunting, but population remains large in a variety of habitats, ranging from mountains to London suburbs and coastal cliffs. Often lies out in daytime and will hunt then if hungry. Good climber, swimmer, with exceptional powers of scent and hearing. Vixen tends to be smaller and narrower in head than dog, but hard to distinguish. Monogamous, rutting late December–February. Dog brings food to cubs. Rabbits and field voles staple food, supplemented by hares, rats, woodmice, house mice, dor-beetles and other insects, berries, including black-berries, game and small birds and poultry. One litter, cubs emerging within 4 weeks and leaving earth for good 7–8 weeks.

Pine-marten, *Martes martes*. Confined to the N. W. Scottish Highlands where it has slightly increased since the war, and to odd corners of Wales, the Lake District and Ireland where it is rare. Rich chestnut-brown to black, with pure white throat and bushy tail. Generally restricted to rocky slopes and woodland. One litter of 2–5 young, late March or April. Short-tailed voles and other small rodents feature prominently in diet with beetles, berries, insects; also fish and carrion recorded, together with game and small birds.

Stoat, *Mustela erminea*. Widespread and common, fluctuating in number according to abundance of rabbits and intensity of persecution. Thrives in woodland, farmland, marsh and moorland. Hunts by scent during night and day. I have occasionally watched remarkable displays of acrobatics as fascinated birds were enticed near. Rabbits killed by bite at back of neck, and either eaten on the spot or dragged away. No truth in belief that blood of prey is sucked. One litter of kittens in springtime, in a den beneath old tree or in hedgerow bank. Some stoats turn white in winter (ermine coat). Larger size and black tip to longish tail distinguish from weasel.

Weasel, *M. nivalis*. Shorter by about 3 in. than the stoat, and with a short tail without a black tip, the weasel is probably more numerous in most districts, and may occur wherever there are mice and voles. It is a useful friend of the forester, and though sometimes guilty of robbing nests, is seldom a serious predator of game outside the rearing fields. Two litters a year, April–May and July–August. 3–8 young in a litter. Life span about 6 years. Both shrews and moles are frequently killed *and* eaten, though voles usually form the chief prey.

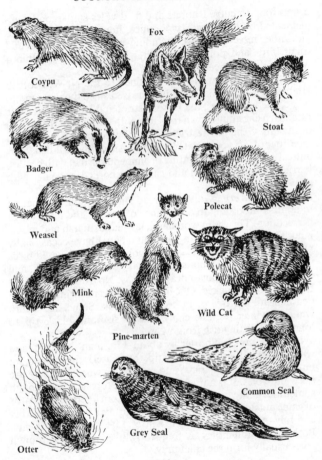

Coypu

Fox

Stoat

Badger

Polecat

Weasel

Mink

Wild Cat

Pine-marten

Common Seal

Otter

Grey Seal

Polecat, *Mustela putorius.* More abundant than the stoat in parts of Central Wales where it can be found in mountain woodlands, thickets and bogs. Possibly present in Devon, Cornwall and the Lake District, but extremely rare, and thought to be extinct in Scottish Highlands. Dark fur, buffish underparts, yellowish-white on muzzle and cheeks. Shorter tail than marten. Two litters of 6–7. First one late April–May after gestation period of 41 days. Rabbits, rodents, poultry and birds probably form bulk of food. Also fish, frogs and snakes.

American Mink, *Mustela vison.* Introduced to fur farms in Britain, from which it has escaped, breeding in wild since 1956 if not before. Teign valley of Devon, Pembroke, Carmarthen, Hampshire, Wiltshire, East Sussex and Scottish lowlands. Dark brown, with small white spot on lower lip and chin, and possibly white hairs on underparts. A powerful predator on game, poultry, fish, small mammals and birds. 120 killed in E. Sussex, 1965–1966, 17 of them in Pevensey Marshes. 5–6 young reared in spring.

Badger, *Meles meles.* Brock. Widely distributed and breeding in all English and Welsh counties and most Scottish counties. Rare in E. Anglia, though recently found to be unexpectedly plentiful in parts of Cambridgeshire. Most abundant in West Country, plentiful in S. and S.E., Common in Ireland, uncommon in most of Scotland. Setts made in woods, copses or quarries and hedge banks, usually within easy reach of stream. Tunnels vary in extent from 10 yd. to 100 yd., with chambers lined with dry bedding comprising bracken, grass and leaves. Two or three families may share a sett in late summer, and frequent moves are made from main sett to minor ones used at certain times. No true hibernation and I usually find badger tracks after a snow fall; but they often remain below ground for a day or two in cold weather. Mates February–May or any time to October, but young are born January–May, mainly during the first three weeks of February in S. England, late February and March in north. 1–5 young stay below ground 8 weeks, and usually venture out in April. They glean own food after 3 months, but remain with sow well into autumn or later. Omnivorous over food. Earthworms, young rabbits, rats, voles and other small rodents, beetles and wasp grubs feature prominently in diet. Moles, slugs, snails, oats and woodland fruits of all kind are eaten. No proof of lamb killing, but occasional cases of poultry being taken. Not generally a serious predator of game. Examination of the yellowish muddy droppings show that earthworms are frequently the main food. Generally beneficial to man. The gassing of badgers is illegal.

Common Otter, *Lutra lutra.* Widely distributed and most numerous in the west, but seldom seen in many districts of S.E. Thick brown fur, long tapering tail or 'rudder' and webbed feet make this species unmistakable. Frequently on the move between one river and another or up and down stream, and a pair may claim six miles of water as their own. Little is known about their breeding, but it may occur in any month of the year, 2–3 cubs being reared in a holt lined with grass, reeds and moss, usually in a quiet backwater. Diet includes game fish, eels, carp, roach, dace, bream, sticklebacks, crayfish, small rodents, beetles, birds and earthworms. Can do much damage to fish hatcheries at spawning times, but not generally thought to be harmful to the angler, though the matter is still controversial. The low density of the otter population, and their heavy destruction of the eels which prey on fish larvae are important points in their favour.

Wild Cat, *Felis silvestris.* Our fiercest mammal, once widespread in the British Isles, and now restricted to Scottish Highlands, where it is increasing. Small mammals, mountain hares, rabbits and birds regularly eaten. 2–4 kittens born early to mid-May. Possibly a second litter.

Seals *Phocidae*

Common Seal, *Phoca vitulina.* Breeds around the Wash and East Anglian coasts, and the E. and W. coasts of Scotland, Shetland, Orkney and Hebrides. Population in the area of the Wash estimated at 2,000 and 400 for S.W. Shetland. Breeds in June, young swimming and diving from birth.

Grey Seal, Atlantic Seal, *Halichoerus grypus.* The larger seal of the North Atlantic, a population estimated to number 35,000 breeding around the British Isles, including Scotland, Wales, and the Farne Islands. Now the subject of much research—and controversy, on account of a suspected increase in the population and damage to fishery interests.

Even Toed Ungulates *Artiodactyla*

Indian Muntjac (Barking Deer), *Muntiacus muntjak.* **Chinese Muntjac,** *M. reevesi.* These two species were introduced to Woburn early in the century, and *M. reevesi* or its hybrid with the Indian species have now spread far afield through the South Midlands and the Home Counties. Charming little reddish-brown creatures, they stand no more than 17 in. high at the shoulder and their antlers are but 4 in. long. They are not easy to find, but can sometimes be seen grazing in forest clearings, or helping themselves to grass, fruit, cabbages or turnips in gardens. They often lie up under holly in winter, when starvation sometimes thins the population. Recently reported from Derbyshire, East Anglia and other counties.

Fallow Deer, *Dama dama.* Probably not indigenous, but flourished here in the 12th century. The 70 odd fallow deer in Epping Forest and the fine herds in the New Forest, Rockingham Forest and on Cannock Chase are descendants of the original herds. Extremely wary and generally silent except in the rutting season in October. They often lie up in day time, emerging to feed at dusk and dawn on grass, herbs, berries and nuts. Will strip bark from smooth-barked hard woods at height of 4-4½ ft. Herds usually move in single file, and in early summer with fawns they sometimes seem to bounce along. Bucks separate from does in summer while antlers grow and establish rutting territories in second week of October, and their groans — a roaring, belching snort—can be heard during the next four weeks.

Red Deer

Fallow Deer

Sika Deer

Roe Deer

Muntjac Deer

Chinese Water Deer

The single fawn or occasional twins are born in May or June. One deer to 70 acres may be a reasonable population for most commercial woodlands.

Sika Deer, *Cervus nippon.* Introduced to a number of parks a century ago, and deer escaping during both the last two wars have founded wild populations, now to be found in about half a dozen English counties and as many Scottish ones. Smaller than the red deer, to which it is closely related. Faint white spots on buff-brown summer coat. Found in mixed or coniferous woodland, wet heaths and alder carr. Male utters strange whistle, rising and falling before ending in a grunt and a half-hour pause. This call is associated with the rut in September–October. Grazes on grasses and herbs, and much hazel.

Red Deer, *Cervus elephus.* Our largest mammal, standing 4 feet high at the shoulder and weighing up to 25 stone, when cleaned of its internal organs. The 170,000 red deer in Scotland occupy open moorland in summer, moving down to the forests and farm estates in winter. Grasses, heather and the shoots of trees form main items in diet, and shares fallow deer's liking for sweet chestnuts, acorns, bramble, ivy and yew. Most active at dusk and dawn, but can often be seen by day—and small numbers, usually descendants of park deer, occur in many English counties. Stags claim own territories and may live alone or in small groups, though large mixed herds can be seen in summer and winter. Stags roar during the rut from early September to mid-October. Life span 20 years.

Chinese Water Deer, *Hydropotes inermis.* Introduced to Woburn, 1900 or thereabouts, and now widespread and increasing in Bedfordshire, Hertfordshire and Bucks. Pale chestnut, white underparts, little bigger than the muntjac. No antlers. Up to 5 fawns are born May–June.

Roe Deer, *Capreolus capreolus.* Indigenous to Britain. Has recently increased much in number, spreading into 16 English counties amd most Scottish counties. Height at shoulder 2½ ft. or less, with bright red-brown summer coat, greyer in winter, when rump is white, and a short tail. Frequently utters a gruff, staccato bark as it bounds off. Nocturnal where persecuted. Eats many berries and leaves, helping to keep down brambles but also eating pine shoots, clover and fungi. Mates in late July and early August, but the single or twin young will not be born until late May. Fraying and browsing often trouble foresters, and culling with the right weapons at the proper season is essential.

Reindeer, *Rangifer tarandus.* This species became extinct in Britain late in the 12th century, but a small herd was introduced to the Cairngorms in 1952 and it is managed under the auspices of the Reindeer Council of the United Kingdom. This species is unusual in that both the bulls and cows carry antlers.

(Close seasons for Deer: See page 283.)

BIBLIOGRAPHY

Burton, M. *Wild Animals of the British Isles.* Frederick Warne, London, 1960.

Cadman, A. *Dawn, Dusk and Deer.* Country Life, 1965.

Matthews, L. Harrison. *British Mammals.* Collins, London, 1952.

Page, F. J. Taylor, Ed. *Field Guide to British Deer.* Mammal Society, 1964 n.e.

Southern, H. N. Ed. *The Handbook of British Mammals.* Blackwell Scientific Publications, Oxford, for the Mammal Society, 1964.

Reptiles and Amphibians

Lizards – Snakes – Amphibians

LIZARDS   *Anguidae*

The Slow-Worm, *Anguis fragilis*. This legless lizard is often mistaken for a snake, though traces of discarded shoulder-girdles suggest that its ancestors travelled on four legs. Usually about a foot long, with a slender dark line down the back of the female, and on each flank. Some specimens are half as long again. Though generally seen on heathland or in open woodland, they often visit gardens where they should be welcomed, if only because of their heavy consumption of the harmful white slug *Agriolimax agrestis*. Snails, earthworms and insects are also eaten. 6–12 young born August–October, and promptly hunt own prey. Hibernates beneath leaves, stones, or in burrow.

Lacertidae Family

Sand Lizard, *Lacerta agilis agilis*. A rarity confined to light sandy soils of Dorset, Hampshire and Surrey where it preys on spiders, woodlice, worms, insects and other food. Heavier build and shorter legs distinguish from common lizard, and a series of dark spots with white centres line the back and flanks. White or creamish underparts, often with black spots. About 8 white eggs are laid in July in a small dip excavated by the female and covered with leaves or sand.

Common Lizard, *Lacerta vivipara*. Frequently found sunbathing on heaths, open woodland or roadside banks, swiftly darting away when approached. Generally some shade of brown, though there is much variation. Preys on spiders, ants, beetles and other small creatures. Drops her 5–8 young in shallow pit, July–August. When caught may promptly shed tail. A frightened lizard will do this even if the tail is not touched. A new tail of sorts soon grows.

SNAKES *Colubridae*

Grass Snake, *Natrix natrix natrix.* Our biggest snake, sometimes 4 ft. long, and easily distinguished from adder by yellow neck-ring, long tapering body, and length of tail. Olive-brown, grey or greenish, with blackish spots on the back. Large shields on long slender head. Particularly fond of garden ponds, where one was observed to eat 17 newts at a meal. It used to be said that frogs formed the principal food, but today grass snakes far outnumber frogs in some parishes. The numerous eggs are laid in compost heaps, rotting leaves or rotting tree trunk, and they hatch 6–10 weeks later. Hibernates. Life span 10 years or so. Not in Scotland or Ireland.

Smooth Snake, *Coronella austriaca.* More like an adder in appearance, with dark spots along back; black patch on head; brown, grey or reddish back. Whitish flanks of belly. Restricted to Hampshire, Dorset, Surrey and Berkshire, though may be overlooked in adjoining counties.

Adder, Viper, *Vipera berus berus.* Short, thick body, broad, flat head, with small shields—the grass snake's are large—and a dark V or X mark on the head, and black zig-zag line along the centre of the back. Common on sandy heaths, downland, sunny moorland, hedge banks and bramble scrub, and even rocky coast and marshy land at times. Lizards, mice, slugs, frogs and newts are eaten, much prey being killed first with a swift thrust of the poison fangs. Highly sensitive to the vibration of approaching feet and tend to be wary. 5–20 young are born August–September. It is physically impossible for an adder to swallow her young. People bitten by an adder should be treated for shock. Not aggressive by nature, but several hundred people

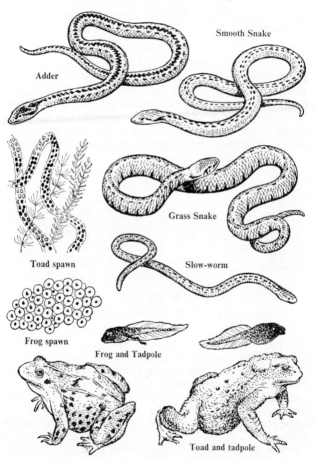

Adder

Smooth Snake

Toad spawn

Grass Snake

Slow-worm

Frog spawn

Frog and Tadpole

Toad and tadpole

221

must have been bitten in Britain during past half century. All but ten soon recovered.

AMPHIBIANS

Salamandridae Family

Crested Newt, *Triturus cristatus cristatus.* Much like a lizard in appearance, our three species of newt are akin to the frogs and toads in developing from an aquatic tadpole. Unlike frogs, however, they retain at all stages a compressed tail. Returning to still waters in March, the handsome male crested newt displays his bright crest before the female, his curving tail rapidly

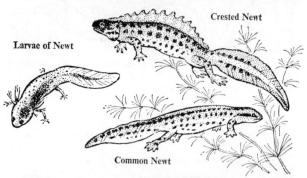

Crested Newt

Larvae of Newt

Common Newt

vibrating. Some 200–300 eggs are laid singly on leaves of aquatic plants. They hatch in about a fortnight and the larvae mature into adults and leave the water late in the summer, hibernating beneath turf or stones or leaves. Our biggest species—6 in. long.

Smooth Newt, *T. vulgaris vulgaris.* **Common or Spotted Newt.** Two inches smaller. Olive brown with dark spots and orange underparts, but much variation. Most common Eastern England.

Palmate Newt, *T. helveticus helveticus.* Local S.E. England, avoiding low-lying Thames valley, but present on higher ground round London. More plentiful than last species in West. Smaller—3 in. long. Ridge of skin on each side of back. No black dots on flesh-coloured throat, unlike smooth newt. Dark web between toes on hind feet of males.

Ranidae Family

Common Frog, *Rana temporaria temporaria.* A species that has dwindled dramatically in recent years, perhaps owing to excessive collecting for laboratories and by children, the filling in of ponds, and the use of pesticides. The migration of frogs and toads to the spawning ponds is a remarkable sight in February and March—and up to the end of April for the toads. The same ponds are used year after year while others are oddly neglected. On emerging from hibernation, frogs soon move purposefully to the breeding pond where each one lays more than 1,000 eggs. The tadpoles are usually transformed into young adults by late May or June. Hibernates in October–November.

The Edible Frog, *R. esculenta,* and the sub-species, **the Marsh Frog,** *R. e. ridibunda,* are recent introductions. The latter, since it was released on Romney Marsh, 1935, has spread widely in this district of the Kent-Sussex border.

Bufonidae Family

Common Toad, *Bufo bufo.* Heavier, larger and a flatter animal than the frog, with shorter legs and warty skin. Most active at dusk and later, often far from water. Huge appetite for ants, beetles and other *moving* insects. Large-scale migration to breeding ponds in March–April often mistaken for that of frogs. **Natterjack Toad,** *B. calamita.* Widely distributed but local in England, Wales and S.W. Scotland. Favours sandy soils for burrowing and lies there in daytime. Narrow yellow line down middle of head and back, and much shorter legs distinguish from the common toad.

Birds

*In the Garden – In Woodland – Heaths and Commons –
On the Farm – Lakes, Reservoirs and Marshes –
Migration*

Bird populations depend upon many factors, none more important than the nature of the vegetation—source of food, cover and nesting sites. The height and density of trees, shrubs and herbs probably matter more than their identity. Yet it is also true that some trees and shrubs are more attractive to particular birds than others.

BIRDS IN THE GARDEN

Birds abhor an excessively tidy garden or, perhaps surprisingly, a too neglected one. The neat formal garden in which every shrub is heavily pruned may offer little food and less cover for wild life. The neglected one, with long grass instead of a lawn, and dense scrub shutting out the sunlight, may offer sanctuary only to the jays, woodpigeons, bullfinches and one or two other species.

A well mown lawn soon attracts blackbirds, thrushes, robins and other ground-feeders, and even the wary green woodpecker may descend to eat the ants. A small garden-pond, preferably no more than a foot or two deep, and surrounded by a varied mass of aquatic plants and insects, may attract a variety of birds at all seasons of the year. In a large garden where it is hoped to attract moorhens, mallard, ornamental wildfowl or kingfishers, a series of slightly deeper ponds, preferably with a gentle slope at the sides and perhaps an island in the middle, will prove a source of much pleasure. Every garden pond needs its snails and oxygenating aquatic plants such as members of the water-plantain family and the water-starworts. Reedmace and flags offer good cover for the birds, though they tend to spread too much, and the leaves of water lilies form useful platforms which gently submerge under the weight of small birds paddling.

Trees and shrubs. Many species already described in this book attract birds to gardens. Hawthorn and rowan should be in every bird garden. Hazel, yew and cotoneaster—avoiding *C. conspicua decora*—are useful, and so are gorse and broom. Honeysuckle seems to attract a rich insect population that is tempting to small birds; and coal and marsh tits and nuthatches are among the birds that welcome the red fruits. Elder is rightly scorned as a hedgerow plant, but it is most attractive to birds, which welcome its cover in early spring, and prey on the insects around it, while blue tits and thrushes delight in the berries. Ivy offers good nesting sites and the berries help blackbirds thrushes and other species to survive the hungry weeks of late winter and spring. A good mixed hedge is always an asset to birds.

In a large garden, an effort should be made to produce a variety of habitats, ranging from the close-cropped lawn and pool to a rich herb layer, shrub layer, young trees and a patch of mature woodland. Birds and butterflies, it should be remembered, are often creatures of woodland edges and open glades and clearings surrounded by belts of thick cover are always welcomed.

Chemicals and Birds. The use of organochlorine insecticides such as chlordane on lawns should be avoided, and DDT is a less potent but persistent substance that should be used as little as possible. Pyrethrum and the more powerful derris have the advantage of not being poisonous to humans or birds, but they should not be allowed to reach fish. Useful suggestions over the whole problem will be found in *Pest Controls without Poisons*, by Lawrence D. Hills (Henry Doubleday Research Association, Bocking, Braintree, Essex, 3s.).

Nestboxes. Every garden should have one or two, especially around a lawn or pond or beside a glade. They should not be less than 4 ft. from the ground, and may face any direction so long as the full force of the sun does not fall upon the young birds. Thus, all my own 17 boxes, in which more than 80 young birds were reared in each of the last two years, avoid a south-facing entrance hole.

The tit tribe welcome boxes about 10 in. deep or a little less, 5–6 in. broad, with a sloping roof and an entrance hole two inches below it, which should be the size of a half a crown for great tits, and as big as a florin for blue tits. Open-fronted boxes or nesting trays are often adopted by spotted flycatchers, robins, pied wagtails and redstarts, but cats, stoats and grey squirrels are always liable to gain entry to these exposed sites, unless they are protected by wire-netting. An open box 25 × 15 × 15 in., erected 30 ft. high in an oak in my garden, and intended for kestrels, was taken over by tawny owls who reared three young in it. But kestrels in Holland and Switzerland do frequently adopt these nest boxes placed on 30 ft. poles around farms and gardens. Clay nests specially baked for house martins can now be obtained and these can be attached to the walls of buildings just below a window sill, or beneath the edge of the roof. It is important that the entrance hole should be no more than 1⅛ in. in diameter, so that sparrows cannot claim it. Many schoolboys enjoy making nesting boxes of varying types. Full details of how to set about it can be found in *Nestboxes*, by Edwin Cohen (British Trust for Ornithology, Beech Grove, Tring, Herts., 3s.). House martin nests can be obtained from Clent House Gardens, Lower Clent, Hagley, Worcestershire.

Food for the Bird Table. It is wise to give little or no food to birds during the breeding season, for no young blackbird or thrush thrives on soggy lumps of sodden dough—though woodpeckers, thrushes and tits in my own garden have access to grated cheese from about the end of June, and the tits bring

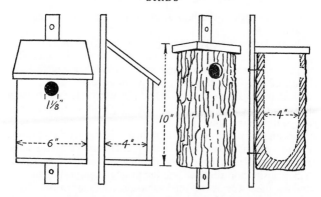

Suggested nesting boxes for Tits, Nuthatches, etc

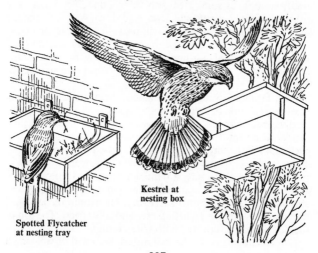

Spotted Flycatcher at nesting tray

Kestrel at nesting box

227

their fledgelings to the house for broken peanuts during high summer.

If ample shrubs and trees are planted, birds should have good natural food in abundance for much of the year. It is a good idea when possible to augment these supplies by feeding birds at set times of day. Like the gulls of Aviemore that meet the one o'clock train each day, they will soon grow accustomed to being fed at a convenient time. Early morning and around midday are peak feeding hours.

Bacon fat hung from a thin branch of a tree where squirrels cannot reach it will attract tits and great spotted woodpeckers. Peanuts, shelled or unshelled, are always demanded by the tit tribe; raisins and sultanas will tempt any blackbird or thrush, and live meal worms will soon tame any robin or thrush. Grain will attract greenfinches. Mashed potatoes are welcomed, oddly enough, by some great spotted woodpeckers. Pastry and other household scraps will always go down well with the tits and windfall apples in winter will prove invaluable for blackbirds, fieldfares and redwings, green woodpeckers, starlings and other birds. In hard weather it is helpful to stir the leaves of the compost heap, or to scrape snow away from odd patches of wet ground.

Water. Drinking water should always be available. In frosty weather it should be frequently renewed; or a nightlight under an upturned plant pot should be used to prevent the ice forming. Glycerine or anti-freeze mixtures must never be used.

Sick and injured birds. It cannot be stressed too strongly that when young birds are found, they should normally be left in peace, for there is usually a harassed parent hidden near who will soon come along and feed them. Only if a bird is injured should it be removed from its territory. Then it should be placed in a spacious box with a little water and some food. The top of the box should be covered with wire-netting.

Grated cheese and packets of mixed seeds will be welcomed

by most species. Budgerigar mixture will suit a seed-eating species, while most livestock dealers stock foods suitable for insect-eaters. Crushed biscuit meal flavoured with honey and soya flour and augmented by gnats, flies and finely minced meat may be a palatable substitute. Game birds are among the species which thrive on hard boiled egg. Live meal worms, available from many dealers, will win the heart of any robin, thrush, or tit, and injured ducks or waders will also eat them. But too many should not be given at once or indigestion results. F. B. Lake's *Treatment of Sick and Wounded Birds*, published jointly as a leaflet by the Royal Society for the Protection of Birds, The Lodge, Sandy, Bedfordshire, and the British Trust for Ornithology, Beech Grove, Tring, Herts. is strongly recommended. Injured hawks and owls should be kept in the dark and sent in a cardboard box to a Receiving Centre of the Devon Trust for Nature Conservation.*

Bird damage. This problem may worsen as the destruction of habitats and the use of herbicides and insecticides make more birds seek refuge in gardens. Every gardener needs to carry out his own research into the effectiveness of different methods of coping with the situation. In gardens well stocked with a variety of natural food, birds may be less inclined to rely on cultivated vegetables and fruit. But, in the last resort, the only effective way of preventing damage is to cage or net the crops, and this is uneconomical except where a few small crops are concerned.

Bullfinch damage to fruit buds, prunus and forsythia, which becomes acute when the ash and birch seeds are exhausted, can be much reduced by Cunitex, according to some growers. Black cotton will stop sparrows tearing at the flowers of primroses and polyanthus. Wild strawberries and raspberries, and odd bushes of red currants earmarked for the birds may help to

---

* Oiled birds should be gently cleaned with Fullers Earth or wood flour, and washed with warm water. See R.S.P.C.A. pamphlet, 'Oil Pollution of Sea and River Birds'.

keep them from the main crops. A large piece of glass swinging in the wind—an old mirror—can prove an effective deterrent if hung above the peas and other crops.

The damage birds do is there for all to see. The good they accomplish can never be proved. One must beware of making extravagant claims. Yet it may be significant that in woodland at Neustrelitz, Germany, trees in ground housing two tit nesting boxes to the acre were found to average 50 caterpillars of the harmful pine looper moth per tree, whereas there were 5,000 caterpillars per tree on adjoining acres where birds were not encouraged. Again the scientist Von Berlepsch claims that during an insect plague woodland with nesting boxes remained green while control plots without any were defoliated.

Below is a somewhat arbitrarily chosen selection of birds associated with particular habitats. The great *Handbook of British Birds* (Witherby) or P. A. D. Hollom's *A Popular Handbook of British Birds*, which is an abridgement of it, should be consulted for more details. Indispensable to any bird-watcher is *A Field Guide to the Birds of Britain and Europe*, by Roger Peterson, Guy Mountfort and P. A. D. Hollom, published by Collins, London.

SOME GARDEN BIRDS

Great Tit, *Parus major*. Our largest tit, with glossy black crown and broad band down the yellow breast. Young are paler. Gregarious and easily tamed. Quick to use nesting boxes. Both sexes build nest. Hen incubates for 13–14 days. Both parents feed young which fly at 18–20 days. One brood. Over 100 calls recorded. Read Len Howard's *Birds as Individuals* and *Living With Birds* (Collins).

Blue Tit, *P. caeruleus*. Our most abundant tit, sometimes travelling in big flocks through woods, copses and reed beds. 5–14 eggs incubated by female for 13–14 days. Young fed by both parents and leave the nest around the 19th day.

Coal Tit, *P. ater.* An attractive species, only $4\frac{1}{2}$ in. long, which should multiply as acreage of conifer woods increases. Frequently in gardens and orchards and often visits bird tables for fat and nuts. Big white patch on nape and double white wing bar distinguish it from the marsh tit. Insects and spiders are much eaten. Nests in hole in or near ground, where 5–14 eggs are laid. Incubation 17–18 days. Young fly at about 16 days. One brood.

Marsh Tit, *P. palustris.* A most confiding creature, with a habit of taking two or three fragments of nut at a time from the bird table or the hand and lodging them in long grass or hedgerows. (Coal tits prefer to bury surplus food.) Glossy black crown and notes distinguish it from the willow tit. Nests in holes in alders, willows and other trees, 7–8 eggs hatching in 13 days. Young fed by both adults for 16–17 days in nest. Sometimes two broods. Less gregarious than coal tit. It favours open broad-leaved woods and well-timbered gardens, not marshes, despite the name.

Wren, *Troglodytes troglodytes.* Second only to the goldcrest as our smallest bird. Quick to perish in prolonged hard frost when small insect prey is scarce. Hard clicking 'Tick-tick' call a familiar sound when a cat is around. Has a song that is astonishingly powerful and sustained for so small a bird ($3\frac{1}{2}$–4 in.). Domed nest in ivy, hedges, shelves of out-houses. 5–6 tiny pale eggs. Hen alone incubates 14–15 days. The young are fed by both parents and fly when 16–17 days old. Two broods. Often roosts in nesting boxes with others of its kind. For a detailed study, see E. A. Armstrong's *The Wren*, 1955, Collins.

Mistle Thrush, *Turdus viscivorus.* **The Storm Cock.** Sometimes nests in gardens high in the fork of a tree or far out on a bough of spruce or pine, but seldom visits bird tables, though in hard weather it will approach the house for windfall apples. Harsh raucous note when excited, but a fine singer whom the novice

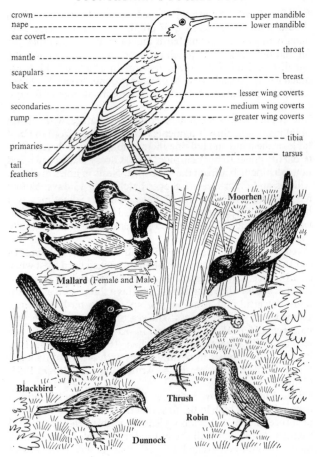

crown — upper mandible
nape — lower mandible
ear covert
mantle — throat
scapulars — breast
back — lesser wing coverts
secondaries — medium wing coverts
rump — greater wing coverts
tibia
primaries — tarsus
tail feathers

Moorhen

Mallard (Female and Male)

Blackbird

Thrush

Robin

Dunnock

may confuse with the blackbird. Two broods, often from same nest. Young fly when 14–16 days old.

Song Thrush, *Turdus philomelos.* Smaller size, browner upper parts and smaller spots distinguish this bird from the mistle thrush. It often has a favourite 'anvil' in the garden where the shells of snails are broken. Hen alone incubates the eggs—for 13–14 days. Young fly after about the same length of time.

Blackbird, *T. merula.* Umber brown female—rufous brown below—and rufous mottled young birds lack the male bird's bright orange bill. Hen builds nest with dry grass lining over the mud, unlike that of the thrush. The 4–5 eggs hatch in 13–14 days. Both parents feed young which fly in about a fortnight. Two or three broods. Recommended: D. W. Snow, *A Study of Blackbirds,* Allen and Unwin, London.

Robin, *Erithacus rubecula.* Our national bird. One of the first at the bird table in the morning and invariably the last one there—and in the garden pool—as winter dusk falls. Strongly territorial, pairing with its former mate in December or later. 4–6 eggs are usually laid during late March–April. The hen alone incubates them for 13–14 days. Both parents feed the young who fly at 12–14 days. Two or three broods. The young are spotted and without a red breast. Eventually they are banished from the parental territory. Some of our robins winter on the Continent. More come to us from Scandinavia. But a large part of our population is sedentary. Read D. Lack, *Life of the Robin.* New edition, 1966. Witherby, London.

Dunnock, or **Hedge Sparrow,** *Prunella modularis.* Slender bill and brown and grey plumage distinguish from house sparrow, of which it is no relation. Less rufous and more spotted young. An attractive but unobtrusive species with a weird display in spring that involves the rapid vibration of the tail. Short, tuneful warbling somewhat similar—but softer and pleasanter—than a wren's. Seed largely comprise winter diet; much insect fare in summer. Nests in hedges or artificial nest sites like a

Willow Warbler

Nightingale

Young
Robin

Blackcap

Marsh Tit

Goldcrest

Fieldfare

Redwing

234

bundle of old pea sticks. 3–6 beautiful blue eggs. Two or, occasionally, three broods.

Greenfinch, *Chloris chloris*. Stout bill, olive green feathers, bright yellow on wings and tail-edges and forked tail are distinctive. Ugly nasal 'Tzwee' call of male, but pleasant song from high in tree or on wing. Flocks often come to bird tables if seed is offered. Berries and beetles also eaten. Two or three broods in hedges and shrubs.

Goldfinch, *Carduelis carduelis*. Bright yellow on the black wings, and the black, red and white bands round the head are distinctive. Young birds have same yellow and white markings on wings, but lack the brilliant head pattern of adults. Dwells in nesting season in gardens and old orchards where it eats seeds and some insects. Charms or flocks much on neglected pastures, roadsides, etc., in autumn and winter. Pleasant trickling song. Two or three families which fly at 13–14 days.

Chaffinch, *Fringilla coelebs*. Surely our most beautiful common bird, with slate-blue crown of male contrasting with pinkish brown underparts and sides of head, broad white shoulder patch, and much white on outer tail feathers. Named the 'Sphink' in Midlands, after its familiar call. Lovely song, from February, varies in style from region to region. Loud, lively and rattling, with flourish at end. Beautiful nest of grass, wool, lichens, etc., bound by spiders web. Incubation by hen for 11–13 days. Young fed by both parents, flying when 13–14 days. One brood.

BIRDS IN THE WOODLAND

Many familiar garden birds like the chaffinch and blackbird were purely woodland species at one time. The traditional coppice woodland with oak standards of southern England is particularly rich in birds and supporting insects and plants, but it is a mistake to believe that our state forests, which are predominantly coniferous, are bereft of bird life.

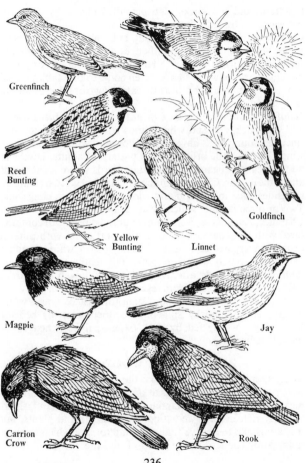

Greenfinch

Reed
Bunting

Yellow
Bunting

Linnet

Goldfinch

Magpie

Jay

Carrion
Crow

Rook

236

When old woodland is clear felled or poor pasture is fenced for planting with young trees, a lush grass-heath flora develops that may soon attract the stonechat, grasshopper warbler and tree pipits. Some sites of this kind have been colonised by the uncommon Montagu's harriers which find ample prey amid the new plantings. When the lack of grazing and consequent growth of grass results in an expansion of the vole population, short-eared owls or, in Scotland, hen harriers may appear.

As a shrub layer develops the habitat may support increasing numbers of small warblers and other birds. Young conifer plantations that deny sunlight to the forest floor generally harbour few birds, but as the crop is thinned and more light reaches the ground, the plant, insect and bird population rises. This is particularly so when the Forestry Commission protect broad-leaved trees and shrubs along the borders of fire-breaks and woodland edges, or where ghylls, stream-sides and other areas are deliberately left unplanted. Some 60 pairs of stone curlews, for instance, flourish in the fire-breaks of Thetford Forest, Norfolk.

Crossbills sometimes colonise mature plantings of Scots pines; and the siskin, once a rarity of the northern conifer woods, has recently spread far across the Scottish Highlands and Ireland, through North Wales, and into parts of England. While the production of timber is the prime aim of the Forestry Commission, it is now official policy to do everything possible to enhance the natural beauty and scientific interest of the countryside, and to promote the welfare of wild life.

Sparrow Hawk, *Accipiter nisus.* Short, rounded wings, long tail and barred underparts, and the habit of darting low along woodland rides and boundaries, or beside hedgerows are characteristic of this species. It favours a countryside of scattered copses of conifers and mixed woods. Persecution and organochlorine insecticides appear to be responsible for a dramatic decline since the late 1950s. Incubation by the female for 32–35 days. Young fly at 24–30 days. One brood.

Kestrel, *Falco tinnunculus.* Our one bird of prey which remains tolerably common, except in much of Eastern England. Easily recognised by its hovering, and long pointed wings, black-spotted chestnut upper-parts and blue-grey head of male. Black band edged with white at end of slate-grey tail. Female is more strongly rufous brown. Nests in old dreys of squirrels, nests of magpies or crows or in hollow trees. Young fly when 27–30 days old, but may remain in vicinity of nest for two or three weeks.

Woodcock, *Scolopax rusticola.* A russet-coloured bird of moist oak, birch or coniferous woods, nesting on dry slopes of wet areas, often near the base of a tree. The female incubates the 3–6 eggs for some three weeks, and is quick to desert the nest if disturbed. The nightly roding flight at tree-top height can be seen before and after dusk from March to late July, the birds flying along regular beats uttering a light, thin 'Tsiwick' call and a weird low croak. Diet comprises earthworms and insects, with other animal matter and some seeds. Two broods.

Tawny Owl, *Strix aluco sylvatica.* Only occasionally, when young are in the nest, does this nocturnal species stir in day-time, though its lethargic hooting in autumn and winter days may be heard surprisingly often if there is keen competition between rivals. A large mottled brown bird, 15 in. long, it spends the day close to the trunk of a tree in woods, copses and well-timbered gardens, often at a height of 30–40 ft. Shrews, woodmice and field voles are the chief foods, but owls in towns tend to catch more small birds. Hen sits on the eggs for almost a month. Young fly after 30–37 days, making loud hissing when pleading for food.

Green Woodpecker, *Picus viridus.* Large size, green plumage and crimson crown, together with the undulating flight, loud, laughing call, and habit of descending to lawns after ants all

Swifts

Swallows

House Martin

Hawfinch

Bullfinch

Wren

Chaffinch

House
Sparrow

Dunnock

Swallows
nesting on kitchen-shelf

239

make it easy to recognise this bird. Breeding in open woodlands and well-timbered parks and gardens, it bores a hole in old trees where 5–7 eggs are laid, hatching in 15–17 days. Young fly at 18–28 days. Much hit by hard weather, but fares well if windfall apples are available. Rarely drums.

Great Spotted Woodpecker, *Dendrocopus major*. Pied plumage and crimson undertail coverts are distinctive. Male has crimson patch on nape and young birds have crimson crown. Loud 'Tchack' call, bouncing flight and hard, hollow drumming in late winter and spring often noticeable. Much more inclined to visit bird tables in recent years. Nests usually 10–25 feet or more from ground, and facing away from nearest road. Glossy white eggs hatch in 16 days. Young fly at 18–21 days. Male takes charge of one fledgeling while female looks after two or three others.

Lesser Spotted Woodpecker, *D. minor*. Barred black and white wings and lower back, lack of crimson under tail covers, and small sparrow-like size distinguish this more local resident of open woods and copses in the south and midlands. Drumming usually softer than that of last species.

Jay, *Garrulus glandarius*. With its bright blue patch on the wings, and russet shaded plumage, with black and white feathers on the crown, this is a most beautiful bird. And a most unpopular one on account of its raids on peas, the eggs of small birds, and the young and eggs of game birds. It also eats mice, spiders and slugs, flapping from tree to tree over woodland rides, but generally remaining near cover. Much natural regeneration of oak is due to their habit of burying acorns in October. Young fly at nearly three weeks.

Long-tailed Tit, *Aegithalos caudatus*. A bird of the bushy outskirts of woods and thickets, both sexes spending up to three weeks building a superb nest of moss and lichen woven firm with much spiders' web and lined with 2,000 or more feathers. 8–12 young fed by male and female and fly after 15–16 days.

High-pitched song and hard low 'tupp-tupp' call. One brood.

Nuthatch, *Sitta europaea.* Unlike the tree-creeper, this bird will rapidly move up or down the trunk of trees without the aid of its tail. Plump body, sharp, powerful bill, bright blue back and chestnut flanks are all noticeable. Utters a loud 'Tcha-tchack' call and a rapid trill. Nests in holes in trees, plastering the hole with mud to reduce the size of the entrance. Generally 6–11 eggs which hatch in about a fortnight, and the young birds fly at 23–25 days. Common in mixed oak woods of southern England and some Midland counties, but scarce in N. Cornwall, Wales and generally absent from Scotland and the extreme north of England.

Tree-creeper, *Certhia familiaris.* A bird of well grown woodland and gardens which often joins flocks of tits or goldcrests in winter. Nests beneath loose bark of trees, laying about 6 eggs in a nest of birch twigs, moss, roots and grass. Incubation 17–20 days. Young fly at 14–15 days. Two broods sometimes.

Blackcap, *Sylvia atricapilla.* Glossy black cap—brown on the female—and larger squat form distinguish this warbler from the smaller marsh tit with which it is sometimes confused. A superb singer of open woodland and copses with bushy undergrowth. Loud scolding 'tucc-tucc' call. Incubation by both birds for 10–11 days. Young fly at 10–13 days. Two broods common in the south.

Garden Warbler, *S. borin.* Similar habitat and strikingly similar song to last species, but chorus lacks the final decided flourish that concludes the blackcap's song. It is more sustained, too. Dark-brown upper-parts contrast with pale buff under-parts. Male makes cock-nests in brambles and shrubs, but the hen does most of the incubating. Eggs hatch in 12 days and young fly at 9–10 days. Usually one brood.

Whitethroat, *S. communis.* Prefers more open surroundings, such as unkempt hedgerows, boundaries of heathland, and gardens with undergrowth. Double-brooded—building nest in

Blue Tit

Tree Creeper

Turtle Dove

Tawny Owl

Nightjar

Wood Pigeon

Great Tit

Great Spotted Woodpecker

Green Woodpecker

Nuthatch

brambles and bushes. Grey cap, white throat and reddish-brown edgeings to wing-feathers are noticeable.

Willow Warbler, *Phylloscopus trochilus.* A charming, slender warbler, uttering its beautiful rippling song from early April to July and again in August and September, and nesting in a wide variety of bushy sites, including open woodland, heath and gardens with a few trees and long grass. The nest is on the ground in hedge-banks, beside woodland rides etc. It is domed and made of moss, bracken, grass and feathers. Young fly when a fortnight old.

Chiffchaff, *P. collybita.* This migrant warbler is equally graceful and can be distinguished from the last species only by the 'Chiff-chiff-chaff' notes, heard from late March to mid-July, and again in September; and by the darker, or even blackish legs.

Goldcrest, *Regulus regulus.* Our smallest bird, nesting in conifer woods, mixed woods and gardens, where a nest of green moss, spiders' web and feathers may be hung on a branch of spruce or pine or some other tree, or lodged in ivy clambering up an old trunk. Feeds on spiders and insects. Population rises in late autumn as goldcrests from Northern Europe cross the North Sea. Two broods by home birds.

Bullfinch, *Pyrrhula pyrrhula.* Stout bill, black cap, grey back, bright red under-parts—dark pink in the female—and the large white rump are unmistakable. Nest of small twigs, moss, lichens and dark roots are placed 4–7 ft. up in thick shrub or hedge. The 4–5 eggs hatch after the hen has sat for 12–14 days, and the young fly when 12–16 days old.

HEATHS AND COMMONS

Many commons comprise open heathland where lapwings, nightjars and snipe nest on the ground, stonechats and grass-hopper warblers breed at the base of the gorse, and tree pipits use the odd solitary silver birch as a song post from which to descend on fluttering wings. Other commons, undergrazed and often neglected, may have been invaded by scrub or mature woodland.

If the prime aim is multiple use of the common, which may include recreation, agriculture, timber production, education and research, the management plan should endeavour to reconcile these objects with the provision of suitable habitats for

Officious notice boards are best avoided on Commons.

birds. Indeed, conservation, which is the wise use of all resources for the benefit of the whole community, should be the first consideration, if the structure of the soil or the biological capital of the area, and its value for amenity, are not to be damaged.

Variety of habitats. This should be a key object of management, for only then can the different and sometimes conflicting interests be served, and a rich reservoir of plants and animals be maintained.

Woodland and scrub. Where the absence of grazing has enabled scrub or woodland to develop, it is often wise—and more economical—to work with nature in managing the ground for forestry, amenity and conservation, encouraging a maximum variety of indigenous tree and shrub species, cutting glades, fire-breaks and woodland rides that benefit both picnickers and wild life, but allowing dense scrub to protect patches of open woodland rich in desirable species. If the common is used for biological education, it is useful to encourage a series of habitats demonstrating the different stages of the plant and animal succession, from open heath or water via herb, bush and scrub colonisation to mature woodland.

Open heath. If grazing, cutting or occasional burning maintain the open nature of the heath, every effort should be made to preserve ample stretches of bog, wet and damp heath—often the most valuable from the scientific standpoint—as well as open dry heath. The wetter areas should never be burned, or the bog plants will eventually disappear and the area will dry out. Grazing on the dry heath may prove helpful to the birds which prefer low, well-cropped vegetation; and the cutting of fire-breaks and the frequent cutting of the too persistent bracken can benefit many species in the long run.

Special measures can sometimes be taken to aid particular birds. A series of small heathland ponds can soon produce a rise in the populations of moorhens, mallard, sedge warblers and other species. By scraping away the vegetation from stretches of damp and wet heathland, it is possible to induce frequent visits, and perhaps nesting, by snipe. An area of open heathland protected from disturbance by walkers and their dogs may attract nesting lapwings. Once a stretch of gorse has been protected from fire for four years, it is liable to be colonised by Dartford warblers in certain parts of Hampshire and Dorset.

Stonechat, *Saxicola torquata.* Black head of male and white on the sides of the neck and on the wings, contrasting with chestnut underparts and dark back are distinctive. Female and young lack the white on the neck and rump. Though badly hit by hard winters and destruction of nesting sites by reclamation or scrub invasion, the bird can be seen in many parts of Britain, especially around the coasts. Heath fires constantly trouble them, but many acres of common have their pairs nesting at the base of gorse or willow scrub, where the hen builds a nest of moss and grass with pieces of dead thistle or gorse, and a few feathers. Two or even three broods, the birds flying at about 12–13 days.

Meadow Pipit, *Anthus pratensis.* A most abundant bird of commons, moors, rough grasslands and marshes, less than 6 in. long, and distinguished from the tree pipit by more olive top part and whiter breast. The same white outer tail feathers. Less often in trees than next species. Song a slender piping culminating in parachute descent from tree. Nests in dip in ground amid heather or grass. Feeds on insects, spiders, earthworms and some seeds. Frequently the cuckoo's foster parent.

Tree Pipit, *A. trivialis.* More stockily built and sleeker than last species and more of a yellowish tinge to breast. Heathland with scattered pines preferred. Rasping 'Teez' call note. Attractive song as it flutters up from a tree and then parachutes down to its perch. Young fly at 12–13 days. Double-brooded.

Yellow Bunting, *Emberiza citrinella.* Yellow head and underparts and white on outer tail feathers are noticeable in flight. Female darker, with little yellow but a chestnut rump that distinguishes it from the more uncommon cirl bunting. Welcomes shrub cover, but not too many trees. Song the familiar 'Little bit of bread and no cheese'. Nests at base of bushes, hedges. Two or three broods which fly within a fortnight.

Reed Bunting, *E. schoeniclus.* Black head and throat and prominent white neck ring of male are distinctive. White outer-tail feathers and buff eye stripe and throat on female. Feeds on seeds of aquatic and marshy plants; nesting in Molinia tussocks, willow stumps and shrubs in wet heathland. Common and widespread, but tends to leave its wet breeding sites in winter for open grassland, arable acres and upland moors.

Linnet, *Carduelis cannabina.* Crimson crown and breast and chestnut back and twittering flight notes distinguish male. Cleft tail. Nests low down in gorse and thorn, the 4–6 young lying in a rough platform of bents, moss, stalks and sometimes a few

Long-tailed Tit at nest

Green Woodpecker

Meadow Pipit feeding young Cuckoo

Barn Owl

Arctic Tern

Redshank

Common Tern

247

twigs. Wool, feathers and hair compose the comfortable lining. Young fly at 11–16 days. Several broods.

Nightjar, *Caprimulgus europaeus.* The strange churring song, continued without a break for as long as five minutes or more, must thrill the most sophisticated observer. Returning from Ethiopia in May, the bird may lay two pale eggs in the identical site on open bracken-infested heath or open woodland that was used in the previous year. Sings on warm summer nights when moths are plentiful, male with white marks on wing and tail, clapping its wings as the mottled brown female approaches. Call 'Co-ic' uttered in flight.

Snipe, *Capella gallinago.* Extremely long straight bill and heavily patterned dark brown upper-parts striped lengthwise down the back. Utters a low hoarse cry when disturbed and flies off in swift zig-zagging flight. 10½ in. long. Bill 2½ in. Feeds mainly on worms, insects and molluscs of wet heathland. Nests among rushes and moor grass near bogs or ponds. Female incubates 19–20 days. Young leave the nest at once and fly in about a fortnight.

Lapwing, *Vanellus vanellus.* Broad black and white wings, flapped fairly slowly in flight, long crest and greenish black and white plumage make identification simple. The familiar 'Peewit' song as the bird slowly ascends, flies more quickly and then tumbles in twisting, turning flight can be heard over their favourite ploughed lands, pastures and moorlands; for though I have classed this species as a heathland bird, faithful to acres where the vegetation is low, it is more often associated with farmland. The 4 eggs are usually laid in April in a nest of grass stems. Male and female share incubation of 24–27 days, and the young fly at 33–42 days. One brood.

Curlew, *Numenius arquata.* Our largest wader, with long curved bill and brown streaked appearance, without the stripes that distinguish the smaller whimbrel. Nests in the moorlands of many counties, both sexes incubating the 4 eggs for almost a month. The young promptly leave the nest when dry and fly after 5–6 weeks.

Black Grouse, *Lyrurus tetrix.* Another bird of the moorlands, though one that prefers the rougher borders and marsh or heather dotted with birch and pine. Black plumage, lyre-shaped tail and white streak on the wings unmistakable clues to black-cock. The greyhen is more rufous-brown—though less rufous and larger than the red grouse—and it is less strongly barred and smaller than the capercaillie. The white wing-bar and forked tail, more easily seen in pictures than in the field, are also diagnostic. Polygamous, males and females assembling at favoured display grounds for the annual spring 'leks'. A resident that has declined much in England, but it can still be found in N. Devon and Somerset, Wales and the border counties of England, the north Midlands and Scotland.

Red Grouse, *Lagopus scoticus.* These dark red-brown game birds are associated with the heather country of N. Derbyshire, Yorkshire and Staffordshire, as well as Brecon, Monmouth, Carmarthen and the English border counties. It has been introduced to Exmoor, and nests throughout Scotland and in every Irish county. Smaller size and unforked tail contrast with greyhen.

BIRDS ON THE FARM

The aim of the most intelligent farmers will be to encourage as much wild life, including game, as is compatible with good agriculture. This object can hardly be fulfilled if every hedgerow and small wood is destroyed, each tree is felled, the marshes drained and the whole area transformed into open prairie. Yet much of our agricultural landscape is antiquated and big changes may be necessary in an age of large-scale machine farming.

If the larger fields are joined by shelter belts and woodland sanctuaries and new small lakes and reservoirs for irrigation are established, the farmlands of tomorrow may still be beautiful though they will be different.

On the poorer farmlands where agriculture is combined with various forms of recreation—fishing, pony trekking, camping and caravanning—that may be most profitable, there should be space for a variety of habitats suitable for wild life. On the more intensively farmed acres of the east and Midlands, farmers may be able to afford land for wild life and recreation only if they are reasonably compensated.

Not all birds on the farm are welcome guests. The farmer will be delighted when the swallows return or the beneficial lapwings breed in his meadows. He may not be so keen on the carrion crow or the flocks of sparrows, still less the woodpigeon.

Wood Pigeon, *Columba palumbus*. This large blue-grey bird with the prominent white patch on the necks of adults and a broad white bar on the wing nests from April to September or even later, breeding reaching its height in high summer. The crude platform of twigs that does duty as a nest is built in any sort of tree or high hedge. The species has much increased in the past century, as the expansion in winter green crops and roots solved the food problem in hard weather, while the young coniferous woodlands offer ample nesting sites. Read R. K. Murton, *The Woodpigeon*. Collins, 1965.

Turtle Dove, *Streptopelia turtur*. This beautiful bird of open woodland, parks and tall hedgerows is mentioned here only so that it may be distinguished from the more cumbersome woodpigeon. It is a migrant, reaching Britain from Ethiopia in late spring and its slighter form, rufous wings, and long black tail with white tips to all but the middle feathers distinguish it from the much bigger woodpigeon. The lovely 'turr-turr' purring may be heard from late April to late July or August. Inoffensive to the farmer and gardener.

Rook, *Corvus frugilegus*. The greyish-white face distinguish adults from the carrion crow, which has a thicker and more dis-

Ringed Plover

Golden Eagle

Sparrow Hawk

Osprey

Pink-footed
Goose

White-fronted
Goose

Greylag
Goose

tinctly curved bill. Nest high in trees built by both sexes with sticks and grasses, leaves and roots, made firm with earth. Female incubates for 16–18 days; young fed by both parents and fly in a month. Food almost omnivorous, ranging over a vast range of animal and vegetable matter.

Magpie, *Pica pica*. Too familiar to need description, for it has increased much in the past half century. Domed nest of sticks and earth lining, to which shiny 'treasures' are occasionally added. An Uckfield, Sussex, magpie lined its nest with 30 shillings in silver and threepenny pieces, the money being filched from a housewife who left it each week for the laundryman, and was bewildered when it vanished.

Jackdaw, *Corvus monedula*. Smaller and more dapper appearance, together with the grey nape and ear coverts and the high-pitched 'Tchack' call distinguish it from rooks and crows. Feeds on insects, worms, young birds and eggs and other animal prey. Often nests in chimneys, holes in trees, quarries, or old nests of rooks. Hen incubates the eggs for 17–18 days and the young fly in their fifth week. Strongly recommended: K. Lorenz, *King Solomon's Ring*, Methuen.

Fieldfare, *Turdus pilaris*. Slate-grey head, nape and rump, dark tail and chestnut back distinguish this attractive and gregarious species which reaches us from Scandinavia in October and November, returning across the North Sea in March and April. Frequently to be seen in open fields of pasture or roots; does not venture far into woods. 'Tcha-tcha-tchaak' notes uttered while in flight.

Redwing, *Turdus musicus*. Chestnut-red flanks, buffish stripe round eye, and smaller size distinguish this thrush-like bird from the fieldfare. Arrives from mid-September; returns to Scandinavia by late April.

Skylark, *Alauda arvensis*. Still one of our most abundant birds, though the numbers singing over the fields are clearly fewer than in W. H. Hudson's day. Song may be heard from late January to early July and again in the fall. The eggs hatch in about 11 days, the hen alone incubating, and the 3–4 young leave the nest by the 10th day, flying ten days later. Two or three clutches. Many of our birds leave their territories in autumn and large flocks of immigrants from Central and Northern Europe arrive.

Swallow, *Hirundo rustica*. One may find this species anywhere in open country, especially near water; but nowhere are its nests more numerous than in old barns and other farm buildings, where its blue-black upper-parts, long tail and red-throat and forehead distinguish it from the white-rumped, short-tailed house-martin. One pair of swallows in my home village nest year after year in the old butcher's shop, rearing two or even three families on a shelf a few feet above the sleeping quarters of the dog. The eggs hatch after a fortnight and the young fly when three weeks old. The nest is more saucer-shaped than a house-martin's and rests on a support of some kind; the martin's nest is of mud and bents stuck to the surface of the building.

Swift, *Apus apus*, which may be seen over any kind of country, and which usually gathers its nesting material in the skies, building in church towers and other village and country town buildings, is not hard to distinguish from the swallow tribe. While the length is only 6½ in., the span of the long, slender, scythe-like wings is no less than sixteen inches. The plumage is dark brown all over. Read Dr. David Lack's fascinating study, *Swifts in a Tower*, Methuen, 1956.

LAKES, RESERVOIRS AND MARSHES

While many birds are threatened by the growing demand to drain the wetlands—by which is meant all marshes and water less than 20 ft. deep—there is no doubt that some species have benefited from the many new reservoirs constructed since the last war. As the nation's consumption of water doubles again in the next twenty years, more reservoirs are likely to be created, a

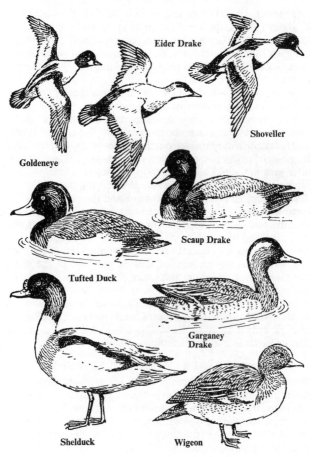

Eider Drake

Shoveller

Goldeneye

Scaup Drake

Tufted Duck

Garganey
Drake

Shelduck

Wigeon

major tragedy for some of the farmers and landowners whose land is flooded, but a real benefit to the wildfowl.

Wet Gravel Pits. These, too, have enabled some species to invade new districts. The steady increase in the population of great crested grebe to more than 4,000 individuals, compared with some 2,800 birds in 1931, has been most marked in areas where new wet gravel pits have been dug.

Improving sites. The value of these habitats can be much improved by judicious planting of shrubs and trees. The Kentish wildfowlers have taken the lead in planting willows and alder for cover by the water's edge, and oak and silver birch for food in the dryer soil behind. Planting of the common bur-reed, *Sparganium erectum*, has proved most profitable in providing food and cover for duck, and other plants favoured include reedgrass, *Glyceria maxima*, hairy sedge, *Carex hirta*, persicaria, *Polygonum persicaria*, water pepper, *Polygonum hydropiper*, orache, *Atriplex patula*, and other species. The water crowfoots, starwort and other water plants such as milfoil and floating reedgrass, *Glyceria fluitans*, also proved effective. For further details, see an article by James and Jeffery Harrison and Peter Olney in the *Thirteenth Annual Report* of the Wildfowl Trust (Slimbridge, Gloucestershire), for 1960–61.

Great Crested Grebe, *Podiceps cristatus*. Our biggest species of grebe, with handsome tippet of chestnut feathers, darkening towards end, on both sexes during the breeding season. Fairly shallow waters of less than 10 ft. and sometimes as little as 3–4 ft., are favoured, so long as they extend to 7 or, at least, 5 acres. It is worth travelling far to see wonderful display in spring. (See the film *A Waterbird's World*, on hire from the Royal Society for the Protection of Birds.) Nest invariably covered with vegetation as bird swims away on foraging expedition. Food comprises fish, insects, and much other animal and vegetable matter. The young acquire independence in 10 weeks. They often ride pick-a-back style on parents' backs.

Little Grebe, *P. ruficollis* (Dabchick). Smallest and most abundant of the grebes, with dark brown plumage and deep chestnut cheeks and throat in summer; paler in winter. Two or three broods may be reared on a variety of fresh waters where there are rushes and flags for nesting cover.

Heron, *Ardea cinerea.* Unmistakable with its long legs, grey back, white neck, and blackish wing quills, and silent pose when fishing. Most numerous in the south-east. May travel 12 miles to fishing grounds.

Mallard, *Anas platyrhynchos.* The drake's dark green head, white neck-ring, and pale grey back is a familiar sight on and around most large or small waters. Mallard will often nest in thick cover some way from water, as on heathland. The young hatch out after some 28 days and are soon led to the water by the duck. Food is mainly plant life, with some insects, worms and molluscs.

Teal, *A. crecca.* Smallest of the duck—14 in.—favouring heathland and moorland ponds. Dark head and horizontal white stripe above wing of the grey male are distinctive. Female has green speculum.

Garganey, *A. querquedula.* A summer visitor from March or April to September or October, which breeds in small numbers from Norfolk to Dorset and a few other counties, before returning to tropical Africa. A broad white band from the eye to the nape distinguishes the drake, and the fore wing is pale blue-grey.

Wigeon, *A. penelope.* Most of our wigeon, numbering about 250,000 in mid-winter, are visitors from Russia and Iceland, and the majority assemble around our muddy coasts and estuaries; but they do also appear on the inland reservoirs; and a resident population thrives in Scotland, while the species occasionally breeds elsewhere in Britain. Chestnut head, grey body and white mark along wing coverts are distinctive.

Shoveller, *Spatula clypeata.* The big broad bill, with dark green head, chestnut belly and flanks, and white breast and scapulars distinguish the drake. The duck is like a small mallard, but with a light blue fore wing. They favour shallow and muddy waters, breeding in most English and Scottish— and some Welsh—counties, and winter migrants come here from the Continent.

Tufted Duck, *Aythya fuligula.* White flanks contrasting with dark plumage of back, front and rear, and the prominent tuft on the back of the head distinguish the drake. The dark brown female lacks the scaup's white patch beside the bill, and there is a faint impression of a crest. Hard weather may bring 5,000 of these duck to the London reservoirs, and the total winter population of Britain may be 30,000, most of them from Iceland and Russia. Our own breeding pairs may not exceed 1,000 pairs. It breeds in most counties.

Greylag Goose, *Anser anser.* A large grey goose with pink legs and no black on the bill. Length 30–35 in. Breeds among the heather in N. Scotland, but mainly a winter visitor from Iceland, frequenting salt and fresh marches and wet grasslands, river meadows, fields of young corn, often far inland.

White-fronted Goose, *A. albifrons.* Orange legs, pink bill, with white band round base of bill, and black patches on the belly mark this species. A winter visitor from Greenland to Ireland and W. Scotland, while *A. a. albifrons* comes from N. Russia and Siberia to the Severn valley and other areas. Feeds on grasses from marsh and wet grasslands.

Pink-footed Goose, *A. brachyrhynchus.* Smaller than the grey lag—24–30 in.—with pink legs, dark neck and black and pink bill. Grazes on the stubble, young corn and potato fields of the Yorkshire and Lincolnshire Wolds, the Severn valley and elsewhere, arriving in September–October and leaving in April and early May.

Canada Goose, *Branta canadensis.* The largest European goose, —36–40 in.—with a long black neck and head marked by a

Bewick Swan

Whooper Swan

Mute Swan with Cygnets

Oystercatcher

Snipe

Knot

Woodcock

Dunlin

Great Crested Grebe with young

white patch from the chin to behind the eye, and a whitish breast. Introduced two centuries ago and now becoming more widespread with more frequent introductions by wildfowlers and others. Feeds on grass and some animal matter, and can be found on grasslands, marshes, lakes and fresh water pools.

Mute Swan, *Cygnus olor.* Our 20,000 or so mute swans are easily recognised by their large size—60 in.—white plumage and orange bill with a black base. They feed largely on aquatic plants, but worms, molluscs and occasional small fish and insects are also taken. They tend to be aggressive at nesting time. Incubation by both parents lasts 35 days. Young leave the nest after a day or so and are fully fledged in about 18–19 weeks. The maximum recorded life span of a wild mute swan is 19 years, compared with 20 years for the rook, the mallard and the starling, 10 years for a chaffinch, and 32 years for a herring gull.

Whooper Swan, *C. cygnus.* The bill is yellow at the base and black at the tip. The straighter neck also distinguishes this migrant from Northern Europe. Winter visitor October–November to March–April. A few remain in Scotland all the year.

Bewick's Swan, *C. bewickii.* Less yellow on the bill than in the last species and there is a sharper division between the yellow and black sections. It is smaller by about 12 in. than the whooper swan. More numerous in Ireland than the whooper, and a regular visitor to Slimbridge, where Peter Scott has been able to distinguish 85 individuals by their bill markings.

Osprey, *Pandion haliaetus.* Can we hope that this rare species, which dwindled to extinction in Britain early in the century, will again thrive here as it did before the Victorians slaughtered so many of them? Thanks to the Royal Society for the Protection of Birds, the species again breeds on Loch Garten, Inverness-shire. Dark upper-parts and pure white under-parts, a white head and a black patch at the side of the head mark this

Herring Gull

Black-headed Gull

Great Black-backed Gull

Nesting

Lapwing

Flight signal

Blackcock displaying

Song flight

Curlew sleeping

fish-eating hawk. Passage migrants from Scandinavia regularly appear in Britain each autumn.

Ringed Plover, *Charadrius hiaticula.* A broad black band over the white breast is the distinguishing feature of this lively little plover, 7½ in. long, together with the white collar, orange bill with black tip, and orange legs. A slender white wing bar distinguishes it from the little ringed plover which was an extremely rare visitor until 1938, though it now breeds in small numbers in various parts of England. The ringed plover breeds inland in various areas of Scotland and England, as well as on the sandy and pebbly shores and coastal marshes.

Redshank, *Tringa totanus.* Orange-red legs, white back and rump, and prominent white hind edges to the dark wings mark this medium-sized wader with an orange base to the bill. Breeding in grassy meadows, lowland moors and water-meadows in most English and Welsh counties, and widely distributed in Scotland, these wary, restless and noisy birds are quick to descend to the muddy shores of our new reservoirs.

Knot, *Calidris canutus.* Vast flocks of these stocky grey and white birds can be seen massed on the coastal mud flats and estuary shores in autumn, and odd ones can frequently be found at inland reservoirs, sewage farms and other wet places. In summer plumage it may be distinguished for its rufous under-parts and shortish bill and it is a good three inches larger than the little **Dunlin,** *Calidris alpina,* most abundant wader of our shores, with a long slightly decurved bill, which arrives in late summer and autumn from Northern Europe. This little wader also breeds in modest numbers about our northern grass moors and peat bogs.

There are certain new reservoirs which also seem strangely attractive at times to the sea birds. Now that the colourful coastal sheld-duck have taken to breeding as far inland as Nottinghamshire, we may not be surprised to see them around the reservoirs. Nor is it any great cause for wonder when the gulls assemble in large numbers at these inland waters—though few share the fate of the London reservoirs which in 1963 became the roosting haunt in mid-winter of 165,000 black-headed gulls. Occasionally the attractive terns or sea swallows, the marine scaup duck or rarities from the other end of the earth may suddenly appear beside any long stretch of water which lies on the great migration routes. But that is worth another brief section.

MIGRATION

No one can watch birds for long without becoming aware of the strange phenomenon of migration. If the short answer to why birds migrate concerns food, and the solution as to how they migrate seems to involve navigation by the sun and stars, we are still left with a thousand and one unsolved problems. The city worker, like the suburban householder and the country gardener, may add new knowledge to the growing tide of information.

There is no space here to mention more than a few points. Briefly, migration in some form or other goes on at all seasons of the year, though reaching its peak in autumn and spring. Rarely is it more impressive than in October, when migrants numbering millions pass over London by night and day. An anticyclone with clear skies may find most of them sweeping on towards their destination. Low cloud, rain or mist may bring a fall of birds—which is why the odd woodcock from Scandinavia or some equally unexpected bird may suddenly appear in a London park. Much of this migration is on a broad front. Most of it is below 5,000 feet, though some birds, particularly waders flying at night, may be much higher than that. Birds flying low may be forced by the geographical nature of the landscape below to concentrate at certain points, such as a pass in mountains and hills, a range of heights like the Pennines or even the Cotswolds, or a convenient stretch of coastline or river valley.

It is an error to believe that migration can only be seen on the coast.

Even as this book was being prepared, a dunlin from East Tilbury was reported from the latitude of the Ural Mountains in Russia. Knots ringed in Lincolnshire turned up in Greenland and a young snipe found in Staffordshire was discovered in Bergamo, Italy. More evidence came to hand that young Manx shearwaters from Skokholm, off the coast of Wales, regularly disperse to the waters off South America. One could fill pages with similar details. One swallow from Cley, Norfolk, for instance, was ringed there in 1935 and discovered near the same site on September 28, 1951, just sixteen years later. It must have migrated 190,000 miles during its quite exceptionally long life.

The whole vast subject is fascinating. Recent books dealing with the subject include Robert Spencer's *Bird Migration* in the 'Instructions to Young Ornithologists' Series (Museum Press, 1963) and my own *Down the Long Wind* (Newnes, 1962). Much interesting material can also be found in Kenneth Williamson's *Fair Isle and Its Birds* (Oliver and Boyd, 1965).

BRITISH BIRD OBSERVATORIES

Fair Isle: The Warden, Fair Isle Bird Observatory, by Lerwick, Shetland. W.*

Isle of May, Firth of Forth: A. Macdonald, Hadley Court, Sidegate, Haddington, East Lothian.

Spurn, Yorkshire: G. H. Ainsworth, 144 Gillshill Road, Hull, Yorkshire. W.

Gibraltar Point, Lincolnshire: A. E. Smith, Pyewipes, Willoughby, Alford, Lincs.

Cley, Norfolk: Booking Secretary, Green Farm House, Cley, Holt, Norfolk.

* Inexperienced observers are strongly advised to write for details—enclosing a stamped and addressed envelope—to those Observatories which have a full-time Warden. They are marked W.

Bradwell, Essex: A. B. Old, Bata Hotel, East Tilbury, Essex.

Sandwich Bay, Kent: J. Webster, 41 Sussex Avenue, Margate, Kent.

Dungeness, Kent: H. A. R. Cawkell, 6 Canute Road, Hastings, Sussex. W.

Portland, Dorset: The Warden, Portland Bird Observatory, The Old Low Light, Portland, Dorset. W.

St. Agnes, Scilly Isles: J. F. L. Parslow, c/o Edward Grey Institute, Botanic Gardens, Oxford.

Lundy, Devonshire: J. Dyke, 8 Rock Avenue, Barnstable, Devon. W.

The New Grounds, Slimbridge, Gloucestershire: The Secretary, Wildfowl Trust, Slimbridge, Gloucestershire.

Skokholm, Pembrokeshire: The Warden, Dale Fort Field Centre, Haverfordwest, Pembrokeshire. W.

Saltee, Eire: F. King, The Orchards, Blennerville, Tralee, Co. Kerry, Eire.

Cape Clear, Eire: H. M. Dobson, Old Barn, Sonning Common, Reading, Berkshire.

Bardsey, N. Wales: G. C. Lambourne, The Cottage Farm, Ipsley, Redditch, Worcestershire. W.

Calf of Man: The Secretary, Manx Museum and National Trust, Douglas, Isle of Man. W.

Copeland, N. Ireland: C. W. Bailey, 17 Hillside Drive, Belfast, 9 Northern Ireland.

Tory Island, N. Ireland: R. G. Pettit, 38 Earlham Green Lane, Norwich.

Rural Sports and Pastimes

*Canoeing – Camping and Caravanning – Cycling –
Falconry – Field Sports (Beagling, Fox-hunting, Deer and
Otter Hunting) – Fishing – Gliding – Mountaineering –
Natural History – Riding – Ski-ing – Shooting and
Stalking – Walking or Rambling*

CANOEING

This sport began to grow in popularity in Britain during the
1930s when the first folding canoes were imported from Germany. The development of British folding and rigid canoes, and
the rapid expansion of the 'do-it-yourself' crafts, using home

construction kits, proved still more important. Canoes can be
used wherever the water is more than nine inches deep and 30
inches broad, a big advantage when one is exploring the small
rivers and derelict canals of Britain. More and more canoes are

being made in schools and youth clubs, and over 160 canoe clubs with 36,000 members, are affiliated to the **British Canoe Union**, 3, The Drive, Radlett, Hertfordshire, and the **Canoe Camping Club**. A further big expansion in the number of enthusiasts is likely, and increasing attention is being given to the problem of granting a public right of way on waterways.

CAMPING AND CARAVANNING

There are thought to be over 1,500,000 family campers in this country, which represents a four-fold rise in the numbers ten years ago. **The Camping Club of Great Britain and Ireland**, 11, Grosvenor Place, London S.W.1 (Tel.: Tate Gallery 9232), exists to encourage and to help all users of the countryside, especially those of limited means, to a greater self-reliance and independence and a desire to care for their rural surroundings. It is supported by specialised clubs catering for caravanners, motor caravanners, canoeists, folk dancers, mountaineers, photographers, and the Camping Youth Club, which offers training in camping to young people and qualifies them to camp alone. The combined membership in 1966 was over 100,000, and members use many of the Club's own camp sites. **The Forestry Commission**, 25, Savile Row, London W.1, the local authorities and the **National Parks Commission**, 1, Cambridge Gate, Regent's Park, London N.W.1—soon to become the Countryside Commission—have taken the lead in providing suitable sites, though many more are needed.

Forestry Commission Camp Sites. These are too numerous to list here, but particulars may be obtained from headquarters or regional offices. (See page 294.) Of the 4 million people who annually picnic in the Commission's Forests—and these include seven Forest Parks—some 600,000 stay overnight at the main camping and caravan sites where charges for a car, tent or caravan are only a few shillings a day. Tobacco, confectionery and some packed and tinned foods can be bought at some of the larger camps, but these are often five miles or more from the nearest provision shops or petrol pumps. Lewisburn Camping Ground in Kielder Forest, Northumberland, is an example. Other camping sites such as Burntshields, Kershope, in the same region, or Burns Cottage, Wauchope Forest, are more primitive, though they do have a water supply. There are also special sites for youth organisations.

Camping in the New Forest. Permits for camping on unenclosed lands in the New Forest are issued on payment of the appropriate small charge, and subject to camping regulations, from

the office of the Deputy Surveyor of the New Forest, Lyndhurst, Hampshire. At week-ends or on public holidays, apply to the Keeper at Bolderwood Cottage, Lyndhurst, or other keepers.

Local Authority Camping Sites. More of these are now being provided in the National Parks and elsewhere. Examples are the restaurant, caravan site and car park at Aysgarth Falls, in the Yorkshire Dales National Park, sponsored by the North Riding County Council, and the combined chalet, caravan and camping site at Neaum Crag set up by the Lake District Planning Board.

Caravanning. It will be seen that many camping sites are shared with caravanners. **The Caravan Club,** 46, Brook Street, London W.1 (Mayfair 6441), was founded 60 years ago and has over 45,000 members.

CYCLING

The heavy increase in motor traffic has much reduced the popularity of cycling, which has declined by half during the past ten years. Yet the **British Cycling Federation,** 21, Blackfriars Road, London S.E.1, claim that 35,000 'serious cyclists' still use our overcrowded roads, enthusiasm for racing is maintained; and the popularity of this recreation in the Netherlands suggests that it might well revive in Britain if a national system of cycle ways were to be established. Some redundant railway tracks might be suitable.

FALCONRY

No rural sport has a more exciting history than falconry, and the tendency for modern exponents of the art to write books about it—often very good ones—has done much to revive interest. Following the dramatic decline of so many of our birds of prey, it is no longer permissible to train home-reared birds in the lore of the chase, but goshawks, peregrines and other splendid creatures are sometimes imported from the Continent for the purpose.

    British Falconers Club—Honorary Secretary: M. H. Woodford, M.R.C.V.S., Summer Lodge, Evershot, near Dorchester, Dorset (Evershot 360). Recommended: *The Goshawk*, by T. H. White, Cape, London.

MORE FIELD SPORTS

Beagling. There are 82 packs of Beagles in Britain, which represents an increase of 20 per cent during the past 30 years. Beagles stand up to about 16 inches at the shoulder and are followed on foot. Hares are also hunted by 26 packs of Harriers—a decline of one third on the number thirty years ago—which are about 21 in. high at the shoulder. They are usually followed on horseback.

An Association of Masters of Harriers and Beagles controls the hunting of hares. No animal that has been handled may be pursued, which means that the artificial introduction of hares into an area for the purpose of beagling is banned. The Association claims that a hunted hare stands a five to one chance of escape from harriers, and a brighter prospect of avoiding beagles.

It is evident that the high population of hares in parts of Eastern England improves prospects for the hunted animals, the quarry often escaping as beagles put up a second hare. Each pack may kill about 20 hares a season. This is not enough on its own to make beagling an effective method of control. The Forestry Commission alone destroyed 37,000 hares—including many mountain hares in Eastern Scotland—by other means during 1964. But the impartial and representative Committee on Cruelty to Wild Animals found that if hunting were abolished the hares previously accounted for by the Hunts would have to be destroyed by shooting, which is often accompanied by a greater degree of suffering.

Deer Hunting. These are the seasons for Red Deer hunting in S.W. England:

August to Mid-October   Big stags of 5 years old or more.

November to February   Hinds (which normally calve in June). (See also pages 283–284.)

Defenders of the sport argue that but for hunting, farmers incensed by damage to their crops would destroy all the red deer with shot-guns, a method likely to cause awful cruelty. (See pages 281–282 for a note on deer control.)

Fox Hunting. Over 50,000 mounted followers go out with the 210 packs of Foxhounds each week from autumn to spring and uncounted thousands follow in cars. The rules of foxhunting are strictly controlled by the Masters of Foxhounds Association which can—and occasionally does—request the resignation of a Master who breaks them. Briefly, these rules include a ban on the hunting of captive foxes; and a fox that goes to ground and is dug out of the earth, as many are, must be killed before being thrown to hounds. The rules permit a fox to be bolted or pursued again 'with a fair and sporting chance of escape'. The Committee on Cruelty to Wild Animals regretted the survival of this practice and urged that the animal, if not left alone, should be dug out and destroyed with a humane-killer—as is frequently done—or killed by gassing.

METHOD AND MEANS. The hunting season opens on November 1st, or about that date, though cub hunting, aimed at educating hounds—and the full grown fox cubs!—may start as soon as the corn has been harvested around the end of August or September. Most hunts are out on two to four days a week until March or April, depending on the size of their 'country' and other factors. A hunt meeting on two days a week probably costs rather more than £5,000 a year to run. In most cases there is a Hunt Committee which raises part of this amount through subscriptions, hunt balls, gymkhanas and the like. The remainder, probably amounting to several thousand pounds, will be met by the M.F.H. or, in a growing number of instances, the Joint-Masters. These men know their countryside and the people who live and work in it with an intimacy attained by few other folk.

The hunt has no legal right to run over private land, and the Master and Hunt Committee are dependent upon the goodwill of the local inhabitants. Among their ranks will be found the people who 'walk' hounds, or rear them, from the age of about

three months to the end of their first year. Others may supply the hunt with 'flesh' for hounds, which are trained and exercised by the professional huntsman and his assistants, the whippers-in. A hound needs to grow used to the scent of cats, sheep or park deer if it is not to be distracted by these scents when out hunting.

Altogether the hunts probably account for about 12,000 foxes a year. At least four times as many must be killed by other means particularly in the more remote hill country of the north and west. For though the fox is a useful destroyer of rabbits, field voles, woodmice and rats, its numbers must be controlled if poultry, sheep, game and ground-nesting small birds are not to suffer excessive losses.

THE FIELD. Their role is both important and, in a sense, a minor one. They are essentially mounted spectators, followers who take no active part in the proceedings—beyond riding across miles of country in the wake of fox, hounds, Master, huntsman and whippers-in. But it is their support which ensures the prosperity of the hunt, and it is their concern for the farmers' crops and fences that largely contribute to the good name in which the hunt is held.

Otter Hunting. There are 11 packs of otter hounds, most of them mainly composed of fox hounds. While the supporting fields of followers on foot have increased since the war, the number of packs has fallen by 40 per cent. The sport is controlled by a Masters of Otterhounds Association. The Committee on Cruelty to Wild Animals found that hunting 'does undoubtedly involve suffering for the otter and the degree of it is rather greater than in most other field sports.' Its supporters point out with truth that shooting is bound to be an ineffective form of control, since few countrymen ever see an otter; and trapping may well involve far worse suffering. Thus, the key question at issue is whether or not there is any real need for the control of otters.

FISHING

The 3 million anglers in Britain are becoming increasingly embarrassed by a shortage of fishing water. While Scotland still has considerable reserves, game fishing resources in England, according to a valuable report on 'Known Demands for Outdoor Recreation' prepared for the second 'Countryside in 1970' Conference by J. F. Wager, are now fully used. Coarse fishing, too, has reached the limits of capacity, though new wet gravel pits offer potential sites.

Many angling organisations are doing splendid work not merely in restocking rivers and lakes, but in fighting the menace of pollution, and it is often due to the pressure of angling opinion that so much progress has been made in cleaning many rivers, though much more remains to be done.

The Fishmongers' Company, one of the Twelve Great Livery Companies of the City of London, whose officials examine all fish coming into London, has set up a representative body known as the **Central Council for River Protection. The Anglers' Cooperative Association,** 76, New Oxford Street, London W.1, has waged a running battle against the pollution menace, and other bodies much concerned include the **National Federation of Anglers,** Secretary: Mr. T. G. Draper, 47, Linden Drive, Alvaston, Derby; and the **Salmon and Trout Association,** Fishmongers' Hall, London Bridge, London E.C.4.

The British Field Sports Society, 137, Victoria Street, London S.W.1 (Abbey 5407) is concerned not only with upholding the rights of fishermen, but also with protecting the interests of Falconry, Hunting and Shooting both in Parliament and in the country. It is concerned with the problems of the individual sportsman and seeks to promote the conservation of wild life and the countryside.

GLIDING

Despite the shortage of gliding sites near the big cities, the new age of leisure has resulted in a growing interest in this pursuit, and more than 20,000 people now belong to the **British Gliding Association,** Londonderry House, Park Lane, London W.1.

MOUNTAINEERING

The first mountaineers a century ago were regarded as a strange and foolhardy band of eccentrics. As more and more university dons and undergraduates practised the sport—some would call it a way of life—interest slowly spread, particularly among intellectuals. Within the last ten or fifteen years interest has multiplied and more than 11,000 people belong to clubs affiliated to the **British Mountaineering Council.** It is concerned with the preservation of mountain and climbing areas and their amenities, the provision of huts and camping facilities, access to hills and mountains, litter, pollution and problems of behaviour as well as with the safety of climbing equipment and technique, the safety of climbers, testing of mountain guides and the effectiveness of maps. With 30,000 youngsters attending courses in climbing each year, this growing popularity of mountaineering is likely to increase. The address of the **British Mountaineering Council** is 74, South Audley Street, London W.1 (Grosvenor 1542), which is also the headquarters of the **Alpine Club.** Recommended: *The Mountaineer's Companion,* an Anthology edited by Michael Ward (Eyre and Spottiswoode, 1966).

NATURAL HISTORY

The Royal Society for the Protection of Birds (The Lodge, Sandy, Bedfordshire) has experienced a fivefold expansion in membership within the past ten years, and most natural history organisations listed in the *Directory* issued by the British Association for the Advancement of Science (Burlington House, London W.1) have had a similar experience to a greater or lesser degree. While no more than about 1 per cent of the 10 million or so people who use the countryside for recreation belong to any organisation, the rapid growth of the 36 County Trusts for

Nature Conservation, which now cover almost every corner of Britain, demonstrates that this mounting interest in wild life extends to an increasing concern for its wise management.

For wild life will survive in the modern world only if it is planned for and its habitats are controlled with wisdom. This increasing provision for wild life may often need to begin at the pre-planning stage, as when arrangements are made for land scheduled for sand and gravel digging to be restored as nature reserves.

The older naturalists used to think that if a valuable site was protected by a fence, all would be well for its plants and animals. Now we know that every habitat needs active management based upon ecological research if its character is not to be transformed by scrub invasion or the drying out of precious wet areas. Nature reserves have an important role to perform as open-air laboratories for research into land management problems.

The Natural Environment Research Council. This is the Government agency responsible to the Secretary of State for Education and Science for pure and applied research into the earth sciences. It includes the Nature Conservancy, the Geological Surveys, the National Institute for Oceanography, and the Hydrological Research Unit. State House, High Holborn, London W.C.1 (Chancery 5541).

Nature Conservancy (19, Belgrave Square, London S.W.1). Established by Royal Charter in 1949, the Conservancy, as a component body of the NERC, provides scientific advice on the conservation and control of the natural flora and fauna of Great Britain, and develops research and scientific services concerned with these functions. The Conservancy is also involved in land management, owning or leasing more than 114 National Nature Reserves.

Council for Nature (c/o Zoological Society of London, Regent's Park, London N.W.1) is the national body representing more than 400 natural history and conservation societies with a membership of over 100,000 naturalists. The Conservation Corps, which it founded, is a body of young volunteers who do splendid work in nature reserves and on other important sites clearing scrub, planting trees, erecting fencing, hedging, digging ponds, etc. Work camps are organised in summer, and weekend tasks carried out throughout the year.

Society for the Promotion of Nature Reserves (c/o British Museum, Natural History, Cromwell Road, London S.W.7), incorporated by Royal Charter in 1916, exists to promote conservation by the creation of nature reserves and by other means. It is the central organisation of the 36 **County Naturalists' Trusts** (including the Scottish Wildlife Trust) whose work it coordinates and assists at national level. The Trusts own and manage more than 300 nature reserves. Their membership is not confined to naturalists, but includes anyone who really cares for the countryside. The address of the Secretary of their Central Committee is Pyewipes, Willoughby, Alford, Lincolnshire.

RIDING

More than 150,000 people in Britain ride, and their numbers continue to increase at a rate which suggests a need in the future for many more bridle paths and gallops. **The British Horse Society,** 16, Bedford Square, London W.C.1 has almost trebled its membership in recent years and enjoys the support of 12,000 people, while the **British Show Jumping Association,** at the same address, has 6,000 members.

Pony Trekking. Within the past ten years, this pastime has gained much popularity, and more centres are opening in good and often remote country. People who have never ridden before can enjoy the experience, for practical training in riding is frequently given. Accommodation is provided, usually for one or two weeks, and the ponies, which are generally of the Mountain and Moorland breeds, are taken at walking pace through dramatic, mountainous country, returning to base each night. When booking, it is wise to enquire if the Centre has been awarded the Certificate of Approval of the Ponies of Britain Club, for this is only granted if the ponies and their care and equipment are satisfactory. Recommended: *The Country Life Horseman's Pocket Book*, by R. S. Summerhays (Country Life, 15s.).

SKI-ING

Ski-ing in Britain is a new major tourist industry that is expanding at a rate of at least ten per cent a year. Almost one third of the 350,000 skiers in Britain indulge in the sport without leaving this country. Facilities for instruction on plastic ski slopes are available in an increasing number of towns, and ski schools in the Cairngorms, Glenshee, Deeside and Glencoe, working in cooperation with the **Scottish Council of Physical Recreation** (4, Queensferry Street, Edinburgh, 2) introduce thousands of beginners to the sport every year. Several state and private schools in Scotland regard ski-ing as a normal part of the physical education curriculum, and the **Scottish Youth Hostels Association** (7, Bruntsfield Crescent, Edinburgh, 1) has organised special ski-ing centres for young people. The **National Ski Federation of Great Britain,** 118, Eaton Square, London S.W.1, and the Cairngorms Winter Sports Development Board, as well as a number of private concerns, are developing facilities for the sport, and British Railways offer reduced fares to Scottish winter sports centres from December 1st to the beginning of May. Ski-ing facilities are also available at Edale and other centres in the Peak District National Park, and in the Lake District.

SHOOTING AND STALKING

More than 400,000 game and gun licences are issued each year, and the success of the Game Fair, held annually in the late summer at different centres, has revealed the existence of a growing public interested in various aspects of this sport.

Conservation and Sport. The most intelligent sportsmen are ardent conservationists, and their prime aim must be the creation and maintenance of varied habitats for wild life. Few developments of recent years are more likely to benefit our wild birds than the growth of good relations between sportsmen and naturalists. Distinguished wildfowlers serve on the Wildfowl Conservation Committee of the Nature Conservancy, and the impressive series of Wildfowl Refuges in Britain owes much to their goodwill.

The Wildfowler's Association of Great Britain and Ireland (43, The Albany, Old Hall Street, Liverpool 3), has its own Reserve and Conservation Centre at Boarstall, Buckinghamshire, as well as other reserves, and its 200 affiliated organisations are encouraged to establish reserves and sanctuaries where shooting is forbidden. W.A.G.B.I., in consultation with naturalists, advocates the rearing and releasing of ducks and geese in former or existing habitats. In the ten years up to 1966, more than 62,000 mallard were released and the greylag goose has been restored to some of its old haunts in north-west England, where it dwindled to extinction two centuries ago.

The Game Research Association, 53, Northbrook Street, Newbury, Berkshire (Newbury 2871), was formed by a responsible group of farmers, landowners and others interested in game conservation, to undertake research into factors influencing the survival and increase of game in Britain. The effects of pesticides, losses due to disease, and methods of combining maximum game production with good farming and forestry are among the matters with which the Association is concerned.

Ely Game Advisory Service, Burgate Manor, Fordingbridge, Hampshire (Fordingbridge 2381), was formerly ICI Game Services. Current research includes the impact of modern farming methods on game, the value of strips of cocksfoot between crops, the advantages of fallow strips beside nesting hedges, the rearing of partridges, and the effects of irrigation on game.

Game Farmers' Association—Hon. Sec.: Mr. John Coles, Home Farm, Hothfield, Ashford, Kent (Ashford 580).

Gamekeeper's Association of the United Kingdom—Secretary: Mr. P. A. Gouldsbury, Pentridge, via Salisbury, Wiltshire (Hadley, Dorset, 370).

Enemies of Game. When the eggs of game birds mysteriously disappear leaving no signs of disturbance, magpies and crows, which search for nests throughout the spring, may be suspected. The shells of eggs bearing an untidy hole at the end or on one side, with fragments of shell attached to portions of membrane inside, may also imply attack from the *corvidii*. Sometimes their bill may penetrate right through the egg, leaving a small hole at the other side, while sometimes the nest is scratched out. Foxes may devour the hen and leave the eggs undisturbed. Saliva-covered feathers found in the grass a few yards away are a sure sign of foxes. A hedgehog searching for anything worth eating will leave behind a tangled mess of broken egg shell and nesting material, while a cat may scatter feathers, wings, head and legs leaving the eggs unharmed. See the *Annual Review* 1965–66 of the Ely Game Advisory Station for more hints.

Firearms Act, 1965. Under this Act, trespassing with a firearm on private land without reasonable excuse entails maximum penalties of 3 months imprisonment and, or, a £100 fine. Carrying a loaded airgun, a loaded shot gun or any other loaded or unloaded firearm in a public place (which includes a public footpath or bridle-way) without reasonable excuse makes an offender liable to a maximum of 6 months imprisonment and, or, a fine of £200 for an airgun; and for other firearms a maximum of 5 years imprisonment and, or, an unlimited fine. The Act applies to England and Wales and, with some limitations, Scotland and Northern Ireland.

Protection of Birds Act, 1954. All birds of prey (owls and hawks) are protected throughout the year under this Act, and special penalties attach to the destruction of the rarer species, and to the removal of their eggs. All the common song birds are protected, though protection has been lifted from the bullfinch in certain fruit-growing districts.

Birds which may be shot at any time of the year by an authorised person:

Cormorant	Lesser Black-Backed Gull	Rock Dove (in Scotland only)
Carrion Crow	Herring Gull	Rook
Domestic Pigeon gone wild	Jackdaw	Shag
Hooded Crow	Jay	Starling
House Sparrow	Magpie	Stock Dove
Goosander (in Scotland only)	Red-Breasted Merganser (in Scotland only)	Woodpigeon
Greater Black-Backed Gull		

Under the Act an 'authorised person' is the landowner, tenant or person having sporting rights, or a person having permission from one of these three or any person authorised in writing by the Local Authority or by certain statutory bodies such as the Nature Conservancy and the River Authority.

Shooting Seasons. Pheasant   *1st. October–1st. February*
Partridge   *1st. September–1st. February*
Grouse   *12th. August–10th. December*
Blackgame   *20th. August–10th. December*
Ptarmigan   *12th. August–10th. December*
Capercaillie   *1st. October–31st. January*
Common Snipe and Jack Snipe   *12th.*
August–31st. January

INLAND: *1st. September–31st. January*

FORESHORE: 1st. September–20th. February
(Foreshore is any area below high water mark of ordinary spring tides.)

Common Pochard	Pintail	Wild geese—
Common Scoter	Scaup	Bean
Gadwall	Shoveller	Canada
Garganey	Teal	Pinkfoot
Goldeneye	Tufted Duck	Whitefront
Long-tailed Duck	Velvet Scoter	All other geese are
Mallard	Wigeon	protected

1st. September–31st. January

Coot	Common Redshank	Grey Plover
Curlew (other than	Bar-tailed Godwit	Moorhen
Stone Curlew)	Golden Plover	Whimbrel

IN SCOTLAND: 1st. September–31st. January. Woodcock
IN ENGLAND AND WALES: 1st. October–31st. January. Woodcock.

Deer Conservation and Control. Many fallow and some red deer escaped from parks during the last two wars and, like the indigenous roe deer, they have found the young woodlands of Britain much to their liking. A herd will increase its numbers by 30 per cent a year, or roughly double the population in three years—to the dismay of foresters, farmers and gardeners who suffer damage to their crops.

It is no kindness to the deer to protect them until they are too numerous for their habitat and starve to death in winter. But control must be carried out by enlightened scientific methods if cruelty is to be avoided. Although it is legal to drive deer to 'guns' armed with 12-bores, loaded with S.S.G.—but not to 'guns' with weapons of lower calibre—the British Deer Society argue that a high proportion of wounded deer too often escape. Proper selection of beasts for the cull is difficult and animals may be dispersed on to neighbouring property where more damage is done. Shooting roe bucks indiscriminately in spring exposes woodland to invasion by strange bucks, and with increasing competition, far more damage to trees will be done than if a single buck is protected in its territory.

The use of shot guns. The use of a 12-bore, loaded with S.S.G., may be justified only when an injured deer is known to be in an area where the use of a rifle would prove dangerous, and where the beast is likely to be shot at close range. Except in close proximity to villages and towns, deer control should be carried out with a rifle. A pamphlet explaining the policy of the British Deer Society on Deer Drives is available from the Hon. Secretary, 43, Brunswick Square, Hove, Sussex.

Control Societies. These are now thriving in Ashdown Forest, the Battle district and the Chichester-Midhurst area of Sussex, in Cranborne Chase and the Poole Basin district of Dorset, in much of the deer country of north-west England, and elsewhere. They have developed in response to an urgent need and with the goodwill of local landowners, farmers and foresters. Experience shows that where there is cooperation between local residents and experienced, unpaid stalkers, effective control can be carried out without the awful cruelty that has too frequently marked the old fashioned and inefficient deer drive.

A Control Society is essentially an association of landowners and farmers which invites practised riflemen to reduce the problem of marauding deer by planned selective control or by an annual cull that matches the rate of increase of the local deer population. The venison is the property of the landowner or shooting tenant.

Forming a Society. It is vital that a Control Society should enjoy the goodwill and support of the Forestry Commission and the British Deer Society, and it is desirable to secure the approval of the County Council, the police, and the Nature Conservancy, and the backing of the County Naturalists' Trust, the National Farmers' Union and, in Scotland, the Red Deer Commission. The British Deer Society's booklet on *Deer Control* (5s. 9d. post free from the Society's Publications Officer, E. H. Down, 'Grey Plovers', Hendon Wood Lane, Mill Hill, London N.W.7) is required reading for all concerned with this issue. Their Control Society Secretary is John Hotchkiss, Stede Court, Biddenden, Kent.

Deer as a Profitable Asset. There is a growing recognition of the potential value of wild deer as a source of income on many estates. Already the Forestry Commission charge a guest stalker between £5–£15 to shoot a roe buck, and between £10–£20 for a fallow buck. The price for a red deer stag in Thetford Forest will not be less than £5 per point on the deer's antlers, and a 16 pointer will cost £100. In parts of Europe a good red deer stag will fetch £1,000, and £100 may be charged for shooting a cull. A potential market exists, too, for venison. In a recent typical year, 'sales of venison' from the Island of Rhum yielded the Nature Conservancy £1,423.

Close Seasons for Deer. These were introduced under the Deer (England and Wales) Act 1963, and the Deer (Scotland) Act, 1959, whose provisions, originally confined to red deer, were extended to other deer under an Order issued by the Secretary of State in 1966.

	ENGLAND AND WALES	SCOTLAND
Red Deer		
Stags	May 1–July 31	October 21–June 30
Hinds	March 1–October 31	February 16–October 20
Fallow Deer		
Bucks	May 1–July 31	May 1–July 31
Does	March 1–October 31	February 16–October 20

Roe Deer

Bucks	No close season	October 21–April 30
Does	March 1–October 31	March 1–October 20

Sika Deer

Stags	May 1–July 31	May 1–July 31
Hinds	March 1–October 31	February 16–October 20

The Forestry Commission voluntarily impose a close season for roe bucks from October 2–April 30 in England.

WALKING OR RAMBLING

The popularity of rambling in this age of the motor-car is demonstrated by the keen demand for accommodation in youth hostels. About a million 'overnight registrations' are recorded each year.

Youth Hostels Association (England and Wales), Trevelyan House, 8, St. Stephen's Hill, St. Albans, Hertfordshire (St. Albans 55215). The prime aim of the movement is to help all, especially young people of limited means, to a greater knowledge, love and care of the countryside.

Scottish Youth Hostels Association, 7, Bruntsfield Crescent, Edinburgh, 1 (Morningside 4755).

Rambler's Association, 124, Finchley Road, London, N.W.3 (Swiss Cottage 5611). This organisation has done much to secure public access to wilder uncultivated moorland and mountain country, and to support the authorities in declaring long-distance routes.

Country Customs and Crafts

Christmas Mummers – Twelfth Night Revels – Shrove
Tuesday Ceremonies – Palm Sunday – Maundy
Thursday – Good Friday: Hot Cross Buns – Rogationtide –
Oak Apple Day – Well Dressing – Abbots Bromley
Horn Dance – Country Crafts

No one really knows why the modern housewife feels impelled to put away the Christmas cards by Twelfth Night; and children who present posies of spring flowers to their Mothers on Mid-Lent Sunday—Mothering Sunday—have no notion that they are echoing the habit of the ancient Romans who took offerings to the Temple in honour of Cybele, the Mother of the Gods.

The past retains so strong a hold over each generation that customs initiated in prehistoric times are sometimes reflected in the doings of modern man, for the country year even today is frequently marked by ceremonies illustrating the grafting of Christian beliefs on to pagan philosophy.

Christmas Mummers. When a group of Nottinghamshire pit-boys were asked, in 1945, how they came to know the words of their ancient play, one lad replied: 'We larn it from them as did it last year.' Until early in the present century hundreds of English villages had their Guisers or Mummers—Tipteers in Sussex—composed of men or boys with blackened faces and strange costumes or streamers who went from house to house on or around Christmas Eve—Eastertide in Lancashire—performing their play. Innumerable versions existed, most of them concerning St. George and the Turkish Knight, who is felled only to be brought back to life by the Doctor with his magical Opplis Popplis Drops.

Other stock characters include Father Christmas, Beelzebub, Little Devil Doubt and Bold Slasher. One Wiltshire version used to end with a dirge for the death of Nelson. The Mummers' Play appeared in Elizabethan chapbooks, but its origins are probably as old as man himself. It may spring from a pagan ritual celebrating the triumph of Light over Darkness at the turn of the winter solstice.

A group of Mummers.

Where it is performed. The Folk Dance and Song Society, in 1951, made a colour film of the Symondsbury (Dorset) Mummers' Play, whose performers learn their parts by oral transmission. The Marshfield Mummers, in Gloucestershire, were revived in 1932, and regular Christmas performances have been staged in recent years at Crookham, Hampshire, Headington and—until 1963—at Andover. The Chailey (Sussex) Mummers are a revival dating from 1950.

Twelfth Night Revels, January 6. 'Christmas goes out in fine style with Twelfth Night', wrote Leigh Hunt, 'and the whole island keeps court.' Elaborate pageants, masques and tournaments marked the day in Tudor and Stuart times, and the was-

- sailing of apple trees on this night continued in some parishes until the first world war. The custom survives at Carhampton, near Minehead, Somerset, on Old Twelfth Night, January 17. Otherwise only the Twelfth Night Cake is remembered—and that has now become the Christmas Cake.

Shrove Tuesday ceremonies. Pancake Day or Good Tide, as it used to be called, gained its name from the thin, flat 'cake' fried after dinner to stay the hunger of those who were about to go to confession on the eve of Lent. It was formerly a great day for cock fighting. Today it is marked by the annual **Shrovetide Football Match** through the streets of Ashbourne, Derbyshire, and by the **Olney Pancake Race** in William Cowper's home village in Buckinghamshire. The race is said to result from an incident in 1445, when a housewife heard the shrivening bell and promptly ran to church still carrying her frying pan and pancake. The Pancake Bell rings at 11.30 and 11.45 a.m.

Palm Sunday. The ancient practice of carrying palms to church on this day, or of distributing them in church, has been much revived in recent years. It was practised in the 4th century and was introduced to the west by the 9th century.

Maundy Thursday. The custom of washing the feet of the poor on this day—in remembrance of the washing by Christ of the disciples' feet—began in the medieval monasteries. The Wardrobe Book of Edward I records the gift of money to 13 poor persons whose feet had been washed by the Queen. Today H.M. the Queen is frequently present at the Royal Maundy service, usually held in Westminster Abbey, when the Maundy Money is given to as many poor men and women as there are years in the life of the reigning sovereign. The coins are specially minted. The Queen carries a posy of small flowers, a reminder of the days when herbs were borne to combat infection from fever and plague.

Good Friday: Hot Cross Buns. It has long been customary to eat these on Good Friday, and they were supposed to be made with dough kneaded for the Host and therefore marked with the cross. They were said to keep for twelve months without becoming mouldy. Today, some commercial firms do in fact keep their hot cross buns in the deep freeze for more than twelve months without their going mouldy!

Rogationtide. Just as the Church has adopted and adapted the Plough Monday ceremonies, a plough now being brought into some churches for blessing on the first or second Sunday after Epiphany, so the old **Rogation** or **Gang days,** when the bounds were beaten, are often remembered today in country churches. In some parishes, choir and congregation walk in procession through the fields for the blessing of the crops. These country services of Plough Sunday and Rogationtide are particularly well observed in Wiltshire, Hampshire and Sussex, and the annual Plough Sunday Service in Chichester Cathedral attracts a large congregation.

Oak Apple Day, May 29. It was long the custom to wear an oak apple in the button hole on this day, in honour of the triumphal return of Charles II to London in 1660. It is still observed as Garland Day in Castleton, Derbyshire, when there is a procession round the village, led by a band, and including a large and impressive garland. This ceremony, too, is said to be in honour of Charles II, but it is clear that its origins are far more ancient.

Well Dressing at Tissington, Derbyshire; Tuesday before Ascension Day. This ancient folk art is carried on in at least fourteen English villages, most of them in North Derbyshire. At Tissington the work is undertaken by a team of 6–12 persons who prepare elaborate pictures of Biblical scenes, using flowers and mosses, and a remarkably high standard of craftsmanship is achieved. The origins of the custom may well lie in the pre-Christian propitiation of the water spirits.

Abbots Bromley Horn Dance. Wakes Monday, following the first Sunday after September 4. This ancient Dance of unknown origin is performed by six men whose heads are half hidden by the antlers of reindeer.

The Horn Dance at Abbots Bromley.

For more information, see *The Country Life Book of Old English Customs*, by Roy Christian (Country Life, 35s.).

COUNTRY CRAFTS

What does our countryside not owe to successive generations of rural craftsmen, many of them embodying a tradition of good workmanship that is almost as old as man. For there were highly skilled flint knappers before metals had been discovered, and the first blacksmiths began to develop their craft in the Bronze and Iron Ages.

Almost every village and country town displays abundant evidence of the incomparable skill and taste of craftsmen in wood, stone and iron; and nowhere is their work seen to better advantage than in the hundreds of country houses now open to the public. Even half a century ago most English villages possessed their own blacksmith, wheelwright, saddler, turner, tailor, thatcher, mason and many more, and it is sad that changing social and economic conditions and the coming of the

Blickling Hall, Norfolk, under the care of the National Trust.

technological age should have banished most of them from the rural scene.

Yet that is not the whole story. There are still many thriving rural businesses and a substantial number of blacksmiths,

Knole, Sevenoaks, Kent, is another National Trust property.

saddlers, basket-makers and other craftsmen have adapted their skills to new conditions.

The Rural Industries Bureau, 35, Camp Road, Wimbledon Common, London S.W.19 (Wimbledon 5101), was founded in 1921, on the initiative of the Development Commissioners, to serve as a central planning and technical body implementing a national policy for rural industries. Working through the voluntary grant-aided Rural Community Councils, the Bureau

The **modern craftsman** may need to cope with farm machinery.

provides individual instruction in manual techniques and the use of machine tools, and runs an Advisory Service that deals with the design and building of rural workshops, the development of new methods and tools, and other matters. *The Rural Industries Loan Fund*, using resources provided by the Development Commissioners, exists to assist with the building of workshops and the purchase of equipment. There is a separate *Scottish Country Industries Development Trust* in Scotland.

Blacksmiths. The decline of the farm horse has not generally put him out of business. Like the **saddler,** he has profited much from the increasing popularity of riding, and the majority of blacksmiths become involved in the making and repair of wrought ironwork. The gates of Penshurst Place, Kent, recently restored by a Sussex smith, a new communion rail for a convent chapel

A modern blacksmith at work.

at Mayfield, Sussex, and new gates for the Royal Holloway College, Englefield Green, may be quoted as examples of good work produced in the last few years.

The Underwood Industry. It is not often realised that there is still some demand for ash and chestnut coppicing. Some 3 million yards of chestnut fencing may be needed in a single year, and the industry, with a turnover of three-quarters of a million pounds, requires 20,000 to 30,000 acres of chestnut coppice.

Boat-Building. The last ten years have seen a rapid expansion in this rural industry—more than 500,000 people go sailing— and standards are rising.

Furniture making and restoration. Some small country firms and individual craftsmen find a ready market for their goods from architects and corporate and institutional bodies. At the request of the Historic Buildings Council and the Ministry of Public Building and Works, the Rural Industries Bureau have trained many craftsmen in the restoration of furniture and chattels for historic houses. Examples of their work may be seen at Hampton Court, Knole Park, Kent, Audley End, Essex, Polesden Lacey, Surrey, Castle Ashby, Northamptonshire, and many other famous houses.

Thatching. The shortage of thatchers in many districts has been acute for some years, and the patience of householders is not inexhaustible. Moreover the rise in costs and high insurance premiums have combined to persuade some owners to use alternative roofing materials. Yet the desire of wealthy city folk to seek a place in the country, and their readiness to spend money on restoring houses that would otherwise be condemned, have saved many fine examples of village architecture from destruction, and many old houses are thatched each year. The shortage of apprentices is a problem. Yet with many thatchers facing years of hard work, even that problem can be overcome.

Watch-making and repairing. This may serve as an example of the small industries and crafts that are being developed in the villages, and which frequently make a valuable contribution to

Watch repairing.

our export drive. More information about these and other country crafts may be obtained from the Rural Industries Organisers at the offices of the Rural Community Councils, or from the Rural Industries Bureau.

MORE USEFUL ADDRESSES

MAIN OFFICES OF THE FORESTRY COMMISSION

Headquarters: 25 Savile Row, London W.1 (Regent 0221).
Senior Officer for Scotland: 25 Drumsheugh Gardens, Edinburgh, 3 (Caledonian 4782).
Senior Officer for Wales: Churchill House, Churchill Way, Cardiff (Cardiff 40661).
Director of Research: Alice Holt Lodge, Wrecclesham, Farnham, Surrey (Bentley, Hampshire 2255).

CONSERVANCY OFFICES IN ENGLAND

North-West: Upton Grange, Upton Heath, Chester (Chester 24006).
North-East: Briar House, Fulford Road, York (York 24684).
East: Brooklands Avenue, Cambridge (Cambridge 54495).
South-East: Danesfield, Grange Road, Woking (Woking 91071).
South-West: Flowers Hill, Brislington, Bristol, 4 (Bristol 78041).
New Forest: The Queen's House, Lyndhurst, Hants (Lyndhurst 2801).
Dean Forest: Whitemead Park, Parkend, Lydney, Gloucester (Whitecroft 305).

CONSERVANCY OFFICES IN SCOTLAND

North: 60 Church Street, Inverness (Inverness 32811).
East: 6 Queen's Gate, Aberdeen (Aberdeen 33361).
South: Greystone Park, Moffat Road, Dumfries (Dumfries 2425).
West: 20 Renfrew Street, Glasgow, C.2 (Glasgow Douglas 7261).

CONSERVANCY OFFICES IN WALES

North: Victoria House, Victoria Terrace, Aberystwyth (Aberystwyth 2367).

South: Churchill House, Churchill Way, Cardiff (Cardiff 40661).

Commons, Footpaths and Open Spaces Preservation Society, Suite 4, 166 Shaftesbury Avenue, London W.C.2. Our oldest amenity body, founded in 1865.

Council for the Preservation of Rural England, 4 Hobart Place, London S.W.1.

Association for the Preservation of Rural Scotland, 15 Rutland Square, Edinburgh.

Field Studies Council, Devereux Buildings, Devereux Court, Strand, London W.C.2. This pioneer organisation runs a number of residential field study centres where highly qualified staff conduct courses in field biology, geography and other subjects. They include:

Flatford Mill Field Centre, East Bergholt, Colchester, Essex.

Juniper Hall Field Centre, Dorking, Surrey.

Dale Fort Field Centre, Haverfordwest, Pembrokeshire.

Malham Tarn Field Centre, Settle, Yorkshire.

Preston Montford Field Centre, Nr. Shrewsbury, Shropshire.

Slapton Ley Field Centre, Slapton, Kingsbridge, Devon.

Orielton Field Centre, Pembroke, Pembrokeshire.

Scottish Field Studies Association, 141 Bath Street, Glasgow, C.2., runs its own field study centre at Kindrogan, Perthshire.

National Trust for Places of Historic Interest or Natural Beauty, 42 Queen Anne's Gate, London S.W.1. Founded in 1895, the Trust is unique in holding land and buildings in perpetuity.It has 160,000 members and owns some 400,000 acres.

National Trust for Scotland, 5 Charlotte Square, Edinburgh 2. This body has been ahead of most amenity societies in developing its information services.

Index

Abbreviation: d = line drawing